GW00569267

BSA GOLD STAR
AND OTHER SINGLES

OSPREY
COLLECTOR'S
LIBRARY

BSA GOLD STAR
AND OTHER SINGLES

The Postwar Gold Star;
'B', 'M', 'C' ranges;
Bantam; Unit Singles

Roy Bacon

First published in 1982 by Osprey Publishing Limited
27A Floral Street, London WC2E 9DP
Member company of the George Philip Group
First reprint spring 1983
Second reprint winter 1985
Third reprint summer 1986

British Library Cataloguing in Publication Data
Bacon, Roy
    BSA Gold star & other singles. – (Osprey
    collector's library)
    1. BSA motorcycle – History
    I. Title
    629.2'275   TL444.B2
ISBN 0-85045-447-6

Editor Tim Parker
Design Roger Daniels
Filmset and printed in England by
BAS Printers Limited, Over Wallop, Hampshire

Contents

Foreword by Brian Martin

It is not very often that I am persuaded to write a foreword for a book, but in this case it pleases me to think that someone has gone to great pains to research with accuracy the facts to produce a comprehensive study of the development of the BSA Gold Star and post war single cylinder motorcycles.

There have recently been written several books by different authors on the demise of the British motorcycle industry, and BSA in particular, and the various names and personalities concerned. The blame for the failure being placed in various directions depending upon the opinion of the individual author concerned. Those books alone make it so refreshing to have this book; written with great accuracy about the actual motorcycles.

In concentrating on motorcycle facts rather than on the personalities, Roy Bacon has succeeded in describing the development of the early BSAs and pieced together the circumstances leading to the awarding of a 'Brooklands Gold Star'. Also the subsequent christening of one of the most famous machines in the history of production sporting motorcycles, the BSA Gold Star—a machine to become even more famous in the post war years as the most versatile motorcycle ever made. What machine could be a winner in road racing, scrambles, trials, International Six Days etc., with only the selection of the correct combination of cam, piston, tyres, gear ratios and exhaust system?

In today's world of specialization in all sports there is no longer room for such a machine. All branches of motorcycle sport now require a machine specially developed for its own specific needs, although there are still some of the later B50 engines giving a good account of themselves in a number of modern events.

Roy has put the subject before both general reader and BSA expert with such clarity and interest that each is informed and injected with enthusiasm at the same time without either being confused or bored.

So much information and 'hard to put down' reading and reference will awaken the interest of anyone interested in motorcycles and BSA singles in particular.

Brian Martin
ex BSA Competition Manager,
Andover, Hampshire
October 1981

Opposite page **Brian Martin negotiating water on a Gold Star in the 1956 Lamborelle trial which he won. An avid row of spectators check his progress**

Acknowledgements

This is always such a difficult part of a book to write where one tries to thank the many people without whose help it would not have been written. Writing about BSA single cylinder motorcycles was a most interesting task but without that outside help it could not have been made a complete story, and it is a pleasant feature of the two-wheeled world that information and pictures are passed around so freely in the best motorcycling tradition. I am most grateful to all who have helped.

To ever cheerful Brian Martin who I have seen at so many shows over the years and who kindly wrote the Foreword. To Dick Lewis who spent some hours helping me with engine and frame numbers at his Weybridge BSA shop, Bob at Blays of Twickenham who did the same, Michael Laidler of the Vintage Motor Cycle Club who sent me more numbering data together with machine specification material, and Jack Harper of BSA who checked the numbers from his records and supplied me with missing data on the pre-war C12.

Most of the photographs used in the book came from the files of the magazines and I am again indebted to Bob Berry of *Motor Cycle News* and Mick Woollett of *Motor Cycle Weekly* for their help. I also have to thank Mike Nicks of *Classic Bike* for the loan of all the BSA shots in his files. Other material came from the archives of the National Motor Museum at Beaulieu, the Post Office, the Imperial War Museum, the London

County Council—London Fire Brigade or were Crown Copyright. Many of the pictures originated from BSA themselves having been sent out as publicity or feature shots over the years.

The final selection of pictures was made from all those collected by the editor and I, not without some difficulty, and all pictures returned to their owners after use. Some carried the imprint of a freelance photographer and in all cases I have tried to make contact to clear copyright. If by chance my letter failed to reach you or I have unknowingly used an unmarked print, I can only apologise.

The freelance photographers and agencies whose pictures were used are: G. T. Atkinson, Cecil Bailey, Barbara Bellingham, Ian Buckden, Malcolm Carling, Ray Gregory, Brian Holder, Tom March, Nick Nicholls, Donald Page, Polly Palmer of Bri-Tie Motorcycles and the BSA Owners' Club, Roger Piron, Russell Studio, Bill Salmond, Peter Strong and Studio Cave.

Finally, my thanks go to Osprey Publishing, and to Tim Parker, their editor, for his continued help and guidance in the writing of this book.

I hope you will enjoy the final result.

Roy Bacon
Hampton, Middlesex
January 1982

1 | Ancestry

The very first BSA built in 1910 was a single and founded a tradition of solid, reliable and dependable transport that was to last for over 60 years. From that belt drive, side-valve model sprang a line of sturdy motorcycles that were to keep the company at the front of the industry for so long and generate the slogan, 'One in four is a BSA'. The single was soon expanded into a range and was joined by a vee-twin for the 1920 season.

The firm had flirted with Brooklands and the TT just before the war gaining a surprise win at the track when Kenneth Holden made his debut there in 1913. In the Isle of Man they were less successful with only one finisher in 1913 but six the following year. After the war they returned to the TT in 1921 but suffered a total disaster with dreadful trouble in practice and every machine retiring from the race. That experience was to keep them from international road racing for the painful collapse of a ten year reputation in a single race remained etched in all minds for a very long time.

If racing was expensive and too chancy there were other ways in which to promote the name and BSA took to these with entries in major trials, six-day events and early scrambles. In all of these they were successful and to further show off the excellence of the product in its standard form and in average hands, became involved with demonstration tests and so in time with the Maudes Trophy.

Always the accent was on proving the

standard product and showing the excellence of the spares and service aspects of the company. Competition was much at the level at which the sporting clubman could participate, again emphasising the standard product whether for touring or sports, and playing down speed and any special works items.

So BSA grew and prospered with machines that suited the bulk of the buying public. Machines such as the Round Tank and the Sloper, two which became classics, were backed up by a range of singles and vee-twins, in a selection of capacities and a variety of touring, sports and de-luxe guises. Often they had features which were advanced for their day but never to the point where these would dominate the machine. In the main all the models were conventional and simply well designed for the mass production techniques of the day, well made from good materials, properly assembled

A BSA classic of its time, a 1928 Sloper in this case with sidecar attached. Fitted with electric lighting and neat leather toolbox

and passed out through a tight quality screen. Nothing startling or much to make a headline but the reputation that a BSA kept on going grew and grew.

Motorcyclists may talk of the super-sports machine they would like but in the end they open their wallets for a conventional model to get them to work. BSA supplied just that and let other firms struggle to produce the technical innovations that the public clamoured for but never bought in bulk.

This policy enabled BSA to ride out the depression years by careful housekeeping while many small companies went to the wall. As the thirties ran on and business picked up the Small Heath firm had its technical innovations, such as the prototype fluid flywheel and preselector gearbox, fitted to a 500 cc single for the 1933 Motorcycle Show. BSA soon realised that riders liked changing gear, especially as footchange mechanisms became more common, so that anything that had a touch of automation was unlikely to catch on very well. Honda were to find the same thing out some 45 years later, but they could afford the poor selling 400 automatic, in 1933 BSA could not risk taking a chance so the line up of machines remained as before. Singles and vee-twins, side and overhead valves, three or four speed gearboxes and a solid reputation for reliability. The public continued to drool over the Norton and Velocette camshaft engines but went out and bought their BSAs.

The company did list the Blue Star versions of its standard models but the differences were all done by switching components during assembly which enabled the extra performance to be offered at a minimal charge and without any real disruption to the production line. There was also a special model available with piston, ports, carburettor and magneto to suit racing but the rest of the machine was box standard. This was a tradition the company would return to time and again as it was both successful and cheap.

The Blue Star models first appeared for the 1932 season and were distinguished by an enamelled star on the timing cover. This indication of high performance internals originated from the Sloper which in 1929 had been made available in a tuned version. To enable dealers and the factory to more easily tell which engines had the quick cams and high compression piston they stencilled a red star on the timing cover. From small beginnings came a lengthy line.

In 1935 King George V celebrated his Silver Jubilee on the Throne and for 1936 BSA introduced their Empire Star models, along the lines of the Special, as sporting machines. Early in the year the 500 cc version was put through one of their endurance demonstrations with 500 miles round Brooklands at an average well over 70 mph followed by a 1000 mile road trip taking in a good selection of the well known West Country, Welsh and Lakeland hills on route. All completed successfully on one set of tyres and without the need for any spares.

Successful though BSA were in the middle 1930s period, it was with a range of machines that had become rather complex and which still had some roots in the vintage years. In 1936 a move was made to change this and came about when Val Page joined the company from Ariel. Page was possibly the most gifted engineer to work in the British motorcycle industry, quiet and gentlemanly in manner but with a breadth of experience that had an enormous effect on the machines designed in and around Birmingham for some 40 years, and prior to that at JAP in London.

In the industry his path often crossed that of Edward Turner and the two had first met at Ariel before Page moved to Triumph in 1932. When Turner took over at Meriden in 1936 Page moved to BSA but was back at Ariel by 1939, where he stayed. In time BSA acquired both Ariel and Triumph with Edward Turner becoming managing director with control over all these and other plants. Page was to climax his career with the brilliant Ariel Leader design.

The prototype 500 with fluid flywheel and preselector gearbox shown at the 1933 Motor Cycle Show. Final drive on right

Back in 1936 he took a hard look at the complex range of BSA machines, left the vee-twins alone and set down the outline of the single that was to run on until the time came for unit construction. The wet sump built into the front of the crankcase, the forward mounting of the mag-dyno in vintage style, exposed valve gear, and the forged steel frame backbone all went to be replaced with dry sump lubrication, saddle mounted oil tank, electrics tucked in behind the engine, and a simple tubular frame. The whole range took on a much more modern style which, with the addition of telescopic forks and rear suspension, was to carry it along for over 20 years.

The new range of singles comprised a dozen models so seemed complex but in reality consisted of two basic ranges, the B and the M, both using the same basic design of engine. The B range comprised seven models in 250 and 350 cc capacities and available with side or overhead valves with the latter in a variety of tuning states. The range was essentially the lightweight end of the scale and was built for solo use, not sidecar. The M range was for heavier duty with cycle

parts beefed up to suit and engine capacities of 350, 500 and 600 cc. Again, both side and overhead valves were offered, not however in all sizes, and the 500 ohv model was available in two states of tune and finish.

The four 350 cc models, all based on engine dimensions of 71 × 88 mm, were the main part of the B range and consisted of the B23 with side valves and four speed, hand operated gearbox, and three machines with overhead valve engines all of which could be had with the then popular twin port cylinder head. The sports B26 had the same handchange gearbox as the side valve model while both the tuned B24 Empire Star and the B25 Competition models had footchanges for their four speeds. The B25 was the trials machine and as such came with a high level exhaust system and trials tyres of 21 in. diameter front and 4 in. section rear.

To supplement the 350 cc machines were a trio of 250s, one, the B20 with side valves and the

other two with overhead. All were based on engine dimensions of 63 × 80 mm and looked like slightly smaller versions of the 350s. All had four speed gearboxes but only the more highly tuned B22 Empire Star had footchange, the B21 copying the side valve job with hand control.

In the M range a further 350 cc model was produced but with the longer stroke of the 500s. This was the M19 de-luxe with engine dimensions of 68·8 × 94 mm and it had the footchange gearbox. Four other M models backed it, three of 500 cc capacity using 82 × 94 mm dimensions and one stretched out to 85 × 105 mm to give the 600 cc M21 with side valves. These engine dimensions came from the old 600 cc Sloper engine and were soon discarded for 82 × 112 mm so making the M21 a lengthened stroke version of the side valve 500. This was the M20 and both side valve machines had hand change while the two 500 cc ohv models were foot operated. The M22 was a sports model and similar in style to the 350 cc B26, while the M23 was the Empire Star with the tuned engine.

All these engines followed the same basic layout that characterised them throughout their life. The most noticeable feature of this was possibly the oil pump which was set in the bottom of the right crankcase half which bulged out to accommodate it. This bulge necessitated the famous kink in the lower right frame tube and made all the engines awkward to fit in other frames, a feature of annoyance to many potential users over the years.

That feature aside, they followed convention for the times in many ways. The crankcase was cast in aluminium and split vertically on the centre line of the cylinder. The crankshaft turned in a drive side ball race and timing side plain bush in the B range, while the M range had the benefit of a timing side roller and both a ball and a roller

Post Office messenger delivery boys on their BSA machines in 1933. Well before the red Bantams of the postwar era (The Post Office)

race on the drive side. The crankshaft was of built-up construction with roller big end. The small end was bushed and the piston a standard four stroke with a dome or flat top to give the required compression ratio for each model. What was less obvious was the thought and care behind the simple facade which brought the reliability and long life to the machines. For instance, cylinder liners were made in austenitic iron to improve bore life and this in turn required that the correct piston ring material be found and tested. It was.

The timing chest was cast into the right crankcase half and carried the gear train that drove cams and magneto. Each cam was carried on a shaft with a gear which was driven from a single pinion on the end of the crankshaft. Inboard of the timing gear was a skew gear which drove the oil pump. The camshafts rotated in bushes in the crankcase and the outer cover. The inlet cam gear meshed with an idler and this in turn drove the magneto gear. The idler shaft ran directly in the crankcase and was ported to give timed crankcase breathing. While the timed breather was an up to date feature which other makes often did not adopt for many years until forced to by oil leaks, the use of aluminium as a bearing was not such a good idea without positive pressure lubrication. The following year the case was bushed which overcame the wear problem that was arising.

The magneto carried the dynamo on its back,

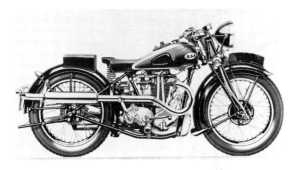

Above **Post Office Engineering Department BSA and sidecar with neat ladder stowage (PO)**

Top **Forerunner—Blue Star of 1935 with forward magneto and wet sump**

Left **1934 Post Office delivery combination (PO)**

both pieces being made by Lucas and the whole assembly was held down by straps to a platform cast into the rear of the crankcase. A single cover enclosed the whole of the gear train and provided a feed into the crankshaft for the lubricating oil via a quill.

The valves, whether side or overhead, were moved through the medium of flat based tappets which worked in guides in the crankcase. In the side valve engines the tappets carried adjustors which operated directly onto the valve stems but the overhead valve models had push rods and rockers in the valve train as well. They retained the adjustment at the tappets so all models had their valve clearance set at the same point and in the same manner. Access to the tappets was by

removal of a small separate cover and on the B range this was fastened to the crankcase but on the heavier M models it was positioned above the crankcase mouth level. It thus screwed directly to the cylinder casting of the side valve models but to the push rod tunnel casting of the machines with valves above the piston.

The tunnel became a feature of the engines over the years being of a flattened cone form. The first type had less taper than subsequent ones and fitted between the crankcase and the separate alloy rocker box. It had lugs for bolts at its base and was ribbed round the top in contrast to the arrangement used later. The rocker box itself was of straightforward design and contained the exhaust valve lifting mechanism which was fitted in the cylinder barrel on side valve engines. The rocker box was lubricated from the return oil pipe and drained down to the crankcase via an external pipe. The box was fully enclosed by a separate top cover.

The cylinder head and barrel were both cast iron, the barrel being air hardened. Both were held down by special bolts anchored into the top of the crankcase and screwing into the underside of the cylinder head, a form of fastening used by BSA for many years. The side valve engines were more conventional with separate heads and stud fixing of the barrel to the crankcase.

All engines used dry sump lubrication, new for the year, with the oil tank mounted on the saddle tube. Connections were straight forward and the return pipe terminated just below the filler cap inside a mesh filter which could easily be lifted out for cleaning. An additional filter was fitted in the bottom of the crankcase below the oil pump to guard against debris entering it. The tank incorporated a vent pipe and a drain plug.

Amal carburettors were standard to the range with an air cleaner offered as an extra. Exhaust pipes were pushed into the port and were downswept except on the competition orientated B25. This was also the odd man out in that it had a tubular silencer and a fishtail exhaust. The

other machines either had a tubular silencer (B20, B21) or a Brooklands can with fishtail. Upswept exhaust pipes were available for a number of models as were twin port cylinder heads. Where the twin port head was fitted, upswept pipes were normally supplied along with tubular silencers.

All the engines had a cam lobe shock absorber built onto the output sprocket and drove the clutch by a single strand primary chain enclosed in an oil bath case. The clutch on the B range ran in oil with cork inserts and had two plates at the 250 cc side valve end of the scale rising to three for the B22 and B23 and four for all the 350 cc overhead valve models, including the M19. All the other M range machines had dry clutches.

The wet clutches had four or six small springs to clamp the plates together, each compressed by nuts which could be adjusted to give the required load and to ensure the pressure plate lifted squarely. On the B25 fabric inserts were used so that the oil level was important on that model, too much and the clutch slipped, too little and the chain wore quickly.

The dry clutches used a single large spring loaded up by a big ring nut done up with a C spanner. The whole clutch sat on a separate centre, itself keyed to the gearbox mainshaft. The clutch sprocket ran on rollers with an oil flinger behind it to help prevent leaks out of the back of the chaincase, this being pressed steel with the outer held in place by many small screws. The clutch assembly was encased in a dome shaped pressing attached to the sprocket by a series of screws. The clutch was operated by a lever on the far side of the gearbox with a built in screw adjustor.

The gearbox of all models contained four speeds and followed traditional British motorcycle practice with top gear, direct drive and the intermediate ratios all going through two pairs of gears. The output sprocket on its sleeve gear was concentric with the mainshaft carrying the clutch and, like it, on the left side of the machine.

The layshaft lay behind the mainshaft with the selectors and the cam drum they slid on above the gears. The sleeve gear ran in a ball race as did one end of the mainshaft, the other running in bushes in the sleeve gear. Bushes served for the layshaft and some of the gear wheels. Gear engagement was by sliding dogs and achieved by rotating the cam drum. This merely had two pins driven into it which worked in slots cut in the two selectors so that they were forced to slide along the cam drum as it rotated.

The rotation was done in one of two ways. The hand change used a lever attached to the side of the petrol tank with a gate and linked to the gearbox. The footchange was of the positive stop type and enclosed under an outer cover, between it and the gearbox end cover. This compartment also housed the kickstart mechanism with the face ratchet and its spring loaded driving gear on the end of the mainshaft where the quadrant on the kickstart spindle turned it.

The gearbox shell was a straight forward aluminium casting with two mounting lugs on its underside and an access hole in its top. This was covered by a small plate. The casting contained both filler and drain plugs for the lubricant.

Heavy and lightweight boxes were used for the M and B ranges, both very similar in appearance and operation but with slightly different internal ratios.

The engine and gearbox were fitted into a cradle frame built up from forged lugs and tubing. The B models had a lighter construction than the M which also incorporated sidecar lugs in the forgings. Both types of frames followed the same lines with single top, down and saddle tubes forming the main part of the frame with the rear wheel supported in pairs of upper and lower chainstays, the latter running forward under the engine. The chainstays were bolted into position to the top of the saddle tube and the bottom of the front downtube. The lower end of the saddle tube was bolted to the gearbox mounting plates and these ran down and back

Graham Walker riding the WB30 over the rough. From this wartime 350 cc prototype came the postwar 'B' range in its many forms

under the box to attach to the lower chainstays at two points. Each plate had two slots in it for the gearbox lugs to pick up on, the slots allowing box movement for primary chain adjustment. The front of the gearbox plates acted as rear engine mountings and the crankcase was supported at the front by a pair of smaller plates.

One variation in the design of the two frames was that only the M type had the famous kinked cradle tube on the right side to clear the oil pump, this section being omitted on the lighter frames.

Front forks were girders, again in two weights for the two ranges, all with single central spring, and adjustable friction dampers. On the M range the dampers were controlled by a large hand knob while the B models made do with a wing nut. The fork movement was claimed to provide constant wheelbase and all models were rigid at the rear, which was normal practice for the time.

The wheels were spoked with single leading

shoe drum brakes and on some models the rear wheel was quickly detachable. The front wheel drove the speedometer and all models had a rear stand. Many also had a front wheel stand which used the mudguard stay for that duty. Steel mudguards were fitted, both carrying number plates and a toolbox was mounted on the right of the rear guard stays on all models with a second one on the left on the more expensive machines. The battery went on the left to balance the oil tank with the dynamo control unit under the saddle. A pillion pad was supplied with some models but was an extra for others. All silencers went on the right and drive chains with their guards on the left. Horns were mounted on the front down tube just below the petrol tank and the headlamps were fixed to the forks so moved with them along with the speedometer head. All the M range had a tank top instrument panel as well as the dip switch on the handlebars. They were also fitted with a ratchet for the front brake lever, this being a small button pressed in to lock the brake on and used when parking if a sidecar was fitted. It had a fly-off action in the same manner as a sports car handbrake of that period.

Other controls were conventional with clutch and valve lifter on the left with the ignition lever, and throttle and choke lever on the right. The gear pedal was on the right along with the kickstarter and the rear brake pedal on the left with a direct link back to the drum.

The finish of the machines was basically black with chrome plating of the exhaust system, headlamp rim, handlebars and minor controls. Only the petrol tanks relieved the black which otherwise extended to the wheel rims on many machines. The three Empire Star models did have chrome plated rims and this finish extended to the chaincase, mudguards and parts of the hubs and brakes on the competition B25. Plated rims were available as an option on all the models not so fitted as standard. The tanks of the machines with side valve engines were finished in green with gold lining and these models had the option

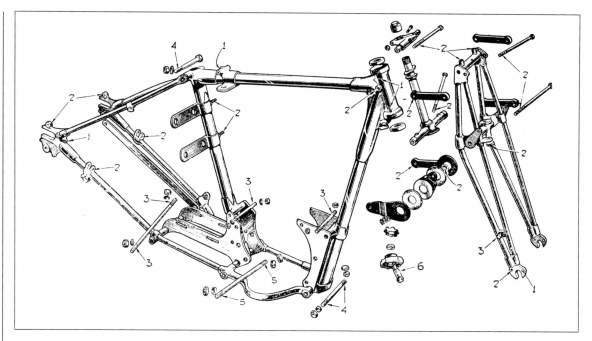

The Empire Star frame from pre-war with built up construction typical of the period. The right rail has the famous kink

of tanks finished in chrome plating with green panels. This latter finish was standard for the rest of the range with the Empire Star models having their own green colour to distinguish them from the less sporting machines. The Star models and the B25 had a star badge on the tank side in place of the prosaic BSA the other machines used. All models had a piled arms transer on the oil tank.

The singles were backed up by two vee-twins and five sidecars in sports and touring finishes and for the whole range was listed a good collection of extras. Footboards could be had in place of rests and had their own special line in legshields. Various speedometers were listed and could be had with a maximum speed needle to record this vital fact. A stop light, pillion seat, pillion rests, rear carrier and adjustable footrests were on offer, when not supplied as standard, along with exhaust systems, crankcase shields, air cleaners, bigger section tyres and steering dampers.

So the new range was launched to the trade at Small Heath and shown to the public at the last major motorcycle exhibition to be held in Olympia before the shift, in 1937, to Earls Court.

Before that took place events occurred at Brooklands, as described in the next chapter, the result of which was an additional model in the 1938 lineup, the 500 cc Gold Star. Of less impact was the announcement in January 1938 of a new 250 cc side valve single, the C10, which was to lead to a series of popular lightweights, as discussed in more detail in a later chapter.

Apart from the two extra models the range continued into 1938 with few alterations and it is a good indication of the brilliant work of Val Page that the changes needed as the result of the first year's experience were minimal. The use of bushes for the idler gear has been mentioned, an easy change and one that could be and was incorporated in all the existing engines. On all models the horn was moved to a mounting on

the left side of the front engine plates so doing away with the need for a horn lug on the frame down tube.

The most noticeable change was to the overhead valve engines and concerned the push rod tower and rocker box joint. This had proved to be prone to oil leaks and was redesigned to incorporate the familiar gland nut with castellations. The top of the tower thus became a simple turned diameter fitting into a hole in the underside of the rocker box and the joint was sealed by a gland ring compressed by the nut. On the early machines the nut was internally threaded and screwed onto the rocker box but this arrangement was reversed later on so that the rocker box was tapped to become the nut and the gland nut was threaded externally. Thus the nut appears to be much more sub-stantial on the early engines although the later design is to be preferred as it is less prone to damage.

These points aside, the alterations for the year mainly concerned the finish although the three B range 350 cc ohv machines changed their carburettors to the horizontal body Amal type, which also meant using the special float chamber to suit. Finish was brightened up with the choice of red or green tank panels and wheel rims with chrome plating and centres to match the tank colour for some models. Others turned to chrome rims with black centres and several models had the oil tank chrome plated with black panels.

The B25 competition 350 gained a crankcase shield and Brooklands style silencer but lost its toolbox, while the two ohv 500s changed their silencer shape a little.

The biggest new item in the range was the Gold Star and this had an all alloy engine and was offered in three forms for road, competition and track use. The finish was a chrome tank with matt silver panels and the famous Gold Star badge.

In the early part of the year BSA staged a major demonstration in an attempt to win the Maudes

Trophy. This was a cup presented by George Pettyt of Maudes Motor Mart in 1923 to the ACU for them to award for demonstrations of strictly standard machines run under observation. At first it went to Norton, for four years, while BSA concentrated on runs that made news and brought them publicity. Their first, in 1924, was to run samples of all their machines up Screw Hill in Wales, a very steep hill with a loose shale surface and six hairpins. They then did an assault up Snowdon which was successful despite very bad weather conditions. In 1925 they sought to prove that their spares were available and fitted. To do this the ACU was called in and ordered all the parts shown on the parts list for one model from a number of dealers they chose from the dealer list. Nearly half were available over the counter and all arrived in 72 hours. In less than five hours the machine was assembled and then taken for a 100 mile ride from London up a good selection of steep hills on the downs. At one stage the clutch was adjusted as it bedded down. Three months later the test was repeated, not with a new model, but with a 1914 machine and this was equally successful.

Similar demonstrations took place over the years to bring out the strong points of the BSA to the people who mattered, motorcycle buyers. All were designed to highlight reliability, adequate performance, good fuel consumption, spares being available and fitting, and thus all the reasons why the general public selected a machine and paid for it.

The 1938 Maudes attempt began with the ACU selecting two BSA dealers from the list of over 1000 and obtaining a 500 cc Empire Star from Sandums of Tottenham and a 600 cc M21 from Godfrey's in Great Portland Street. The side valve machine was taken to Birmingham by the ACU, fitted with a sidecar and appropriate gearing, all under observation, and then rejoined the Empire Star at Wembley Stadium. On Sunday, February 20, the two machines moved off with R. A. Harris driving the sidecar and Ted

Mellors on the solo. They ran down to Shrewsbury that day at 30 to 35 mph, which was the only running-in the solo received, and moved on to Bwlch-y-Groes in Wales the following day. This was a notorious hill climb some $1\frac{1}{2}$ miles in length with an average gradient of 1 in 7. The surface at that time was not tarred. Each machine made 20 climbs and descents. To ensure observation was continuous the solo followed the sidecar and was forced down to second gear at one point when the chair selected bottom for one of the hairpin corners. With the climbs completed the machines repaired to Brooklands in Surrey for a six-hour speed test. The original targets of 300 and 200 miles for the two machines were soon seen to be low and were reset to 350 and 250 miles. Three stops for replenishments were made in no great rush and both machines completed more than their new targets, the figures being 351 and 276 miles to average 58·59 and 46·12 mph. The solo did a lap at 72·71 mph and the sidecar one at 50·583 mph. This high speed run was followed by a well earned meal for the riders, who then did some acceleration and brake tests plus a flying start quarter mile which produced 78·94 mph from the solo and 56·25 from the sidecar.

Following all this the two machines returned to Wales, the clutch on the M21 was adjusted and a further 20 climbs and descents of the hill were reeled off. This brought them to Friday, and Saturday was occupied in the drive back to London in poor weather conditions. The machines were locked up for Sunday but on Monday morning at 10·30 am stood at Highgate Archway ready for a flexibility test. They were started, put into top gear and the gear controls removed. The aim was a trip across London, first north to south, and then east to west, all in top gear. For this part David Munroe, the BSA experimental chief, took over the sidecar and off the machines went. Munroe had a stop at Herne Hill to adjust his clutch and when near the top of the very steep approach to Crystal Palace decided that the

much abused item had been caned enough so turned his machine downhill. Mellors, on the solo, romped up the hill. The party then moved on to Canning Town and once again removed the gear controls and the two machines ran through the heart of London to Hammersmith. The hardest part for the Scottish Munroe was reported to be the sight of a halfcrown in the road at Kensington Gore and not daring to stop to pick it up in case he stalled the engine!

All told the solo covered 1250 miles and the sidecar 200 more in the test following which the machines were stripped and examined to be found to be in the fine fettle, the only signs of the hard work done being a settling of the exhaust valve spring of the 500, slight pitting of the exhaust valve seat on the 600, and severely charred cork inserts in the back clutch plate on that machine. And they had good reason to be charred for many felt that it had been asked to do too much.

For this excellent demonstration the company was awarded the Maudes Trophy for 1938.

1939 brought further changes to the range with the disappearance of the B20, whose position had been taken over by the C10. The B22 Empire Star 250 also went, although the B21 remained in both standard and de-luxe forms, it being accompanied by a new ohv 250, the C11 based on the C10 design. In the 350 cc class the M19 was dropped but the others continued, the side valve model in both standard and de-luxe forms, while the B24 changed its name from Empire to Silver Star. All the 500s continued, the M20 following the pattern of the B23 and being available in two guises while the M23 copied the B24 and became a Silver Star.

The side valve engines had a minor change to their valve guides which had been in two separate sections since 1937 and were changed to single long items. Nearly all models received a major change in the timing chest, only the standard versions of the B21 and B23, along with the M22 remaining as they were. The rest

changed to a fixed spindle design for the cams and idler to run on, the three spindles being pressed into the wall of the crankcase. Each cam and the idler gear were fitted with bronze bushes and the shafts were supported solely by the case wall so the outer cover became an unstressed part. To prevent the shafts bending they were supported by a precision steel plate which bolted to all three spindles and to the crankcase at three points. It also carried a bush to support the mainshaft and prevent it bowing under load.

At the same time the camshaft lubrication was improved by using special bolts to hold the plate on the camshaft spindles. These were drilled along their length and had extended heads which fitted into seals pressed into the outer cover. Behind these seals were drilled passages connecting to the main oil feed to the crankshaft, this being via a quill as before. At the same time the cams were changed in form to incorporate quietening ramps that extended nearly round the entire base circle and the tappets offset slightly so that they rotated in use to equalise the wear.

Externally the horizontal carburettors were changed back to the normal type and some of the silencers changed models if not their shape. Handchanging of gears all but disappeared only being kept on the standard versions of the C10, B21 and B23. With the need to remove the gear change gate from the side of the petrol tanks the

chance was taken to revise the tank shape and capacity for many of the models. The tanks also received new kneegrip rubbers in most cases.

All models, except the B21 standard, B23 standard and M22, received new oil tanks with an increased capacity of 5 pints and most also had the toolbox moved to a position between the chainstays on the right. This included the Gold Star which lost its tank top box but gained an instrument panel as did the de-luxe M20 and the rest of the M range.

Valanced mudguards were fitted to both Silver Star models along with the big side valve machines and the rear only of the Gold Star. Finishes were also altered with the green and red being dropped for a general finish using black, silver and chrome plating in a variety of combinations. Maroon lining was used on a couple of models and all the oval tank badges changed to a round form with BSA on it, although the star models continued with their special badges.

Prices remained the same and for some models were even reduced.

Another complex Maudes Trophy test was devised for 1939 and the BSA efforts were matched by Triumph and Panther. While the tests interested the public the eventual outcome was overshadowed by the approaching clouds of war as the year progressed. In the end the trophy went to Triumph but BSA won it back in 1952

The Gold Star was derived from the M23 Empire Star here seen in its 1937 form

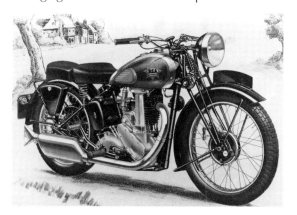

using their Star Twin model and kept it for 10 years before it went to Honda.

The likelihood of war was fully appreciated by the BSA board as early as 1937 and it was their foresight and initiative which laid down plans for a great expansion in what the initials stood for—Birmingham Small Arms. It was to their credit that they pushed ahead with these plans in the face of Government indifference so were more than ready when the need became obvious to the officials. As with the guns so it was with the aircraft that used them, the Hurricane, and with the motorcycles.

Under these external forces it was not surprising that the 1940 range was greatly curtailed and, of course, few machines were built as production had only just begun when war broke out. The whole of the B range went and was replaced by two models the C12 and B29, both 350s, but with side and overhead valves respectively. The C10 and C11 continued along with a single M20, the M21 and the M23 Silver Star.

There was considerable standardisation of parts among the models left in the range and of the two new ones the C12 was very similar to the C10 while the B29, known as the Silver Sports, was of particular interest for it was to become the forerunner of the postwar singles. It had the normal BSA engine dimensions of 71 × 88 mm but owed more to the old M19 than the B range. It used the stiffer M-type crankcase and, like all the larger models, had a timing cover whose top side ran straight from engine up to magneto with the tappet inspection cover attached to the push rod tunnel. Thus it looked like an M23 until one came to the cylinder head which was cast in iron with the rocker boxes integral. These contained a further innovation in the form of hairpin valve springs which laid across the head in the two valve chambers which joined over the push rod tunnel. Each was sealed by a separate lid and a small plate in the side of the rocker box gave access to the top end of the push rods for

location. A special tool was provided in the tool kit to compress the valve springs and so release the valves.

For the rest the B29 was as the B26 and had the lighter frame and forks while being the only single not to have a tubular silencer. A small number were complete ready for despatch when war broke out and these were among the stock which was promptly requisitioned, painted matt olive green and sent into service. Any that went over to France were left there in the Dunkirk evacuation so met the same fate as many of the machines impressed at that time.

The model was not forgotten at Small Heath and the design was used as the basis of a light 350 prepared at the request of the War Office for use in bad conditions. It was required to be easy to handle, which it was, and used the B29 engine with a tubular silencer and a rather small front brake. It carried a bulb horn on the forks by necessity as the lights were direct with a generator mounted on top of the magneto in place of the usual dynamo. A dry battery was housed in the headlamp for parking. The machine was coded B30 or WB30 and fitted out with panniers and headlamp mask while the finish was the usual olive green. The War Office were delighted with the results of the tests on the prototype and quickly ordered 10,000 more. None were built however, as the order was changed to the standard WD 500 cc M20 to avoid complications of spares and service in the field.

So ended the early days of the dry sump single but most of the 1940 models were to come back after the war, only the C12 and M23 not making it, along with the near vintage vee-twin.

The B29 was to be the key for although no more hairpin springs were to be seen, a foundation for the future had been laid.

A 1939 Silver Star B21 seen as renovated in 1980. Very typical early 'B' range timing cover with tappet plate and push rod tower

2 | Gold Star

The Brooklands gold star is a small lapel badge in the form of a six-pointed star enamelled dark blue with the border and the number 100 in its centre in gold. It was awarded by the British Motor Cycle Racing Club, otherwise known as Bemsee, to anyone who completed a lap at Brooklands on a motorcycle at over 100 mph during a race. It was not an easy thing to earn for the track was rough and bumpy while machines had rigid frames, narrow tyres and minimal front suspension. Anyone who won one could wear it with pride.

Many were won on Wednesdays, for during the 1930s meetings were often held at the track in the middle of the week and it was one such that occurred on 30 June 1937. These were normally rather leisurely affairs with as much discussion as racing but on that day the programme contained the entry of Wal Handley on a 500 cc BSA.

This caused considerable speculation for Handley had retired at the end of 1934 after a long and successful career which had brought him four TT victories and the first TT double in 1925. Then there was the machine, a very standard Empire Star from all appearances and certainly not a make associated at all with racing, Brooklands, or Handley.

The inspiration for the entry came when Frank Cope borrowed a works Norton and won a gold star. This led to a number of Small Heath staff wondering if such a feat was possible with an

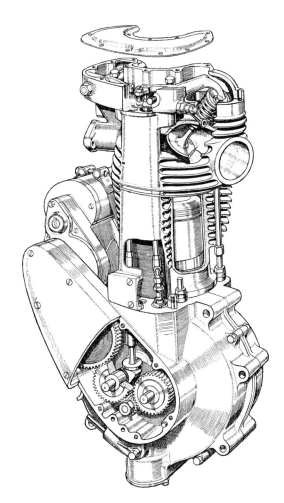

The start of the line, the 1938 Gold Star M24 all alloy engine

Empire Star, and with the boss, Joe Bryan, in tacit agreement, plans were laid. The main scheming was done by David Munroe and sales manager Stan Banner, but soon Val Page and his assistant Herbert Perkins were involved while Len Crisp and Jack Amott prepared the machine, Jack being a cam expert who always had his pockets full of cams ground up to his own ideas.

The recruitment of Handley was done by Bert Perrigo one of the great men of BSA history who was a brilliant competition rider in the late 1920s and 1930s, and later filled many senior roles in the company. Into all these he brought his drive, expertise, good humour, and enthusiasm which was just as keen when the writer met him in the 1960s as it was in his youth.

The appearance of the BSA at Brooklands may have surprised the spectators but the officials and timekeepers were well aware that the machine was fast. BSA had plenty of experience in building quick engines and often produced these for ISDT and other events. For the track the Empire Star was set up with a piston giving a 13:1 compression ratio and so ran on alcohol fuel. A racing magneto was fitted and the power output was around 33 to 34 bhp. The compulsory Brooklands can was attached, footrests and controls modified and the gearing changed to suit the track.

With the necessary pre-race trials and the use of a top rider the handicapper was not caught napping and Handley was set off on the nine-

B.S.A. 500 c.c. O.H.V. Gold Star
Model M 24

The now famous B.S.A. Gold Star — the fastest standard sports machine you can buy. It is fitted with **quickly detachable rear wheel.**

£77. 10s.

Competition model £5 extra.

Speedometer extra.

All machines supplied with speedometer unless otherwise ordered.

Engine. Single cylinder single port O.H.V. 82 mm. bore x 94 mm. stroke. 496 c.c.; individually built and bench tested; aluminium cylinder and head; valve seat inserts; cylinder liner. B.S.A. dry sump lubrication with 5-pint oil tank under saddle; oil indicator on engine; enclosed O.H.V. gear; roller bearings on both drive side and gear side of mainshaft, new design silent timing gear; improved tappet construction facilitating adjustment; Amal T.T. carburetter.

Transmission. Engine shaft cush drive; front chain ⅝ in. x ·305 in., with oil bath; rear chain ⅝ in. x ⅜ in. with lower run guard; five plate clutch embodying fabric inserts, on double row ball bearing centre; B.S.A. four-speed gearbox; enclosed foot gear change; gear ratios 4.8, 5.2, 8.15, 11.8. Wide ratio gearbox optional.

Frame. Triangulated cradle type; 531 tubing; front fork shock absorber with finger adjustment; steering

damper; 3¼ gallon tank; new knee grips; Dunlop Universal tyres, 3.00—20 front, 3.50—19 rear; 7 in. dia x 1⅛ in. wide brakes; spring-up rear stand; lifting handle on rear guard; **quickly detachable rear wheel;** front stand; adjustable footrests.

Equipment. B.S.A. flexibly mounted handlebar with special controls; racing twist grip throttle; ratchet lever for front brake; adjustable Terry saddle; metal tool-box with complete tool kit; inflator; gear-driven Lucas 6-volt Magdyno lighting set with compensated voltage control; tank instrument panel; anti-vibration battery; electric horn; valances to front and rear mudguard; licence holder; provision for pillion footrests.

Finish. Black and chromium; chromium tank with matt silver panels; chromium wheel rims with matt silver centres. Wheelbase 54 in.; clearance 4½ in.; saddle height 28½ in.

second mark with a number of other fast riders. The race was over three laps of the outer circuit, that 2·767 mile track with its two heavily banked left hand turns separated by the railway straight and the fork with its right kink past the Vickers sheds. Throughout the first lap Handley was weaving his way through the field that had started ahead of him and he took the lead on lap two, to increase it to several hundred yards by the end of the race. His average for the race was 102·27 mph and his fastest lap 107·57 mph, so another gold star was claimed.

Handley went out again that day in a two lap handicap and was set back to six seconds behind

1939 catalogue page for the Gold Star which has the extra bolts either side of the push rod tunnel and the tank top instrument panel

scratch. At first all looked well as again he began to carve his way through the field. Unfortunately, as he went onto the Members banking for the second time T. F. Pullin changed direction on his 500 cc Excelsior Manxman just as the BSA was about to pass. The front of the BSA caught the back of the Manxman and the impact fetched Handley off in a heavy fall while Pullin managed to stay aboard his machine, although he suffered a broken ankle in the accident.

Handley escaped with cuts and bruising but that was the end of racing that day for the BSA. In fact the one race was sufficient and when the new sporting 500 was announced in the 1938 programme it was inevitable that it should continue the star name tradition and become the Gold Star.

That first model was typed the M24 and, although based on the Empire Star model, had a good few alterations. For a start both the cylinder head and barrel were in light alloy, the first with screwed in valve inserts and the second a liner. Furthermore, the push rod tunnel was incorporated into the cylinder casting and its line continued up into the head. The usual access plate was fitted at the base of the tunnel for tappet adjustment and the separate rocker box retained.

On the outside of the head was hung an Amal TT carburettor while the silencer was of the tubular pattern, unlike the M23. It was a low level system as neither the twin port head nor the high level silencer were offered. The compression ratio was raised to 7·8:1 thanks to the alloy engine, the iron one being limited to 7·2 on petrol. Each

engine was built up and tested to give 28 bhp at 5250 rpm and if it failed to reach this figure was reworked until it did. This practice was to continue throughout the life of the Gold Star and later owners received a copy of the power readings with their machine.

The transmission was the same as the Empire Star except for the gearbox shell which was in Electron, a magnesium alloy even lighter than aluminium, and the addition of a lower chain-guard. The gearbox weight saving exercise was extended to the frame which followed the lines of the M23 but was made in a light gauge, high tensile tubing with the heavy sidecar lugs omitted. No sidecar gear ratios were quoted either, just to make certain the point got home that the Gold Star was a sporting machine and would not enjoy being harnessed to a chair.

The remainder of the machine was Empire Star down to the tyres plus a crankcase shield, special petrol tank and special finish. The tank was unusual in that it had a tool compartment built into its top with a hinged lid. The finish was chrome plating for the tank with matt silver panels carrying the Gold Star badge. The oil tank

On the test bed. A pre-war engine undergoing its power testing and running at 4700 rpm. Carburettor is an Amal TT

1938 Gold Star with toolbox in top of petrol tank exhibited in April 1981 as 1939 model although external features are for first year

was also plated but with black panels while the wheel rims had black centres to the chrome finish.

In addition to the standard road machine two others were also listed, a competition and a track racing model. The first was simply a Gold Star with competition tyres, narrow chrome plated mudguards, an upswept exhaust pipe and plated chain case and guards, both rear chainguards being retained despite the intended trials use.

The track racing version sported a high compression piston for use with alcohol fuel and was fitted with a double float chamber and special fuel pipe connections. With a compression ratio of 12·5:1 a power output of 36 bhp could be obtained. A racing magneto was fitted and a lever throttle, this being quite normal for Brooklands where you opened it up and then just hung on. No kickstarter was fitted and the controls were positioned for racing. It came with a Brooklands silencer and was offered with or without the front brake, the rear one being directly controlled. All this added £10 to the price and pushed the maximum speed over the 100 mph mark.

Above **The first postwar Gold Star at the 1948 Earls Court show surrounded by BSA top brass including James Leek and Bert Perrigo**

Right **A pre-war Goldie as seen at the owners' rally in 1978. Listed as 1939 model but with earlier two screw tappet cover**

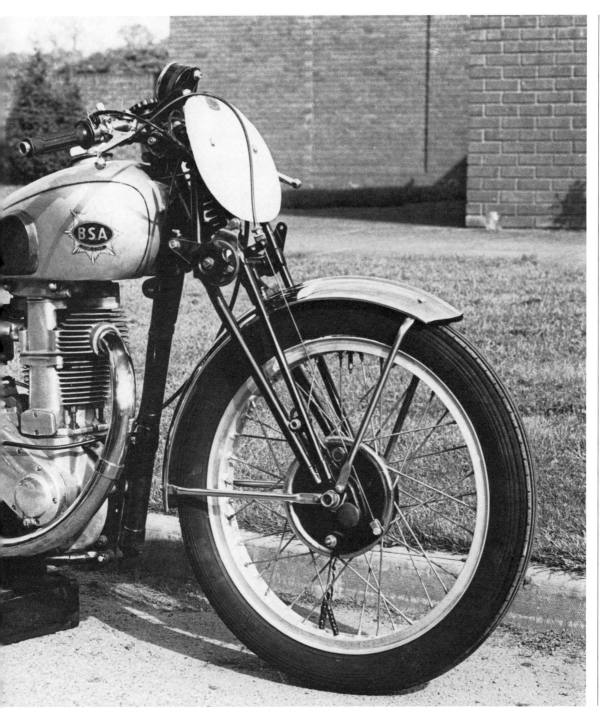

It is very unlikely that any of the track models were ever made and even the road machine met with a lukewarm reception due to two factors, the BSA stolid and reliable image and the advent of the Triumph Speed Twin at the same show. The Gold Star failed to draw the enthusiast who aimed for a company with a racing background, while the tourist preferred the more sedate Empire Star if he could not get his name down for the exciting new Triumph which looked more like a twin port single than a twin.

The BSA very quickly underwent a change to the engine with the addition of a boss either side of the push rod tunnel at the head to barrel joint. These had all the appearance of having been added on hastily to the casting to cure an oil leak and the change was already in use on the model road tested by *Motor Cycling* in March 1938.

The machine went well enough being timed over the quarter mile at 91·8 mph in one direction with a mean of 89 mph. 72 came up in third with 48 in second at some 6300 rpm which was a good engine speed for a long stroke single in 1938. Fuel consumption came out at 62 mpg. Braking and acceleration were praised as was the handling but this was perhaps over complimentary about what was really just a much faster M20. The alloy engine caused the weight centre to shift and riders of the day found the Empire Star easier to cope with although that fell short of Norton and Velocette standards. The alloy engine with its sharp cams proved to be noisy in use and it was only the bark of the exhaust from the small silencer which covered the noise of the valve gear rattle. All told this did not make it a popular machine in town for riders or others.

With these shortcomings plus a gearchange that was acceptable rather than good the Gold Star impact could have been minimal but the light weight and low down punch from the engine made it a winner in the trials of the period and it quickly achieved a good reputation in this field.

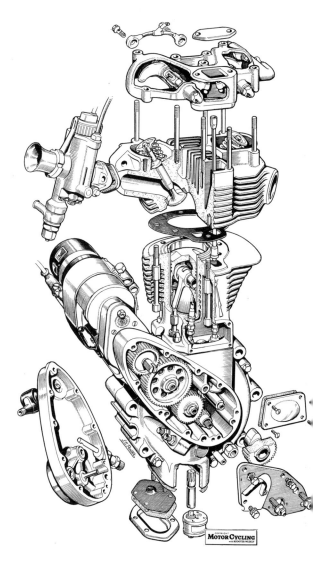

Above **The 350 cc Gold Star engine for 1952 with separate rocker box and die cast head and barrel. Fitted with shorter connecting rod and oil breather shroud on cam spindle support plate, a feature transferred to the timing cover in production. Small fin type ZB**

Right **1954 type BB of 350 cc in swinging fork frame used from then on. Fitted with new type gearbox, dualseat and oil tank**

The Clubman Gold Star in its plunger frame form. This is a 1952 model with the austere petrol tank brought about by the nickel shortage

1957 Clipper B34, the USA version of the alloy engine competition B34 with central oil tank. Very similar to trials Gold Star

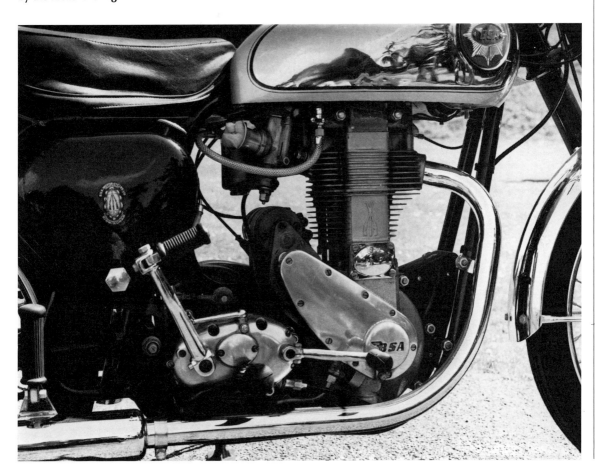

A lovely period shot of a Goldie and boy with dreams—
did they come true? The BSA's front rim shows signs of
hard use. It was later learnt that the boy was the late Tom
Herron, a great road racer

This kept the model in the lists for 1939 when along with most of the range it received revised timing gear, a larger oil tank, a standard toolbox, tank top instruments and a new petrol tank. A minor change was to the tappet access plate which received four screws to hold it, while the rear mudguard was valanced although the front was not. The rear tyre size went up a little and its wheel was driven via a close ratio gearbox housed in an aluminium casting. The Electron case was no longer to be had but the wide ratios were still available as an option. The M23 Silver Star did it the other way round for 1939 with the wide ratios standard and the close ones an option. The rear wheel was quickly detachable with a single through spindle.

With the new tanks the machine's appearance was noticeably changed although the

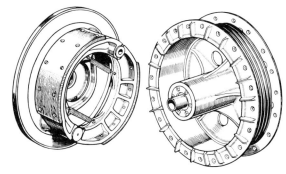

The famous 190 mm front brake. Full width alloy drum with cooling holes in the web, very wide alloy shoes with single operating cam

colour remained black with the petrol tank chrome plated with matt silver panels carrying the gold star badge. Wheel rims matched with chrome and matt silver centres. The oil tank and toolbox were lined, the tank no longer plated.

Although the catalogue gave the finish as silver this did not stop BSA showing a gold finish to the tank on the front cover of the show report

Bill Nicholson riding a 1954 trials model at the owners' rally in 1980. His first for two decades but the touch was still there

1962 standard scrambler fitted with normal oil tank, centre stand and open pipe

issue of *The Motor Cycle* for 1938. Gold lining is also applied to the oil tank, toolbox, and the valances shown as being on both mudguards, again at variance with the catalogue. That front cover advert also shows a two screw tappet plate, although the push rod tunnel does have the two extra bolts and is not the type as shown on the very first Gold Star model.

In a sense academic for a year later the model had gone from the range and it was to be one war and nine years before the Gold Star was to be seen again.

After the war production was the first essential and BSA soon had a small range of machines available for the public. There was a great upsurge in interest in competition in those immediate postwar years and in turn this brought a cry for machines built for competition use. BSA met this at first with competition versions of their road machines and also produced a variety of special engine internals to further improve the performance for trials and scrambles.

Work to improve the performance of the engines was limited by the standard material of cast iron used for head and barrel, although the works machines had alloy items as early as 1946 either to push up the power, lower the weight, or both. For the 1947 Manx an alloy engine was prepared based on the B29 suitably modified internally. The race itself was hardly successful with the rider running out of fuel but the machine went well enough to encourage its use as the basis of a fast road machine.

The new Gold Star first appeared at the 1948 motorcycle show at Earls Court and was based on the road and competition 350 cc models then in production. The engine, however, featured an alloy head and barrel, and these parts incorporated the push rod tunnel just as on the pre-war M24. The head and barrel were held down by four special through bolts which anchored into the crankcase and screwed up into inserts in the cylinder head, as was normal BSA practice for ohv machines postwar. In addition a further four special bolts joined barrel to head by screwing into a further four inserts in the head. One of these bolts was situated between the push rods in the tunnel in the side of the barrel. A whole range of options was available for the engine specification and affected the compression ratio, port sizes, cams, valves, valve springs and carburettor type and size. This option range was extended throughout the machine and gave alternatives for the gearing, gear ratios, petrol tank size, tyre type and size, and the electrical equipment. This last could comprise a Lucas racing magneto supplemented by a battery lighting set and electric horn, the Lucas magdyno from the standard road

Control layout of road model Gold Star on test for *Classic Bike* **in 1980. Taylor-Dow two way fork damping has been added**

Right **a 1956 stunt demonstration on a Gold Star carried out by the Cytrix display team, later to tour in the USA with the Hollywood Motor Rodeo**

The duplex frame with oil pump kink used by most of the larger BSA machines

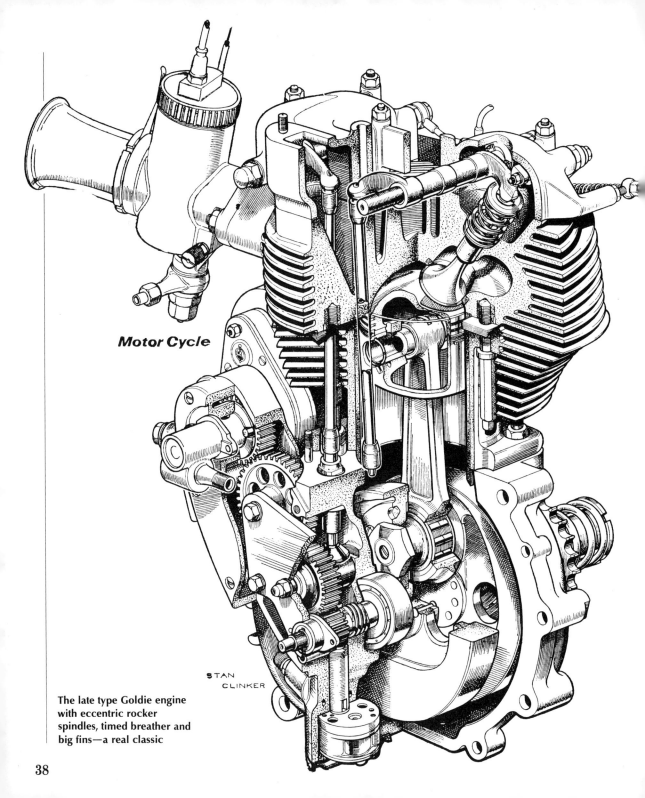

Motor Cycle

STAN
CLINKER

The late type Goldie engine
with eccentric rocker
spindles, timed breather and
big fins—a real classic

The 500 cc Clubman Gold Star in all its glory with clip-ons, rearsets, reversed gear pedal, swept back exhaust and the twittering silencer

machine or a racing BTH magneto.

While all these variations did allow BSA to build machines suitable for touring, trials, racing or scrambles using the same basic set of parts, it did impose some restrictions. One of these concerned the cylinder head ports which were designed to suit the trials machine and retained the standard shallow downdraught angle, both features which imposed a restraint on the production of maximum power. Initially all that could be done was to bore out the inlet port and fit a larger racing Amal carburettor for the racing engines which were then in the minority.

Despite all the options much of the machine was from the B31 or B32 with the transmission and gearbox using standard parts in the main. The folding kickstart lever from the competition models was used but the clutch and box were standard aside from the internal ratios.

The front half of the frame was the same open diamond as used by the tourers with single top, down and saddle tubes brazed into lugs. The rear half of the frame was bolted on at the saddle nose and the bottom of the seat tube and comprised two pairs of cross-braced chainstays joined to the plunger suspension forgings. The rear suspension units had compression and rebound springs but no damping other than that

provided by grease and friction. Rigid frames were available for use in trials but were normally never supplied for racing. The only exceptions were for Daytona in 1954 and American flat tracks in 1956 and 1957. The scrambles machines normally had rear suspension. The front suspension was by the BSA telescopic forks and both wheels were common to the tourers, the rear being the standard quickly detachable type. The standard tyres fitted were Dunlop Universals of the same size as used on the B32 but others were available to suit requirements.

Many of the cycle fittings such as the oil tank, toolbox, exhaust system, seat and headlamp were standard parts from the B31, while the B32 was the source of the wide, flat, chrome-plated mudguards and the chaincase and chainguard in the same finish. The frame and forks were in the usual black but the tank was chrome plated with matt silver panels lined in maroon and carried the special Gold Star transfer on each side. The list price was £166 10s 0d plus £44 19s 1d purchase tax, to which had to be added £5 1s 8d for the speedometer.

In May 1949 *Motor Cycling* road tested the Gold Star in two of its possible forms, first as a tourer and then in its Clubmans racing form. In its road guise it proved to be much like the B31 but with better acceleration, a higher top speed of 78 mph and a noisier engine and exhaust. Handling was excellent, assisted by the spring frame, and the brakes matched the performance. For the test a rev-counter was fitted, driven from the magneto gear by a right angle box bolted to the outside of the timing cover, a position and arrangement that was to be used by all Gold Stars throughout the series.

For the second half of the test the machine was returned to the works and modified to the specification to be used in the Clubmans TT. The engine received a new piston, cams, cylinder head and carburettor, the gear ratios were changed and the change pedal turned round while, to keep the conventional up-for-down

English change, the internal mechanism was reversed. Externally the footrests were moved back to the alternative lugs provided on all Gold Star frames, a short foot brake pedal fitted, the speedometer removed and the machine returned to the magazine complete with two spare Champion plugs and the recommended exhaust pipe extension for use in place of the silencer when racing.

The model was tested in its Clubmans form at an airfield, for at that time it was permitted to remove silencers in the race. Along with the other changes this lifted the maximum speed to 90 mph or just over despite the full equipment still carried. Using the airfield as a circuit, after the speed runs had been carried out, showed that the handling and brakes were quite up to their task and the use of close ratios in the gearbox had improved the gearchange, never the best point on the BSAs of that era. The effect of the racing cams was to remove all power below 4000 rpm but from there up to the recommended 6500 rpm it was as clean as a whistle and keen to run even higher up the scale.

The model went on to prove the point by winning the 350 cc Clubmans that year and was to dominate the whole series.

For 1950 a 500 cc version, the B34 Gold Star, was added to the range and was a replica of the 350 apart from the engine which was based on the B33 dimensions. A new feature on both machines was an 8 in. diameter front brake with a finned cast iron drum mounted on a pressed steel hub.

The two Gold Stars continued unchanged into 1951 but late in the year the cylinder head of the 500 was altered to give a separate rocker box. This allowed the head, rocker box and cylinder barrel all to be die cast, which improved finish and accuracy while reducing production costs. At the same time the design of the valves and cotters was changed as there had been cases of the stems breaking at the sharp corner of the groove. A simple semicircular groove in the valve

was adopted with the cotters shaped to suit and this overcame the problem.

In April 1952 the 350 cc engine followed the 500 and appeared with separate rocker box die cast, as were the head and barrel. Any suspicion that the separation of head and rockers would reduce rigidity was removed by the nine studs used to hold the box to the head. Of more fundamental importance was an increase in the downdraught angle of the inlet port and a small decrease in the included valve angle which gave a slightly more compact combustion chamber. Also the valve size was increased and the semicircular cottar groove adopted. Furthermore, the exhaust valve material was changed to Nimonic 80, a nickel alloy originally developed for gas turbines. A further major change was to the connecting rod which was shortened by half an inch, and this in turn reduced the barrel length by $\frac{11}{32}$ in. so it lost one cooling fin going from ten to nine. In the lower half the crankcase webs were increased to stiffen the assembly but otherwise there were few changes from the standard M type arrangement. The valve gear, its drive, the timing gears, oil pump, rocker oil feed, big end lubrication quill, all remained as before, alterations being minor or to materials.

The flywheels of the Gold Star engine were of a different shape to the road engine and polished but were built up in the same way with forged wheels and pressed in mainshafts secured by a ring of rivets through a flange on the shafts. The big end thrust washers were also rivetted to the flywheels and the crankpin was keyed to the drive side for location of the oilway drilling. The pin had shoulders and tapers which called for close tolerance machining but gave a rigid and secure assembly.

While the valve train was unaltered the timing chest did incorporate a couple of features, one the rev-counter drive which was taken from an extended magneto gear nut, and the other concerning the oil breather. This was still the same untimed disc that relied solely on crank-

Above **For the USA, a Catalina model scrambler with the high rise bars demanded by that market**

Left **Few Goldies get hitched but this one in France also has a big fin head on a small fin barrel and competition mudguards**

a pressing fixed to the timing gear spindle support plate but this was soon changed for one cast as part of the outer cover which kept the problem at bay for a year or two.

Aside from the engine, some changes were made to the rest of the machine and included the addition of a de-frothing tower in the oil tank, the lowering of the dualseat, the adoption of an eccentric pin for rear brake pedal height adjustment and changes to the kickstart pedal and footrest on that side to allow the rider to tuck away better. A four gallon tank was added to the specification list as a further extra.

In May 1952 *Motor Cycling* repeated their 1949 exercise with the new style 350 cc Gold Star in its full Clubmans trim. It thus had a 7·8:1 compres-

case pressure to move and was built into an assembly originally mounted in the crankcase wall. Around 6000 rpm it was unable to move quickly enough to cope and, at high speed, oil losses became excessive. In an attempt to cure the problem it was moved to a point in the underside of the outer timing cover where it was fitted with a short pipe. This was better but not good enough so the pipe end was sealed and cross-drilled while the assembly was shrouded to keep the oil away from it. At first the shroud was

sion ratio, 1 and $\frac{3}{32}$ in. TT9, road racing cams and valves to suit. The complete lighting equipment was carried along with a silencer, and the four gallon tank and a dualseat were fitted. The folding kickstarter, reversed gear lever and short brake pedal all went with the rearset footrests, the right one of which folded up to let the kickstart past. Sprockets were chosen to give a 5·28:1 top and the close box fitted then meant the bottom gear was 9·86:1. This, taken with the wide inlet tract, meant it was not too well equipped for town use but by taking care with the throttle and ignition controls this could be managed. A rev-counter was mounted in solitary splendour on the fork crown and the handlebars were clamped to the back of the crown using the standard fixings. They were swept forward and then down but while this gave an acceptable touring stance, when flat on the tank the clutch lever was nearly out of reach and both wrists were uncomfortably bent.

After some work on the roads the tester repaired to an airfield, removed the silencer and attached the exhaust pipe extension. This resulted in some mid-90s timed runs and the next move was to take the horn off as its position on the left saddle lug forced the rider's leg well out into the wind. This resulted in 94 mph on a slight down gradient but against the wind, and 97·9 mph uphill and helped by the breeze.

Handling and braking were tried round the perimeter of the airfield and found to be up to the performance, although the rear wheel movement was lively on bumpy corners as it still had no damping. The front end stayed firmly in touch with the ground and gave the usual precise BSA steering. During the circuits the engine ran smoothly from 4300 to over 7000 rpm, 7400 coming up in second if wanted. Below 4000 it went woolly and it had a flat spot at 3500. Normal practice was to slip the clutch and hold the engine at 5000 rpm while it was fed in.

The finish of the test bike reflected the then current shortage of chromium, for nearly all the parts normally plated were finished in matt silver, the exhaust system being the only major item to remain with the plating. This was, however, only a temporary problem and, when the 1953 range was announced, the plating was back and the machines assumed their former glory. At that point no changes were given for the Gold Stars, but in November a further release brought news of major alterations to gearbox and frame.

Both these originated from work done by Bill Nicholson, an Irishman who had joined the BSA experimental shop in 1946 and had considerable success in trials and scrambles. He had built his own frame with swinging fork rear suspension for 1947 but had to return to plungers for policy reasons. His plungers had oil damping hidden inside them although they looked standard. In 1951 he built a duplex rigid frame for trials use and later that year a swinging fork version for scrambles. He spent the rest of the year working to make the rear Girling units function to his satisfaction and for 1952 replaced the damping internals with his own design. These ideas later went into the production Girlings.

The new BSA frame was of the swinging fork type based on this work and of all-welded construction. The substantial, single top tube was braced by a smaller tube beneath it. Duplex down tubes ran down from the headstock, under the engine and curved up to meet the top tube. The right one had the famous oil pump kink in it to clear the crankcase. The duplex tubes were cross braced beneath the engine and above and below the fork pivot, while each carried a further rear loop to support the top of the rear spring units, the seat and rear mudguard. A small loop joined this loop and the main frame below the fork pivot and served to support the pillion rests. The engine was carried by a pair of small plates

The classic Clubman with all the usual fittings including the 190 mm front brake and alloy rims. Signs of an oil leak on the silencer

A Taylor-Dow special pictured in 1977 and fitted with DBD34 engine canted forward in Reynolds frame built by Ken Sprayson

at the front and combined engine and gearbox plates at the rear. These fully encircled the gearbox and each side comprised an upper and a lower plate, making four in all. The swinging fork was of tubular construction with forged ends to carry the wheel and it pivoted on pressed-in Silentbloc rubber bushes. The rear units were large diameter Girlings with three position preload and were available with a variety of springs to suit different uses.

The engines were the same units as before with separate rocker boxes but the gearbox showed signs of further Nicholson work. He had found that, while the standard box worked well enough on the road, it was inclined to miscue in the heat of scrambles. The clutch also left

something to be desired. Early work involved an A7 shell of the type that bolted to the back of the twin engine. The mounting plate was cut off and lugs welded on. The A7 clutch was also converted to suit the single and in time this work evolved into the final Gold Star gearbox. It followed the same lines as that built for the twins and later used on the B range with a more compact design with shorter shafts. The selectors were moved by a camplate mounted on the front wall of the shell and this was turned by a simplified positive stop mechanism. To accom-

modate all these changes, late in 1952, a new shell was designed and this fitted the new frame.

At the same time the pressed steel chaincase was changed for a cast aluminium alloy one, the outer part of which was highly polished. The gearbox mainshaft seal remained the same in principle as did the method of mounting the inner case to the machine. The outer was still attached by a large number of screws and carried a combined filler and inspection cap. It presented a much sleeker appearance than the old case with its domes over shock absorber and clutch.

To these mechanical changes had to be added various cycle ones to suit the new frame. A new six pint oil tank was tucked into the right frame loop and matched by a toolbox on the left with the battery between them. The dualseat was fitted as standard and the machine came with either a rev-counter or a speedometer. Footrests could be positioned for touring or road racing and a further substantial pair were available for scrambling, which clamped to the frame main and cross tubes. The new models became referred to as the BB types from their 1953 code of engine number, all earlier units being ZB types regardless of rod length or whether the rocker box was separate.

While the cycle parts had reached a form in which they were to stay, the engines, or some of them, were due for a major facelift. The BB type was to run on in the touring and scrambles machine and also for a few special racers built for Daytona. However, the machines built to Clubmans or road racing specification received a new engine unit from early in 1954 to become the CB type, and by then they accounted for the bulk of the Gold Star production.

The new machines were dramatically different in appearance with massive finning to head and barrel set off by the essence of the late type Goldie, the swept back exhaust pipe. Inside the engine the combustion chamber was little affected in the 350 but the 500 was altered in downdraught and included valve angles on the lines taken by the smaller engine in 1952. Also the connecting rod was shortened some more and, in fact, so much that the flywheels of the 500 had to be machined oval so that the piston skirt cleared them. BSA went to some lengths to ensure that everyone realised that this had no effect on the balance of the engine.

The crankshaft was modified with the crankpin material being changed to EN36 and its locating keyway, in the drive side, being removed. From then on the position of the pin was checked with alignment marks, this being done to ensure the oil holes were not blocked off. The drive side mainshaft of the 350 was also increased from its earlier constant diameter to a stepped form with the inner bearing increased in size. It thus fell into line with the 500 so that the lower halves were the same apart from the oval turning of the flywheels of the bigger engine.

Inside the heavily finned barrel ran a shorter piston than before, while the cylinder head was equally well finned to match. It was held down in a slightly different manner as, although the wellknown crankcase to head through bolts were used, there was now a fifth one in the push rod tunnel in place of the usual shorter bolt of which there were only three. Thus the head still had its eight bolt fixing but now divided into five through bolts and three short ones.

In the rocker box was a new method of adjusting valve clearances with eccentric rocker spindles which allowed all the old adjusters to be discarded so reducing valve train weight. The rocker spindles were locked with nuts and continued to be hollow and fed with oil from the return side via a pipe and a pair of hollow bolts.

A further change in the engine concerned the breathing, for the old design could no longer keep up with the engine speed. The new breather was a timed rotary one set in the timing cover and driven by the magneto pinion. It was spring loaded against the cover, ported to breathe into an outlet in the underside of the cover, and also

drove the rev-counter drive box by a small slot in its end. It was to remain unchanged for the rest of the model's life.

The engine was fitted with an Amal GP carburettor and remote float chamber which for that year was suspended from a horizontal rubber mount. It was fitted into the swinging fork frame, now equipped with slim-line Girlings, along with the gearbox and this item received needle rollers for the layshaft in place of the bushes used before.

One useful addition to the specification was clip-on bars which carried welded on lever pivots and bolted directly to the fork stanchions. The standard clamps were retained and used for touring or competition bars, the same clamp bolts carrying the clip which locked the steering damper knob.

In May 1954 *Motor Cycling* once again road-tested a 350 cc Gold Star in full Clubmans trim both on the road and the race circuit. Carrying full equipment but with the open exhaust extension in place it reached 102 mph still accelerating with third gear good for 97 mph. On the road the addition of the silencer held the engine speed down to 5700 rpm and the machine to 82 mph. Still not a bad speed for a fully equipped bike and in that form it would tick-over at 900 rpm and lost the power band effect the open pipe produced. It was also exceptionally economical when used for running about, the result of an efficient engine and tall gearing.

Handling was aided by the optional light alloy rims and the new frame handled well on fast bumpy corners. The wellknown brakes continued to stop the machine on cue. Faults were minimal and one concerned the position of the kick-starter which could dig into the rider's shin. The rocker feed oil pipe connection leaked onto the machine and the new breather dripped onto the exhaust pipe as it lacked a drain pipe to the union.

All told it continued in the style as before.

During 1954 and into 1955 the BB version of the Gold Star continued to be produced for use other than Clubmans and road racing, while in 1954 a rigid frame version of the 500 was built for the Daytona races. The CB type also continued into 1955 but, during that year, became superseded by the DB, virtually the final version.

The DB engine looked the same as the CB with massive finning but contained a number of fundamental changes. The most important of these, but applied to the 350 only, was to the cylinder liner, which became much thicker and was reversed in its assembly to the aluminium fin muff. Thus it sat and located onto the crankcase mouth and carried the cylinder head on its upper

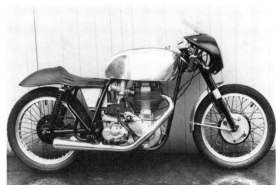

Left **DBD34 engine room. This model has a Concentric fitted which helps the slow speed running and enhances the roadster model image with the forward footrests and gear pedal**

Below **A Goldie prepared by Eddie Dow for racing but retaining most indentifying features**

end with the fins just for cooling, although they still contributed to the overall engine stiffness. The head joint continued to be stepped with the well known peel-off gasket sealing the outer gap, while the liner fitted accurately to the head.

The oil fed into the crankshaft was also revised as part of an exercise to fit a plain big-end. This demanded real oil pressure so the normal quill was removed and a hollow bush pressed into the crank end. This ran in an oil seal contained in the timing cover and behind it was the main oil supply at pressure. The plain bearing was not adopted but the revised oiling system greatly improved big-end life so was used from then on.

Smaller changes concerned the head fixing which reverted to the four through bolts and four short bolts. The fifth through bolt in the push rod tunnel had proved to be too inaccessible to be properly tightened. The flywheels were reduced in diameter a little and those in the 500 became round again.

Outside the engine the float chamber support was changed to a vertical mounting, clip-ons became standard for the Clubmans and a new silencer with very special internals was adopted. This was the forerunner of the much beloved twittering Goldie system, the name coming from the odd noise it made on the over-run and an essential feature for any genuine Gold Star silencer.

The brakes also received attention to improve their ventilation by the addition of six holes in the back of both front and rear drums. These were then blanked off by light steel pressings, rather like car core plugs, which could be removed by the owner if so desired. The rear brake drum received an alloy muff incorporating the cooling fins which replaced the earlier ones machined direct in the hub. To suit the Clubmans TT regulations a speedometer and rev-counter were fitted side by side on the fork crown.

In June 1955 *Motor Cycling* finally managed to get their hands on the 500 cc Gold Star for a test and began this with a ride from London to Liverpool to catch the boat to the Island where the machine was pressed into general duties. For these it carried normal bars and footrests while performance was restricted by a non-standard silencer. While in the Isle of Man the clip-ons, rear sets and standard silencer were fitted and transformed the performance. Top speed came out at 110 mph still accelerating and third was

Road testing a DBD34 in 1980 for *Classic Bike*, **Royce Creasey gets the Clubman well over for the camera. Fast and noisy**

good for 105. With the close ratios fitted even second produced 87 mph but of course quite a lot of clutch slipping was needed to get the machine on the move. The brakes worked well, the machine handled and complaints were restricted to the noisy silencer and none too easy starting—both attributes directly traceable to the use for which it was built.

The 350 cc Gold Star was now in its final engine form but the 500 still had one more step to take in 1956 when the DBD type appeared. The main change was the fitting of the $1\frac{1}{2}$ in. GP, the largest size Amal made. In addition it had a larger headed inlet valve and different flywheels. Apart from this it was a copy of the DB which continued on into 1957.

For 1956 both sizes of machine were fitted with the megaphone shaped silencer derived from the previous year's one, and producing the correct twitter on the over-run. The gearbox gained needle rollers in the sleeve gear and this type was marked on the gearbox by an additional figure '2' along with the 'T' for layshaft needle bearings and the ratio letters. Thus came about the extra close ratio box, type RRT2, all the best Goldies are fitted with.

Another front brake made its appearance, the famous full width 190 mm unit with alloy hub bolted to iron drum with the shoes carried on an alloy backplate. To top the machine off was another optional fuel tank in light alloy taking 5 gallons to ensure no extra fuel stops in the TT.

That really brought the Gold Star to the end of its development for no DBD version of the 350 was built and little or no further changes took place. At the end of 1956 the touring versions were both dropped and 1957 saw the 500 in DB and DBD forms, together with the DB350, available in Clubmans, road racing, and scrambles builds. Late in 1957 the 350 was dropped from the lists altogether along with the road racing 500, so in 1958 only the larger capacity Clubmans and scrambles machines were built.

In 1959 the 350 returned in a curious manner for it was not listed as a machine in its own right but as a 500 fitted with the 350 engine. The 500 was only built with the DBD engine and both Clubmans and scrambles versions were listed, the later with the option of a central oil tank developed from the works scramblers and already in use on other models.

1960 saw the 350 listed as being built to special order only, still as a 500 with the smaller engine fitted, and both scrambles versions fitted with a two gallon tank as standard. This continued through 1961 and into 1962, although very few 350s were built in that year. During 1962 the 350 was finally dropped but the 500 continued, using the DBD engine, in both Clubmans and scrambles forms into 1963.

Sadly, this was to be the final year and during it production of the Gold Star came to an end. In many ways it was inevitable for the performance was no longer competitive in road racing, the Clubmans TT was long since gone and the scrambler was being superseded by much lighter two-strokes. From a practical production viewpoint the model had become far too specialised for a firm as big as BSA to build. It shared many of the jigs and fixtures with the road singles and with them replaced by a unit construction design, the Gold Star numbers just became uneconomic. Added to that was the end of production of the Lucas magneto and dynamo which meant that a major change was needed to fit an alternator. Finally it was realised that the engine had really reached the end of its development in its original, simple single, form.

From a business point of view it was correct for BSA to drop the Gold Star but its passing was mourned by enthusiasts. Fortunately for them Eddie Dow, who had been involved with the model through most of the 1950s, kept many machines going from his shop in Banbury. For the factory it was the end of the single with the twitter.

3 | 'B' range

Even before the war was over BSA had announced a four model programme, which appeared in the press early in August 1945. Three machines were much as in 1939 but the most sporting of the new range was a fresh model which had its roots in the 1940 line up. This was the B31, an overhead valve single of 350 cc based on the B29 and thus the sturdily built M series crankcase. This did of course fit in well with the production of the two M models in the range at the time but also was to bequeath a really robust lower half which could be exploited over the years.

The new model followed the lines of the pre-war M series and used the traditional BSA engine dimensions of 71 × 88 mm. Unlike the B29, it was fitted with double coil springs to restrain the valves as these proved to be as good as the hairpins and much easier to accommodate in the one piece iron cylinder head. The valve pockets in the head were capped by light alloy lids each retained by four screws and the front one carried the exhaust valve lifting mechanism. A further small plate was fixed to the side of the head by four screws and gave access to the top ends of the push rods and the inner rocker ends during assembly.

The other major change from the pre-war models lay in the adoption of telescopic forks with hydraulic damping and a friction steering damper. The remainder of the cycle parts were from the earlier designs with rigid frame, saddle, dry sump oil tank on the right, battery on left,

and toolbox between the chainstays behind the oil tank. The petrol tank had a three gallon capacity and housed the speedometer head just behind the steering column with the filler cap to one side. The speedometer was driven from the gearbox which contained four speeds engaged by a positive stop mechanism and fitted with a four-plate clutch which had Ferodo inserts and ran on a double row ball bearing.

A new design of brake was used along with the older type of hub. The rear hub was not quickly detachable at that time but both it and the new design used at the front were fitted with die-cast aluminium brake shoes. No rear stand was provided but both centre and front ones were, the latter doubling as a mudguard stay.

The following week details of two BSA patents were released, one concerning the gearbox positive stop mechanism and the other a quickly detachable wheel. The second of these was of especial interest as it reduced the essential parts to a minimum and the basic idea is still used on many modern machines. The brake drum and sprocket were formed in one with a single ball race and this assembly was clamped to the frame by a large nut. To the drum was bolted an internally splined ring and it was this which mated with an external spline on the hub itself. This hub ran on a pair of ball races and carried the two spoke flanges, both the same size. The splines were disengaged by sideways movement of the hub so a gap had to be left between it and

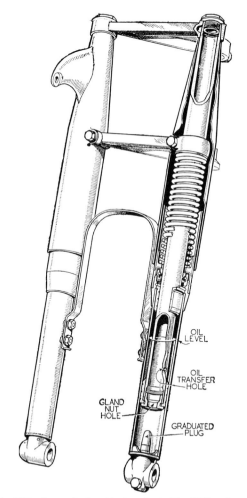

OIL LEVEL

OIL TRANSFER HOLE

GLAND NUT HOLE

GRADUATED PLUG

The BSA telescopic front forks adopted in 1945 and used for many years and models

the frame which was filled with a distance piece. A single long bolt went straight through the hub and screwed into the drum carrying bolt to secure the whole wheel in place. It was a design to be blessed if you suffered a rear wheel puncture.

This was not the last word on the rear hub, for in May 1946 another patent was published to cover the famous crinkle hub with straight spokes. In this the centre tube carrying the bearings was mounted in another tube whose ends were flared out into a crinkle pattern. The two tubes were held together by rivets which could, and did, work loose and shear under really heavy loads in later years but were quite adequate for a touring 350. The crinkle pattern gave the correct angle for the spokes to cross over one another in the lacing pattern, while the natural die release angle ensured they laid into the rim centre. The drum side was of a larger diameter than the other to allow the assembly of spokes past the hub shell.

At the front end a new hub was needed to fit the telescopic forks and this was built up from a number of steel pressings on a tube carrying two ball races and a hollow centre. The ends of the centre were threaded and carried nuts, one of which clamped to a ball race and the other did the same, but also held the brake backplate in position. Through the centre went a spindle with a distance collar on the side away from the brake and this was clamped into the left fork leg by a cross pinch bolt. The end of the spindle carried a left hand thread and screwed into the right fork leg so that wheel removal was very quick and easy.

The forks themselves were simple and robust with external springs under the shrouds and hydraulic bump stops. The design was to prove very successful and popular for all manner of machines, both from the BSA range and outside it, and was used by many special builders over the years. It comprised in essence two tubes with bearings, an oil seal and control over the oil flow.

To this was added the fittings to attach it to the machine and also carry the headlamp and mudguard. Head race adjustment was easy and nearly 6 in. of fork deflection were available.

During late 1946 a further patent was taken out for a refinement to the front forks which added a valve, an additional internal spring and a long tube with a series of metering cross holes. This was designed to give progressive damping on both bump and rebound and indicates the type of advanced thinking indulged in by Perrigo and Perkins on BSA's behalf.

In March 1946 *Motor Cycling* published a road test on the B31 and found it cruised very comfortably at 60 mph with a maximum of 73 mph. Fuel consumption was seldom below 75 mpg and often much more frugal. There was nothing really exceptional in the performance but it was delivered in a smooth easy manner that, coupled with good handling and a comfortable riding position, enabled 45 mph averages to be accomplished without fuss. The new brakes were excellent and worked well in all conditions. Criticisms were minor and concerned the saddle position for tall riders, the gear lever position, and a small leak from the oil tank cap.

Before this test, in January, a new single cylinder model was announced, the B32 competition version of the road machine. While it used much of the B31 in its make-up, it had a distinct sporting appearance with high level exhaust system and silencer, competition tyres and chrome plated mudguards, stays, front stand and rear chainguard. The gearing was lowered to suit trials and scrambles and, while the machine was fitted with magdyno and headlamp as standard, it was also available with a separate magneto and a battery lighting set to special order. A crankcase shield was fitted and the machine used the standard rigid frame and telescopic front forks.

In January 1947 the range was expanded further when the public demand for a 500 cc edition of the popular road single resulted in the

Above **Competition model fitted with alloy head and barrel, full lighting equipment, raised silencer and saddle**

Top **London Fire Brigade ladies on a world tour with plunger framed singles of 1953 type. Typical 'B' range role that they excelled in**

Right **The 500 cc B33 all iron engine with its push rod tunnel and mag-dyno. The Monobloc dates it as 1955 or later**

Right **The famous BSA crinkle hub introduced in 1946 with straight spokes. Very quickly detachable**

Below **Component parts of the 'B' range engine shown in exploded if cramped form on BSA service sheet 301, a great asset to the home mechanic**

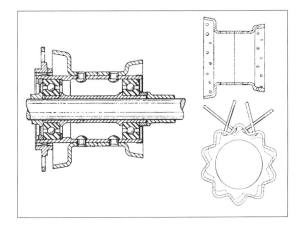

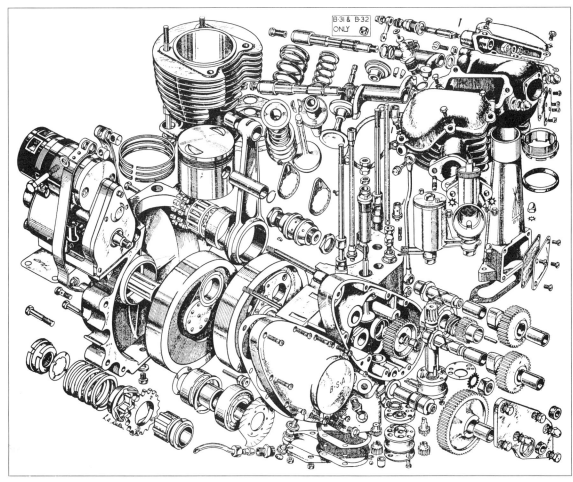

B33. This was an enlarged version of the B31 with engine dimensions of 85×88 mm and the increase in bore size made for a nearly square unit. A heavier flywheel was fitted, but in other respects the machine was a repeat of the 350 with raised gearing and a slightly fatter rear tyre.

In May *Motor Cycling* had one on test and liked it as much as the 350. They found it as fast in third as the 350 could manage in top and good for 82 mph in the fourth ratio. Fuel consumption still bettered 70 mpg, and the overall performance was extremely lively. The added speed failed to disturb the brakes, which remained fully on top of the situation at all times. The transmission worked well and the machine was generally quiet both mechanically and from the exhaust.

It was hardly surprising that the 500 cc road model was joined by a competition version, the B34, in April that year and this followed exactly the same lines as the B32 that had preceded it. It too was tested by *Motor Cycling* both on the road and through a number of trials sections from which it emerged with flying colours. The gearing was perhaps a compromise at one tooth down from the B33, and the tester suggested that two down and a spare sprocket for road use would make the machine even nicer. Both sprockets were available.

In July it became easier to distinguish the B33 from its smaller brother as it gained a half-inch wide matt silver stripe down the centre of each mudguard.

For 1948 a number of changes were incorporated, with drain plugs appearing in oil tanks and at the bottoms of telescopic fork legs, domed headlamp glasses being adopted and standard handlebars used for all models. The speedometers of the B group machines left the petrol tank and took up a much better position on a small bracket bolted to the centre of the top fork yoke. The upper foot of the drive cable to the speedometer was armoured for protection. The competition models received folding kick-start pedals and no doubt these were quickly bought and fitted to all the existing machines in the field.

Aside from some options in the finish to petrol tank and wheel rims, that was it. In these days production was the essential thing so alterations were kept to a minimum and only introduced where they caused little or no disruption to the business of making machines.

Early in 1948 *The Motor Cycle* had the chance to road test a B31 and recorded the same maximum speed as their opposition. They summed the machine up as sound with a good all-round performance, and this is a fair assessment. Criticisms were levelled at the heaviness of the front brake, exposure of the magneto points to the vagaries of the weather, and the awkward centre stand which highlighted the absence of a lifting handle. BSA never were very good at stand design.

1949 brought few changes to the overhead valve singles, although the dynamo was improved and the plunger frame became available for any of the B model range. The clutch, gearbox, front forks and hubs all became common on the B and M ranges. All models were equipped with a sealed beam headlamp and the 350 cc competition B32 was given a further option of an alloy head and barrel. These were a copy of the iron parts so the separate push rod tunnel was still retained as it had been on the works machines which had enjoyed the 20 lb weight saving since 1946.

The 500 cc B34 was given the same option in 1950 after the appearance of the similar size Gold Star, while both it, the B32 and both road models continued unaltered in their general build. The optional finishes for the road machines continued to be available with green tank and wheel centres for the 350 and red for the 500.

1951 left the road models alone but brought in a modified competition frame with a steeper head angle. The following year saw the alloy barrels and heads changed to the Gold Star

pattern with integral push rod tunnel but otherwise only brake details were changed. A 2 gallon alloy petrol tank became available as an option for the competition machines.

March 1952 finally brought a change to the petrol tank styling and finish which had remained unaltered since 1945. The new style did away with the need to chrome plate the tank and may well have been encouraged by the shortage of the material at that time. The tanks were painted all over and carried a round BSA badge which extended back in a wing pattern to the kneegrip. The badges were finished in chrome plate and yellow while the tanks themselves were in green, blue, red, matt silver and black, depending on the model, the road 350 being in green and the 500 in red. The competition models remained as before in their chrome plate and silver.

In the middle of the year *Motor Cycling* once again road tested a B31, this time with the optional plunger rear suspension, and found it little changed. Top speed was within one mph, cruising still took place at 60 and consumption never dropped below 70 mpg. Starting was easy but gear changing less so, while the machine snaked on one fast bumpy corner. Comfort was assisted by the dualseat and, as always, the centre stand was too high and hard work to use. I know for I owned one of these models and it performed much as the tester wrote, although mine always behaved itself even over some atrocious, downhill, bumpy curves. My one was equally reliable and, as I had racing linings, my brakes were even better than those of the test machine, good though they were.

With 1953 came an easement of the chromium supply problem and the reappearance of plating together with a change of colour and style. The two road models received cowls to their headlamps which faired them to the forks

and carried the lighting switch on the left and the ammeter on the right, albeit in a position in which it could not be read from the saddle. The headlamp was itself changed to the type with underslung pilot lamp, a useless idea that few riders liked.

At the other end of the machines a new number plate appeared with boxed in sides, a

Every East Sussex patrolman got a spare on this occasion for the 14 men have 28 B31s to ride. The Inspector walked or went by car

Lucas 525 Diacon stop and tail lamp, and a round reflector at the base of the plate. The petrol tank mounting was changed to insulate it from the frame, while engines received more fins on the cylinder and finned collars on the exhaust pipes.

All wheel rims became chrome plated while the 500 received an 8 in. front brake and a valanced front mudguard which carried the front number plate on its sides. Internally the 500 connecting rod was shortened by $\frac{1}{2}$ in. and carried a split skirt piston. The gudgeon pin hole in this was $\frac{1}{2}$ in. lower than its solid skirt predecessor so the overall engine dimensions remained unchanged.

Externally an improved toolbox was fitted to any machine equipped with the plunger rear

The B31 in the form built in 1956 and 1957 with full width alloy hubs and cowled headlamp. Mag-dyno was replaced by alternator in the following year and cowl, brakes and stand all changed

suspension and the petrol tanks received large, chrome plated, side panels which encompassed the 1952 style badge together with the kneegrip. The colour for both road models was maroon for all painted parts with the option of black except for the tank which retained its maroon colour regardless. The competition models took the chrome plating, matt silver panels and polished aluminium of the Gold Stars and so lost their distinguishing green or red tank sides.

In March 1953 *The Motor Cycle* road tested a B33 and found it good for 80 mph while retaining all the known assets of the simple reliable single. The larger front brake proved to be even more potent than its predecessor and the well

valanced front mudguard was a boon in wet weather.

1954 brought a more radical change with the adoption of a swinging fork frame by the competition models and those road machines destined for export. At home they continued either rigid or with plungers. The new frame followed the lines of that used by the Gold Star and was of all-welded construction. With the

Above **Two young men about to set off on their BSA singles—destination New Zealand**

Below **The competition model B34 in 1957 with alloy engine and central oil tank which made it a copy of the Gold Star**

new frame went the polished aluminium alloy chaincase and the competition machines were all built with alloy heads and barrels and fitted with magnetos. The tank styling of all the road models was modified to simple large chrome plated side panels with round piled arms badges. The tank fixing became a single bolt screwed into a lug in the top of the tank frame tube and covered with a rubber bung carrying the BSA symbol.

Within a year the swinging fork frame had become an option for the home market road machines and with it went the Gold Star type gearbox fitted with the standard ratios. Fitted at the same time were the new Monobloc carburet-

tor, a new rear mudguard on the 350 and a new rubber air cleaner connector on the 500. A steering head lock was fitted into the top fork crown and all models had plastic fuel pipes and a two-lobe engine shaft shock absorber. Where the new frame option was not taken up the plunger frame was supplied, so the rigid machines were no longer listed at all.

However, the competition models did turn to a rigid frame which was based on the duplex type and was all welded. The front part followed the usual lines with kinked right lower tube to clear the oil pump but these tubes then ran back to the rear wheel to join two further chainstays which ran up to the top tube. A single saddle tube supported the oil tank and the mounting plates above the gearbox. With upturned silencer the models were to be one of the last of the big four stroke singles used for trials.

1956 brought further changes for the swinging fork frame became standard for the road machines along with a dualseat and new, full width, alloy brakes in both wheels. In each the adjuster was built into the shoe fulcrum not the lever and the shoes were wider than before. A three-piece rear chaincase was available as an option and the colour choice was maroon or black with chrome tank panels still carrying the round piled arms badge. The competition jobs continued without change.

The Motor Cycle road tested a B31 with swinging fork frame during the year and found it little changed from 1946, although a good deal heavier. It started, ran, steered and stopped in a smooth, serene and reliable manner just as always. It offered very full equipment with chaincase, prop stand, ammeter and comfortable dualseat but still the centre stand took a real heave to pull the bike up onto it.

1957 brought little change to the road machines but the competition ones acquired the swinging fork frame once more and with it a central oil tank tucked well out of harms way. They thus became a replica of the Gold Star but

with the small fin engine and B31 crankcase, while the oil tank was to be fitted as standard to the Gold Star scrambler later on. Late in the year the models were dropped for they now had no role to play in the model line up and were really only a complication.

The road machines continued on and for 1958 received quite a number of changes. The most complex of these concerned the electrics for the old magdyno was replaced by an alternator in the chaincase and coil ignition. With the rotor on the end of the crankshaft the shock absorber had to be moved so the clutch was modified to incorporate a three-vane damper. The magneto drive remained, for in place of the old unit sat a small contact breaker and advance unit with a neat cap. With this change came a new wiring loom and the combined lights and ignition switches were positioned to the right of the speedometer, balanced by an ammeter on the left. All were carried in a new cylindrical headlamp cowl which was attached to a flat upper fork shroud within which the horn was sited.

The hubs were new with ribbed, full width, cast iron drums and these carried brakes of the same size as the 1945 B31. Both were cable operated, the cables having knurled adjusters, and the rear was worked by the brake pedal pivoting in the hollow fork spindle with a small lever on the right end to work the cable. The rims of the back plates and hub end covers were polished. The rear chain was made wider and the centre stand altered to roll-on feet which improved it somewhat.

The finish also changed with frame and forks in black while the mudguards, petrol tank and oil tank were almond green for the 350 and gunmetal grey for the 500. In both cases the chrome plated tank panels were still fitted along with the round tank badges.

A B33 was tested by *The Motor Cycle* and proved to retain all the charm of the British single, thumping along up to the legal limit with

little regard for hills or headwinds. Top speed was 81 mph one way but speed was never what the B range was about. Reliable, year in, year out motorcycling was its forte and one it excelled in to the end of its days.

Rather sadly these were now drawing near for quicker, lighter, unit-construction replacements were to come from Small Heath and the easy flow of weighty power that is the great charm of any engine with heavy flywheels and soft valve timing was to be replaced by revs. Not to everyone's liking but late in 1959 the B31 was dropped from the model list.

For 1960 the B33 carried a new tank with pear-shaped badges, handlebar adjusters for the clutch and front brake, and an altered rear brake but only because these features were common with other models in the range. That year it too was dropped to bring the old fashioned but charming 'B' range of road singles to an end.

Left **The 1956 quickly detachable, full width, light alloy rear hub. The optional full chaincase gave access to the four hub nuts**

Below **1958 to 1960 single in final form with alternator and points. This is the B33 fitted with chaincase and the cast iron hubs**

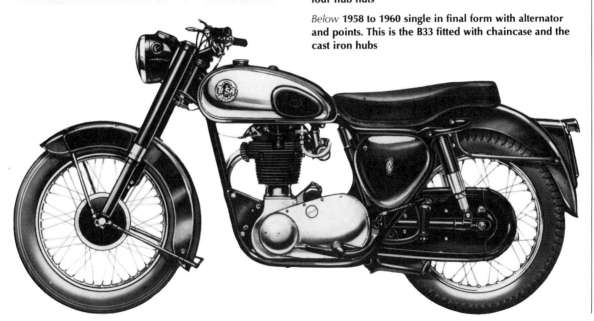

4 | Side valve and sidecar

When the new range was announced for 1937 it was the most natural thing at the time that it contained machines with side valve engines in frames designed to cope with the stresses of sidecar use. The prospective buyer could always plump for the big vee-twin but this was rather an old design and a little large for many owners, who preferred the simple single with its immense slogging power derived from the valve position and a pair of heavy flywheels.

BSA catered for this market with two models, the M20 and M21, of 500 and 600 cc respectively. The smaller model used the same engine dimensions as its more sporting ohv brothers, while the early M21 retained the 85 × 105 mm of the old wet sump engine before changing to 82 × 112 mm for 1938 to become a long stroke version of the M20. Both engines were to retain these dimensions throughout their lives.

For 1938 both models continued with the changes to the idler gear bushes and horn position as on other machines, while the finish of chrome plating with green panels for the petrol tank became standard.

1939 brought the new timing gear with fixed cam spindles common to most of the range and a new de-luxe M20 alongside the standard one. Both M20s and the M21 received footchange gearboxes and also the larger oil tank, re-positioned toolbox and new petrol tanks. Both the de-luxe M20 and the M21 were fitted with tank top instrument panels, valanced mud-

The 500 cc side valve M20 in 1946 when the finish in black and silver was as spartan as the ride with girders and saddle

For the sporting sidecar owner BSA fitted the B33 engine to the 'M' frame to make the M33 with brighter tank in 1948

guards and quickly detachable rear wheels, while the standard M20 used a tubular silencer. The finish of all three machines was changed from the previous year and the tanks carried the round badge as used in 1939 in place of the earlier oval shape.

The two versions of the M20 failed to last into the 1940 range, which was much curtailed but contained five side valve models out of a total of eight, the five being the 250 cc C10, 350 cc C12, 500 cc M20, 600 cc M21 and 1000 cc vee-twin G14. The two big singles were little changed except that both had tubular silencers, the tank finish was again changed and the tank badges were oval once more. The valanced mudguards and tank top instrument panel were both retained.

The performance of these side valve machines

was not exactly startling as was shown by road tests conducted by *Motor Cycling* in 1938 on a combination M21 and in 1939 on the solo version. The solo reached a maximum of 69 mph and cruised comfortably around 45 to 50 mph, while the outfit managed 54 mph maximum although it would cruise at 45 mph. However, in those days of limited traffic, no motorways, and few by-passes these were acceptable figures for the people who bought the machines. Consumption was 56 mpg for the solo and 48 mpg sidecar, which is not unreasonable for low compression side valve engines hauling along a fair weight.

Oil consumption was minimal and the low down pull and engine flexibility all that could be desired. As was usual in those times, the machines were forced through some mild trials

for often owners lived on farms or had similar problems of rutted lanes to navigate to reach their front door; motorcycles were expected to cope with this type of going and deal with it in the worst depths of winter.

And then BSA went to war. The small arms section of the company had been resurrected in 1935 after many years of idleness and the very special rifle machinery was taken out of store. The men with the special skills were found and brought back to BSA to form the nucleus of a very large organisation spread over many factories.

During the war it poured out an incredible quantity of munitions and along with them came reconaissance cars, armoured cars, bicycles and, of course, the motorcycles. Before the war they had already begun supplying the M20 and also some 250 cc machines for training purposes and at the outbreak produced the B30 as already described. However, in the end the Ministry stuck to the M20 although BSA themselves considered it heavy, rather clumsy to use and not to have enough ground clearance. The authorities felt that one model would avoid complications with spares and service while the M20 was known to be simple, very tough and reliable. The records show that 126,334 BSA motorcycles were supplied to the War Office during the conflict.

The machines were simply khaki coloured M20s with a headlamp mask and canvas pannier bags on steel frames. Pillion seats and footrests were fitted for it was required that officers up to a certain rank could be transported by bike rather than staff car if necessary. For the western desert a rubber hose connected the carburettor to a special Vokes air cleaner carried on the top of the petrol tank, but the rear chain had to take its chance in the sand.

The dispatch riders, known as Don Rs, were really by definition individuals for all had to have the initiative to find their way across country to a map reference in the dark with neither lights or signposts. This was in sharp contrast to the usual army style of 'orders is orders' and it was to be expected that riders took to looking after the machines they rode. In turn this led to minor and unobtrusive changes and a keen desire to hang onto a particular bike. Often this could be done by swapping parts so that a single machine would finish up with all the dud parts and could then be consigned to the workshops. At this point machines were stripped and rebuilt with the first items from the stores so there was no continuity of engine and frame numbers, much less gearboxes, forks or electrical parts.

When the war ended the army had a vast surplus of machines on its hands and many were stored in dumps to be sold in batches to the trade. With a public clamouring for any sort of machine there was a ready market waiting to snap these up and they were sold in their army form in some cases, while in others some attempt was made to give them a civilian appearance. Often this was little more than an all-over coat of paint and the removal of the most obviously military parts. They served a need at the time but before many years had past most were traded in or swapped as more glamorous mounts became available. Few now remain, although the volumes of spares that some dealers bought up seem to be unending.

1953 version of the sidevalve model when it had gained the standard headlamp cowl and underslung pilot lamp used on other models. These and the chrome plated tank panels look strangely at variance with the 'M' range image

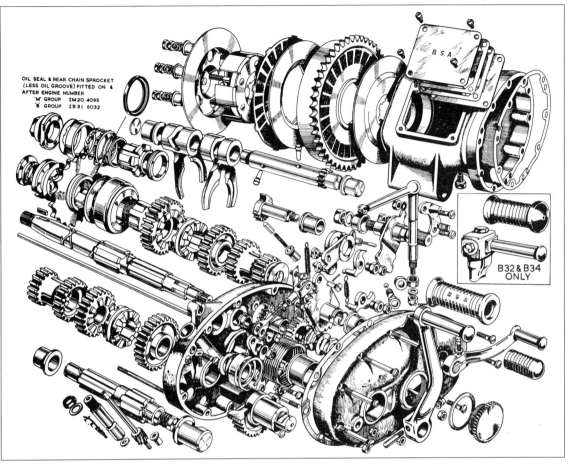

OIL SEAL & REAR CHAIN SPROCKET
(LESS OIL GROOVE) FITTED ON &
AFTER ENGINE NUMBER
'M' GROUP   ZM20 4095
'B' GROUP   ZB31 6032

B32 & B34
ONLY

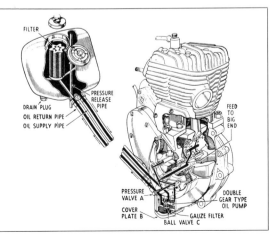

FILTER

DRAIN PLUG
OIL RETURN PIPE
OIL SUPPLY PIPE

PRESSURE
RELEASE
PIPE

FEED
TO
BIG
END

PRESSURE
VALVE A

COVER
PLATE B

DOUBLE
GEAR TYPE
OIL PUMP

GAUZE FILTER
BALL VALVE C

Above **The four speed BSA gearbox used on the 'B' and 'M' ranges from 1950. This is service sheet 602 which shows all the parts in the assembly**

Left **Lubrication system for the side valve engine with oil feed to cam spindles. Overhead valve models used the same system plus a rocker oil line**

After the war the M20 reappeared as part of a four model programme in August 1945. The machine was the WD model and so based on the 1940 machine with minimal changes. These amounted to such details as an engine steady running back instead of forward, different toolbox catch, luggage grid on the rear mudguard which, like the front, no longer had valances, and another style of petrol tank no longer fitted with an instrument panel. This item with lighting switch and ammeter was fixed to the rear of the headlamp shell while the tank finish was matt silver lined in black with the bulk of the machine, including the wheel rims, in black. Unlike the army issue there was some chrome plating and the gearbox end cover, timing covers, and valve chest plate were highly polished. The speedometer, like the headlamp, took its chances riding on the top of the girder forks.

Early in 1946 the M21 also returned to the scene and followed the same lines as its smaller brother in specification and colour.

The two machines continued on in this form through 1947, but for 1948 were tidied up a little and had a number of items changed to those already used on the B range. These included the battery carrier, petrol filler cap and toolbox, which lost all resemblance to the wartime items, while the speedometer moved to a central position, the horn and dipswitch copied the ohv machines and the ignition and valve lifter levers were positioned together on the handlebars. The petrol tank shape was changed to that of the B range and, while the standard finish was not changed, there was an option of chrome plating with matt silver panels lined in black.

New for 1948 was an overhead valve version of the M20 produced by fitting the B33 engine into the rigid frame used by the side valve engines and fitted with sidecar lugs as standard. This model was called the M33. It retained the girder forks but was fitted with a quickly detachable rear wheel and the chrome plated optional M20

The M33 with teles and plunger rear suspension. The front down tube has been pulled back for front mudguard clearance

Above **An M20 on service training in the desert sand where one boy signaller is helping another (Imperial War Museum)**

Right **Redcaps from two armies meeting at Tinchbray cross roads in August 1944. The Limeys on the M20 are L/Cpls Hornsby and Baker and their US cousins are PACs Poosednik and Onika (IWM)**

tank as standard. It also had wheel rims chrome plated with matt silver centres, lined black, so looked less sombre than the side valve machines.

It was designed to give the sidecar driver a machine with a little more snap and a *Motor Cycling* road test showed that it did just this with the top speed with sidecar up to 63 mph and consumption better than 50 mpg. Acceleration was brisk in comparison with the sidevalve motors and thus main road averages of 40 mph could be managed without much bother. There was no sidecar brake and this reflected in the braking figures recorded although the front unit tried its best to the point of squealing the tyre even in the dry.

In June 1948 a major change was introduced on all three M models with the adoption of the standard telescopic front forks in place of the girders. To give clearance to the front mudguard on full fork deflection the frame was modified by shortening the downtube and tucking it further back. This gave a small kink to the line from steering head down to the front engine plates. The prices of the machines all rose slightly.

Further rationalisation took place for 1949 with the gearbox for both B and M ranges

becoming common as were the forks and front wheels. There were, of course, many other detail items used on all the heavier models in the whole of the BSA range and in that year these included the Lucas sealed beam headlamp units.

There were no changes to the M range for 1950 but 1951 brought light alloy cylinder heads for both side valve models. These had bolder fins and a phosphor bronze insert to take the sparking plug as a precaution against stripped threads. As on the iron ones, a small plug was still provided to assist setting the ignition timing and the compression ratios remained at 4·9 for the 500 and 5·0 for the M21. A further change introduced for 1951 was that the plunger frame became available for any of the range but at first was only fitted to those machines destined for export.

Early in the year *Motor Cycling* road tested an M20 in its solo trim and with the rigid frame. It was a pleasant enough mount and quite comfortable thanks to a good riding position and the saddle. It proved to be good for 64 mph and cruised well at just under 50, when it returned some 70 mpg. With its massive flywheels, low compression ratio, and soft valve timing the engine was quite happy to pull from low speeds so it was essentially a top gear machine once underway. The brakes were more than adequate for the performance and the whole machine gave the rider pleasant and leisurely travel through the countryside.

For 1952 there were detail improvements to the brakes, the plunger frame continued as an option and was joined by a dualseat if the rider required one. During the year there was the chromium shortage so petrol tanks were painted all over and the round badge with flying wing was adopted by the M range, along with the B models. On both, this was changed to the chrome plated side panels once the supply position had eased.

The 1953 range had a good few changes and the cowled headlight, underslung pilot, new rear

number plate, and improved toolbox for the plunger frame, all appeared on the M models as well as the B. The tank colour became maroon with separate chrome plated side panels but the remainder of the machines stayed black. As the M33 used the standard road going ohv 500 cc unit it automatically acquired the modified unit with shorter connecting rod and altered piston.

The three models in either rigid or plunger frame forms continued through 1954 but with the round plastic tank badges with the piled arms symbol. For the following year they received the steering lock and two lobe shock absorber cam on the crankshaft end used by other machines in the BSA range.

During 1955 *Motor Cycling* road tested two models from the M range, both with sidecars attached, and the first was an M21. Rather as expected it had little changed from the pre-war version with similar performance although comfort was aided by the sprung frame. Braking was aided by a drum on the sidecar wheel so in this area the figures were of an acceptable standard. The second test was of an M33 and again the results were very much as before in all areas. In both cases the pulling of the engine was lusty and the machine completely reliable; exactly as expected from the models.

Later that year the solid, reliable, old M20 was dropped from the model range for its purpose was better served by the other machines, and for 1956 the options were restricted a little. The M33 was fitted with the plunger frame as standard, although this still remained an option for the M21. For seating the ohv model had a dualseat, while the side valve one continued with its saddle, and both were fitted with the 8 in. front brake and a valanced front mudguard. The finish was also modified with the tank in maroon with cream panels and the remainder in black, although the chrome plated tank panels remained available as an option.

1957 brought no further alterations and during

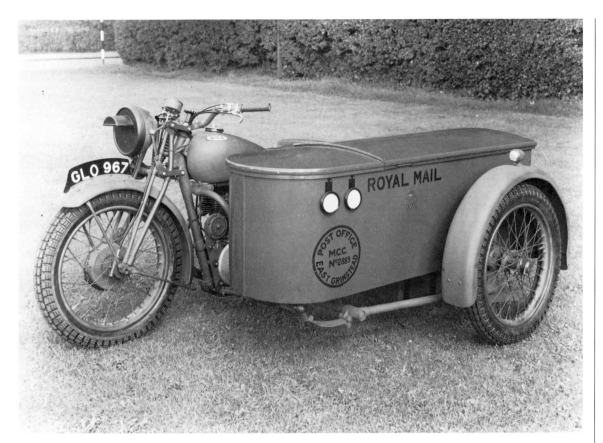

Nice wartime photo of what appears to be a new M20 about to do its bit for the Post Office complete with headlamp mask that made night travel hazardous (PO)

it the M range shrunk once more when the M33 was dropped in August. No doubt one of the reasons was the impending change to AC electrics on the ohv road singles and for the traditional sidecar man the magdyno was as essential to him as his steering damper.

The M21 plodded on its way, rather unmoved by all the changes around it, perhaps carried on by the sheer inertia of its massive flywheels. By the end of 1958 it was no longer listed but was still available to special order, although with plunger rear suspension only. By then it was the only surviving British built side valve and was still in demand by the AA and the armed forces. For these markets it was often given special extra equipment to suit the job it was destined for and naturally the finish was done to match the force

who used it.

It was still there as the 1950s came to a close but only for the specialist users and the occasional rider who still insisted on having a big sidevalve engine to pull him along. It could not really continue of course and, like the Gold Star and the B range, was dependent on the supply of magdynos from Lucas. An alternator version was also built from 1961.

Finally it had to come to an end and, in 1963 the sidevalve 600 was dropped and so the M range was no more.

5 | Lightweights

When the new B range was introduced in 1937 it contained both 250 and 350 cc machines. As both shared many common cycle parts this made the smaller machines overweight for their power, which was unfortunate as they were nice motorcycles. The engines had the same potential as their larger brethren but economics dictated that a 250 cc Gold Star would not then be a financial proposition.

They went on to call for a simpler and cheaper small capacity range and, although the B models continued in ohv form up to 1939, their replacements and the real BSA lightweights first appeared in January 1938.

The first model was the C10, a simple machine with side valve engine, coil ignition and three speed gearbox. In many ways it followed the lines of the B range and used the same oil pump fitted in the same way in the right crankcase half. The use of coil ignition was considered a little unusual at the time and it was controlled by points in a car type housing incorporating a centrifugal advance and retard mechanism. This whole assembly was skew gear driven from the camshaft and lay forward at 45 degrees in its clamp in the timing chest which allowed it to be easily rotated to set the ignition timing.

The timing side was very simply constructed with the camshaft running in bushes in the crankcase and timing cover directly above the crankshaft from which it was driven by spur gears. The lower one incorporated the oil pump

drive worm while the upper was pressed and keyed to the camshaft machined in one with the two cams and the points drive. Above the camshaft a solid pin was pressed into the crankcase wall and carried two cam followers which moved tappets and hence the valves. Access for tappet adjustment was via the normal small plate attached to the side of the cylinder with four small screws.

The engine had the usual BSA dimensions of 63 × 80 mm and a detachable head on the cast iron barrel. The crankshaft ran in a drive side ball race and plain timing bush and was of built up

1939 C11 with oil compartment built into the petrol tank. The cycle parts were common for the 'C' range although wheel sizes did vary

construction with a roller big end. At the rear of the right crankcase half was clamped a dynamo and this was chain driven from the extreme end of the camshaft. Rotation of the dynamo body provided a means of adjusting the chain which was enclosed by a light outer cover.

The mixture was supplied by an Amal carburettor controlled by a hand throttle lever, while the exhaust system was downswept and carried

a tubular silencer. Primary drive was by chain, totally enclosed in a cover, and the engine sprocket incorporated a cush drive. A two plate cork clutch was fitted to drive the three speed handchange gearbox and both these items followed normal BSA practice for the times. The rear chain was on the left as usual.

The frame was a simple diamond of brazed-up tubular construction and employed light girder forks at the front while the rear end was rigid. Wheels and brakes came from the 250 cc B range along with many of the cycle fittings. The tank however was new and contained both petrol and oil, along with an oil filter, in separate compartments. This allowed the toolbox to be fitted to the seat tube to balance the battery on the left, while the horn went above the dynamo, the coil under the back of the tank, and the dynamo regulator under the front. A centre stand was fitted.

The finish was black with green tank and chrome plated exhaust system, headlamp rim and handlebars. The price was £37 10s 0d with the speedometer a further £2 10s 0d.

In 1939 the basic C10 was joined by a de-luxe model fitted with a footchange gearbox. This retained the existing ratios but was fitted with a new style end cover and revised method of clutch operation and adjustment. It also had an oil bath primary chaincase but still retained the lever throttle. Finish was in black with the petrol tank in matt silver with maroon lining. The silencer had an upward tilt, induced by a bend in the exhaust pipe, and the same feature was used on the standard model. This had the same tank finish as the de-luxe and its regulator moved to a position under the saddle.

At the same time an overhead valve version, the C11, was introduced. This shared many of the C10s parts in the engine and used the same transmission as the de-luxe model. The C11 did have a twistgrip throttle.

Its engine had one marked similarity to the 1935 Francis Barnett Stag which had the same

The postwar C11 fitted with telescopic forks, separate oil tank, speedometer in tank, non-standard dualseat but with drip shield missing under carburettor

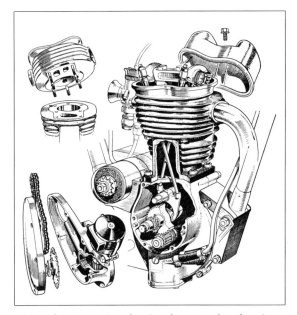

Above **The C11 engine showing the crossed push rods, points housing and dynamo drive. The front oil connections indicate a 1939 model, postwar they ran from behind the pump casting**

Right **Exploded drawing of the C10L engine taken from service sheet 401A. Apart from alternator and points housing little changed since its 1938 debut**

Above **Last version of C10 with points housing in 1953, still with sprung saddle but rigid frame**

layout for the camshaft and a drive to the magneto which sat behind the cylinder. As in the Stag, the C11 had hardened steel rockers pivoting on a single pin above the camshaft and these moved a pair of push rods which ran up in a tunnel cast in the side of the barrel and crossed over within it. Thus the forward rocker was associated with the inlet valve.

The valves lay at a small included angle in the head and were thus roughly parallel to the push rods. The rockers lay across the head and pivoted on pins formed at an angle and as one forging held to the head by two bolts. The rockers were end loaded by springs to prevent rattle and carried adjusters at the push rod ends.

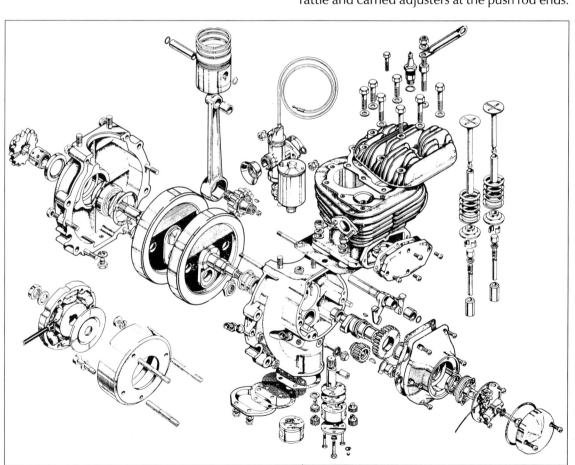

The whole of the valve gear was lubricated by oil mist passing up the push rod tunnel and enclosed by a large cover retained by a single screw. The cover contained the two engine breathers, each a cone containing steel wool which allowed the air out but retained the oil mist. Each valve was held to its seat by two coil springs retained by a collar and cotters.

The cylinder head was originally designed to be cast in one with the barrel but public reaction required that the parts be separate so the head carried seven studs which projected down through the cylinder fins to receive their nuts. The barrel was held by six studs at its flange.

For the rest, the machine copied the de-luxe C10 to provide a sound and reliable ride-to-work bike capable of about 60 mph and 100 mpg. Not the most exciting machine but cheap to buy and run, and very much in the BSA tradition of providing transport for people.

The 1940 range was to contain the C10 and C11, both with the footchange gearbox, and a new and larger model with side valve engine, the C12. This was of 350 cc and followed the same format as the C10 in nearly every detail. One of the few differences was the use of a long bodied Amal on the C12 and not the more usual short instrument. It was geared up one tooth at the engine and was hard to distinguish from its smaller brother.

All three C models ceased production at the start of the war and only the 250s reappeared after it, late in 1945. Both looked much as in 1939 but a change had been made in the position of the oil tank which was no longer combined with the fuel but bolted to the saddle tube on the right side as with the larger models. To accommodate this move the oil pipe connections in the crankcase were moved from their pre-war position at the front of the crankcase to behind it. From there the two pipes ran straight up and

1957 publicity photo of C10L and Bantam Major. The posed setting, the clothes and the offered cigarette are typical of the period

back to the oil tank. A further change to the lubrication system was the fitting of a disc clack valve in the side of the crankcase behind the primary chaincase. A triangular toolbox was fixed between the two chainstays on the right, the gear pedal shape altered, a tyrepump located beneath the petrol tank and the silencer positioned horizontal with the ground without the pre-war uptilted end. Cycle parts remained as before, but the petrol tank was new with an increased capacity and provision for the speedometer to mount next to the filler cap. The finish was black with the petrol tank chrome plated with matt silver panels lined in black, while the wheels had matching rims in matt silver with black lines.

In January 1946 *The Motor Cycle* had one of the new C11 models for a road impression and over 300 miles it proved very satisfactory. It was simple, robust and ideal for its job of commuting with the occasional longer journey. Top speed was over 60 mph and consumption bettered

80 mpg under the hardest of riding. The machine performed well in all departments and had many excellent detail points to make it ideal for its usual buyer—the rider seeking transport without tears.

In April a major change to both models occurred with the adoption of telescopic front forks. These followed the normal BSA form with shrouded fork springs and hydraulic damping which the road tester from *Motor Cycling* fully appreciated late in the year when a lorry dropped some masonry in his path. Otherwise the formal test confirmed the earlier impression of a simple, reliable machine for all seasons. Controls remained at a minimum with the ignition switch in the centre of the lighting one in the rear of the headlamp shell. There were no ignition, valve lifter or air levers so the bars presented a very clean appearance, while instruments comprised the tank mounted speedometer and an ammeter ahead of the light switch.

Above **Control layout of the C10L in 1954 when fitted with the Bantam forks and lamp. The awful horn button remained for years rather than combining with the dip switch**

Left **Drive side of the C10L with case removed to show alternator and clutch. Light alloy cylinder head and cover plate behind cylinder were features. Rectifier under saddle is standard size for time**

No further changes were made that year or the following one, but for 1948 a de-luxe version of the C11 was added which had a special finish with blue tank panels and wheel rim centres. Both ohv machines were fitted with carburettor drip shields to keep any fuel about clear of the dynamo, while all C models received quick action twistgrips. For 1949 the dynamo output was increased and sealed beam headlamps fitted, while all three machines continued in this form through 1950.

The following year brought a number of changes and options with an alloy head being fitted to the C10 and a barrel with increased finning to the C11. Both models had the horn button screwed into the top of the front brake lever pivot block, a position in which it was completely inaccessible to anyone in a hurry. Ergonomics were not the strong point of the British industry around that time. The model options were two in number and available for both side and overhead valve machines, although initially for export only. The first was the provision of rear suspension with a simple plunger system contained in spring boxes. It had no damping, other than friction and grease, and

rather limited movement. The second option was a four-speed gearbox based on the design used for the larger models but fitted into a shell shaped to suit the existing mountings. The extra ratio allowed the rather high bottom gear to be lowered while the gaps between the gears were reduced. The new box shell presented a very clean exterior to the world and internally followed the lines of the medium weight box with regard to layout, gears, selectors, and change mechanism.

For 1952 the machines continued as they were, apart from a sleeve gear oil seal added to the four-speed gearbox, but were listed differently. The basic standard models had rigid frames and three speeds with the plunger frame an option while the de-luxe models were fitted with both rear suspension and four speeds. In all this gave a choice of six possible combinations to the potential buyer, although not all would be found in the showroom.

The effects of the nickel shortage had already been seen in the tank finish but this problem faded by 1953 to leave the C range in maroon with styled, chrome plated, tank panels. At long last the speedometer moved out of the petrol

Left **The four speed gearbox used on the C12 when it was introduced in 1956. The layshaft ran in needle races**

Below **The C12 frame with its hydraulically damped rear suspension units. Note engine plates**

tank to a position on the front forks where it could be read much more easily. A dualseat became available as an option and the rear number plate and its light were tidied up, as on the larger machines. The C11 wheels also changed to match the C10 in size which lowered the effective gearing a little.

In April 1953 *Motor Cycling* tested a C11 fitted with the plunger frame and four-speed gearbox and also asked it to pull along a single seat sidecar. This was to assess the possibilities and was prompted by a budget tax concession. It showed that the machine could cope with the load and geared to around a 50 mph maximum would give acceptable acceleration. The one area where the machine was unable to manage the added weight proved to be braking, which failed to give quick stops and on occasion was augmented by some fast down changes in the gearbox to use the engine braking effect.

Later that year *The Motor Cycle* road tested a C10 with spring frame and, although it ran along well enough as was expected, they did have a number of points to make. They thought the brakes only adequate with the front below par, the horn button in an impossible place, and were none too happy with the transmission. The clutch was only classed as moderately light and gear changes needed some care to ensure quiet, clean selection. Despite the wide ratios bottom still required a fair degree of clutch slip when starting on a gradient. The centre stand was to

the usual BSA standard and so none too easy to use, while its operation was not helped by oil from the crankcase breather blowing onto its left leg.

In October 1953 the range for the next year was announced and both 250 cc machines received their first major engine change. The electrical system was modified with an alternator fitted to the left crankshaft end outboard of the primary drive, a solid state rectifier under the seat and a redesign of the timing side. The side valve engine became the C10L and was fitted with a Wipac generator, while the overhead valve engine received a Lucas unit and the type number became C11G early in 1954.

With no dynamo to be driven, the old style timing cover over the chain was discarded and this allowed the ignition cam and its auto-advance drive unit to be keyed directly into the end of the camshaft. The points plate was fitted to the outer timing cover and enclosed by a small alloy cap. The cam drive, valve gear, and oil pump remained just as before, as did the remainder of the engine with the exception of the crankcase breather. This changed from the disc valve to a timed port connecting to drillways in the drive side mainshaft. With the disappearance of the dynamo a cover plate was added

On stage at the Drury Lane Theatre in the 1956 American musical *Plain and Fancy* **is a C12 in its USA make-up with high bars**

over the gearbox to fill the gap left, while a modified chaincase was used to accommodate the new alternators.

Aside from the engine, the transmission continued with the three-speed gearbox only for the C10L and a three vane shock absorber in the clutch centre to replace the cam lobe device that had been on the crankshaft. The C11G continued with the three- or four-speed boxes and had the same changes to its clutch. While this model continued with the C11 cycle parts the side valve 250 was given a new and lighter frame of all-welded steel tubing with plunger rear suspension and completely different front forks. These came from the Bantam range and had gaiter seals, cowled headlamp and a different front wheel spindle design. Both hubs came from the larger Bantam so the rear was smaller than it had been. An attractive green finish was used in two tones, while the C11G continued the earlier maroon colour.

Some rationalisation took place for 1955 with the two models built as standard with three speeds and the plunger frames, while only the C11G was available with the four-speed gearbox. A number of changes were incorporated including a new camshaft with quietening ramps that became the standard fitment on replacement for all models. The new Monobloc Amal was fitted and fed with petrol via plastic fuel pipes and, on the export models only, air through a new air filter. The pillion rests were changed and the faster overhead valve model gained a 7 in. front brake and a deeper valance to its rear mudguard. The petrol tanks of both models had their seams covered with a trim strip.

The Motor Cycle road tested a C11G early in 1955 and found that the new front brake overcame the earlier stopping problems. Top speed proved to be 62 mph and the machine behaved well during the test. The horn button was still located on the brake pivot block and so well out of reach, but apart from this strange lapse the controls fell easily to foot and hand. It was a comfortable and easy machine to ride so served its purpose well ferrying people about their business and pleasure.

Not for much longer, however, as the model was dropped late in the year to make way for a more modern version, the C12 with swinging fork frame. This used the well developed C11G engine coupled to a new four-speed gearbox also fitted to the C10L. The old three-speed one was dropped. The one item in the engine that was modified to suit the C12 was the lubrication of the valve rockers. To make this more positive a feed pipe was taken from the main oil return just before it reached the oil tank and this was connected to a new rocker cover bolt which was drilled to allow the passage of oil. The rocker support forging was modified with a groove cut along its top so the oil ran through this to the pivot pins and the rocker bearings. After doing its job it drained down the push rod tunnel and in passing augmented the lubrication of the cams and followers. This change could be fitted to any C11 type engine and BSA issued a service sheet to this effect listing the parts needed to do the job.

The C12 frame was a straightforward, open diamond with single top, down and saddle tubes. To this was attached a rear triangle which swept down to carry the rear fork pivot before bolting to the rear of the gearbox plates attached to the saddle tube. The fork pivoted on Silentbloc bushes and was controlled by a pair of hydraulically damped units. Attached to the front of the frame were front forks damped in the same manner and the chassis ran on wheels with new full width, light alloy, hubs with brake drums of the same diameter as before. The electrics were simplified by positioning the main switch on a panel located on the right side behind the oil tank so the headlamp shell only carried the ammeter. Like the larger machines, it was cowled to the forks. The new model was fitted with a dualseat as standard and finished in maroon with cream tank panels.

Right side of the C12 showing the clean lines achieved despite the separate gearbox, also the combined switches in their panel. Whole style of these small machines mirrored their big brethren

The C12 in final form with full width hubs. The horn button is still in its awful position but that apart it was a good machine. Where did the map go when the model rode away?

The C10L continued much as before but did receive deeper finning on both head and barrel. It was fitted as standard with the new four-speed gearbox with its needle roller layshaft bearings. The existing three vane shock absorber was incorporated into the clutch. Electrically, the harness was simplified by separating ignition and lighting switches both of which were mounted in the headlamp. At the front the forks were changed for a more substantial design similar to those fitted to the C12 but the brakes remained rather small, as before. The machine was still fitted with a saddle as standard but a dualseat and pillion rests were available.

In May 1956 *Motor Cycling* tested the C12 and found that it continued the work of the old C11 with easy starting, quiet running, comfortable ride and a consumption figure around the 85 mpg mark. Top speed under good conditions came out at 65 mph and was achieved with an engine speed just over that at which maximum power was produced, which indicated good gearing. Normal cruising was up to 55 mph, although hilly country did force the machine down to third a fair bit. The particular model tested seemed to have a tired front brake for it failed to produce the expected results, although it did have over 60 lb more of machine to stop than the first C11 did. Generally, however, the C12 behaved in the mould of the lightweight BSA to provide good value for money in purchase and running costs.

Both it and the C10L continued unchanged into 1957, the only variation being the option of chrome plated tank panels in place of the painted ones for the ohv model, which was also available with a black finish instead of the standard maroon. The days of small machines with side valve engines were now numbered and so, in October 1957, the C10L was dropped from the range and brought to an end the very long, if unspectacular, run of the 250 cc side valve. It was never its job to be exciting but BSA always managed to produce a good package to suit the job it was designed to do.

The C12 continued on but only for one more year before it too was taken out of production to be replaced by a unit construction machine.

So ended a model run that had spanned two decades to build machines sometimes referred to disparagingly as 'grey porridge', but to BSA they were a success—after all, many people go to work on a bowl of porridge!

6 | Flyweights

The foundation of most successful motorcycle firms lies in their production of bread and butter models. These, by their ability to carry people about quietly and reliably, can be sold in large numbers and so make a vital contribution to the company's finances. They pay the overheads and it is by selling such mundane models that the firm can indulge itself with the more expensive and exotic machines which capture the imagination of the public. All too often such stirring models are either sold at a loss or at such a high price that there are few actual buyers.

The solid base for these exercises usually comes from small capacity, reliable machines. For BSA such an opportunity came in the immediate postwar years when they took the design of the pre-war DKW RT125. This had been offered round the British industry as part of the war reparations but there was little interest. Typical of the attitude of the times was the reception an Army officer received from Villiers. He 'commandeered' a 350 cc DKW in Germany, rode it to the Villiers factory, and they could not be bothered to look at it, much less take it apart. Had they done so they would have found a flat top piston for the Deek had used the Schnuerle loop scavenging port system for some years in preference to the heavy deflector piston.

Top **Early Bantam with headlamp switch, BSA badge on chaincase and incomplete tank badge**

Left **First 125 cc Bantam engine unit with gear indicator on left**

BSA took the DKW design lock, stock and barrel, with its opposed transfer ports, and reversed it so it became a mirror image. In time others were to do the same with Harley-Davidson, Yamaha and Voskhod all following suit, down to fine details. DKW themselves continued with the original after the war and a quarter of a century later the Polish WSK was yet another copy.

The announcement of the BSA engine came in March 1948 with full descriptions of the engine and gearbox unit in the press. At the time it was stated that it had been designed to suit a specific export contract and there was no suggestion of a complete machine or that it would be sold on the home market.

In time it was to prove to be one of the most successful machines ever made in England.

The engine was built in unit with the three-speed gearbox and based on a 52 mm bore and 58 mm stroke, the latter dimension common for all versions of what was to become the Bantam. The engine unit was split vertically on the centre line with a spigot diameter around the crankcase for alignment assisted by two hollow dowels fitted in the top front and rear engine mountings. The flywheels were of a substantial size and this feature did make the engine a little taller than it need have been, but they were full circle wheels and ran on pressed in shafts. The balance weights were forged into them but were completely encircled by the outer flywheel rim, while the hollows formed in the wheels were enclosed by thin steel discs retained in a recess in the flywheel sides by centre-punching. On occasion they were to work loose and would continue to spin for some time if the engine was stopped quickly.

The big end pin was pressed into the wheels and the bearing was a single row of uncaged rollers which ran directly in the connecting rod eye. The rod was a steel stamping with phosphor bronze small end bush in which ran the hollow gudgeon pin retained in the piston by circlips. The piston had a slight dome to its crown and carried two pegged piston rings. It was cutaway on each side below the gudgeon pin to ensure a freeflow of mixture into the transfer ports.

It ran in a cast iron barrel which was inclined forward a little and this carried an aluminium alloy cylinder head giving a compression ratio of 6·5:1. The fins were styled to match on both head and barrel and the sparking plug lay back at an angle on the centre line of the part spherical combustion chamber. The barrel had an exhaust port whose outlet was offset to the right and threaded externally to take an exhaust pipe nut. On the inlet side a short stub was angled to the barrel to be horizontal and carried a clip fitting, single lever, Amal of $\frac{5}{8}$ in. bore fitted with an air cleaner equipped with a strangler choke for cold starting. There was a transfer port on each side of the engine and these were positioned on the crankshaft axis to match passages cast in the crankcase. Each transfer port was angled so that the mixture was directed to the rear of the cylinder away from the exhaust.

The head and barrel were retained on four long studs fixed in the crankcase and no head gasket was used, the joint being flat without any step. The barrel was deeply spigoted into the crankcases so was cutaway on each side at the transfer passages to allow the mixture to flow.

At the bottom of each transfer passage an oil collecting recess was machined and, from these, oilways were drilled to feed the main bearings. There were three of these, two on the drive side with an oil seal between them and one on the magneto side with a seal outboard of it. The two inner mains were thus lubricated by oil passing down the drain holes and this also looked after the seals. The outer drive side main was dealt with by the transmission lubricant. The big end received its oil via slots cut in the rod eye, while the remainder of the engine ran on the oil mist the petroil mixture provided.

On the left of the crankshaft was fitted the flywheel magneto and generator made by Wipac and providing self-contained ignition. The rotor

Left **First Bantam with shovel mudguard, flat silencer, saddle, cable operated headlamp switch and poor stand. A most successful design overall**

Above **Line drawing of 1951 Bantam with plunger rear and fork gaiters. Used by thousands of learners and all over the world**

lay inboard of the stator and was keyed to a tapered part of the shaft. It was surrounded by a simple casting that also carried the clutch lifting mechanism and to this casting was clamped the stator plate with ignition and lighting coils. In this first design the contact points were housed on the outside of the stator plate and protected with a small cover, while the high tension lead was connected via an adaptor held in place by two screws. Outboard of the rotor a pre-oiled bush supported the crankshaft further and to the end of the shaft was keyed the ignition cam. Timing was varied by rotating the entire stator plate.

The drive side on the right comprised a single

strand roller chain connecting engine to clutch. This had three cork plates, six non-adjustable springs, and was held together by one very large circlip. It ran on a bronze bush and was to prove very, very tough. Clutch operation was by a three-start, quick-thread worm which was fitted with a hardened adjustable screw in its centre. This could be set from the left and was pulled by a cable which swept under the magneto into a cast-in socket. A push rod and separate mushroom passed the movement through the centre of the gearbox mainshaft on which the clutch was mounted.

The three-speed gearbox was traditional in that the layshaft sat beneath the mainshaft and the output sleeve gear carrying the gearbox sprocket ran on the mainshaft. Less traditional was the cross-over drive with clutch on right and sprocket on left. The mainshaft ran on ball races with bushes in the sleeve gear and for the layshaft. The two centre gears were linked and moved together under the influence of a simple positive stop mechanism. This included a spindle which carried a small pointer on the left of the

Plunger Bantam with Lucas rectified generating system, battery and switch panel with ammeter in headlamp. Unsprung front mudguard and fully valanced rear but still with flat silencer

crankcase to indicate which gear was engaged. The gear pedal was on the right and had an up-for-up movement, while the pedal shaft ran through the centre of the kickstarter shaft. This carried a quadrant gear which meshed with a ratchet gear engaging with the back of the clutch, so giving primary kickstarting, then a very rare feature and nearly unique for a British machine at that time. The kickstart lever was returned by a clock type spring and this, along

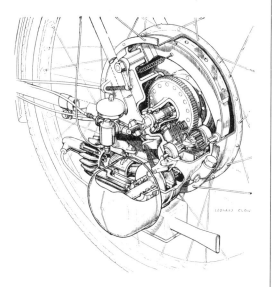

Above **The BSA Winged Wheel bicycle sold in ladies or gents style and fitted with sprung forks**

Right **In-hub Winged Wheel power unit which substituted for the normal bicycle one. Often nicknamed 'Stink Wheel'**

with all the primary drive, was enclosed by an oiltight cover.

Passages between the gearbox and the primary drive area allowed the use of a common lubricant, so $\frac{3}{4}$ pint of oil did for both once it had been inveigled into the small, angled filler in the top of the crankcase. The filler plug carried a dipstick for the level. Both the gearbox and crankcase had drain plugs.

This then was the new 123 cc two stroke engine unit and it was not long before a complete machine was announced. This came in June 1948 when the model DI appeared, soon to be called the Bantam, but at first listed for export only.

The engine unit was fitted to an all-welded rigid frame, BSAs first of that type, with single tube main loop running round the unit, and rear loops for the wheel. The engine was dropped between welded-on mounting plates front and rear with two fixings in each. Lugs on the frame carried the toolbox, chainguard, seat and footrest bar, the rear brake pedal and centre stand pivoting on this.

The front forks were simple telescopics with internal springs but no damping and the legs slid on sintered bronze bushes, grease lubricated, fitted into the fixed, outer tubes. The legs were formed with scrolls in their tops to which the fork springs screwed and these were held in place by top nuts also with scrolls which screwed into the top of the springs. Screwed caps at the bottoms of the fork tubes contained grease seals and, while the top yoke was a pressing, the lower one was a forging with the steering stem brazed into place. A simple bracket for the headlamp was fixed to the bottom yoke, the speedometer was mounted on the top one, and the bulb horn worked through the stem with bulb screwed into the top and flared mouthpiece into the bottom. The handlebars were mounted in split clamps, also on the top yoke, and had the control lever pivots welded into place.

The ends of the fork legs were flattened to accept the nuts retaining the fixed spindle front hub. Both hubs ran on non-adjustable ball races, had 5 in. diameter brakes and steel rims carrying 2·75 × 19 in. Dunlop tyres. A very deeply

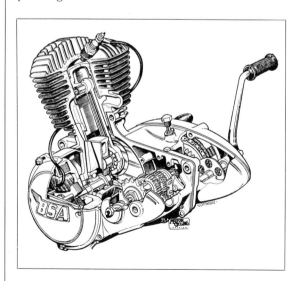

Line drawing of 150 cc Bantam Major engine and gearbox unit. The increased finning on head and barrel was common to both engine sizes

The 1954 Bantam Major fitted with heavier forks than the 125, a tubular silencer and easily grounded legshields

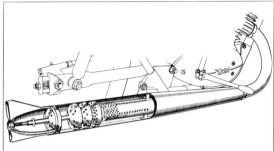

Above **Long silencer with tapered inlet introduced for 1956 150, tailpart as earlier tubular type**

Top **The 1956 Bantam Major swinging fork frame**

The publicity budget for 1956 did not run to much of a wardrobe for the model it would seem. Bike is the Bantam Major

valanced front mudguard was fitted to the fixed fork tubes and this carried the front number plates on its sides. The rear guard valance increased from minimal to deep as it went round the wheel and one of its stays supported a rear carrier. It was also retained by the two bolts that held the saddle springs to the frame, this item also being supported at its nose.

The toolbox was mounted below the saddle just behind the air cleaner and the exhaust system was mounted low down on the right. The pipe swept round to meet a silencer of styled form and thin section that in time became known to all users as the 'flat Bantam'. The fuel was carried in a tank formed as two side pressings welded to a centre section, the welded ridges running over the tank top being a styling feature.

The lighting was direct for the main headlamp with the switch mounted in the aluminium headlamp shell but operated by a lever mounted on the left handlebar and connected to the switch by a cable. A 3 volt dry cell in the headlamp provided power for the pilot lamp.

Finish of the machine was mist green for all painted parts, which included the wheel rims, with yellow side panels to the petrol tank, these having a BSA transfer applied to them. The exhaust system, handle bars and minor controls were chrome plated.

In October 1948 both *The Motor Cycle* and *Motor Cycling* road tested the new model, now with its Bantam name, and came up with some discrepancies in the results. The first obtained speeds of 21, 41 and 47 in the three gears, while the second came up with speedometer readings of 28, 41 and 54 mph with a 12 stone rider aboard. Fuel consumption in both cases was around 120 mpg and both magazines were very impressed with the overall performance of what was Britain's first modern two stroke. Handling, comfort and braking all met with approval and there were few criticisms. It was to take the private owner to discover the high mounted gear

The Beeza scooter shown at the 1955 Earls Court show but not to go into production due to its predicted high costs

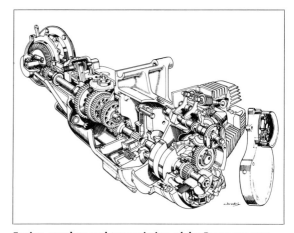

Engine, gearbox and transmission of the Beeza scooter built as one unit with rear wheel and pivoted to provide rear suspension

pedal, semi-collapsible centre stand and high level rear brake pedal pad. The wide gear ratios also left something to be desired, but in the late forties it was a major step forward and was soon proved to be an incredibly tough machine.

It was sold for £60 0s 0d plus £16 4s 0d purchase tax and BSA could not make them fast enough. The Bantam was tremendously popular with all manner of riders all over the world. It was light, it was reliable and, when needed, it was easy to work on. Most of all it could stand up to the punishment novice riders handed out to it and under the worst abuses seldom came to any great harm. Some were seized up, by lack of oil in the petrol in many cases, but went on again with the piston filed down a bit. Others caught out their traditional English riders with the reversed gearchange movement. It was all too easy to forget and change down instead of up when flat in second. Even if you remembered in time and held the clutch in, it felt as if a giant had suddenly seized the carrier and pulled, if you released the clutch you could take all the teeth off the mainshaft gear. Not actually a great problem for spares were cheap and a morning's work would see the machine healthy once more.

The single model continued through 1949 but 1950 brought a number of alterations and additions. The first of these was a plunger frame as an option to give the machine rear suspension. It was based on the normal BSA design and both load and return springs were concealed under spring covers with the movement undamped apart from the effects of grease and friction. With it came a rear mudguard with deep valance that ran right round its length. At the same time the front forks were fitted with gaiters and a competition version was introduced with turned up silencer, raised saddle, modified footrests, and a wider section rear tyre. It also had a folding kickstart lever, lowered gearing and a forward sloping decompressor fitted to the cylinder head. This was screwed into a hole tapped to a plug thread so inevitably some riders tried reversing the two items and experimenting with twin plugs. Less obvious were the taper roller bearings fitted to the front hub.

On all models the centre stand lost the clip which had held it up and received a spring attached to a pivoting C-shaped link to give an over centre effect. As the stand stop bolted to the frame was too thin and both it and the stand

The Dandy scooterette also shown at the 1955 show and which did reach production. An ingenious design that was too clever in parts

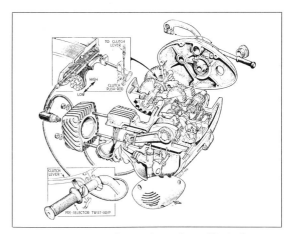

Dandy engine unit with preselector box of limited appeal. The trade disliked the central points which were inaccessible

wore, so it ceased to hold the wheels aloft. It passed through a phase when both wheels and stand balanced the machine evenly to reach a point where the centre stand became an inadequate propstand. Owners welded on extension feet and the process continued.

The road machines were also available with a Lucas alternator, 6-volt battery hung on the left side and matched by the toolbox which was moved over to make room for it, and a rectifier housed alongside the toolbox. A new side casting was used to house the generator and with the arrangement came coil ignition with the points fitted beneath a small cover and opened by a cam on the end of the rotor shaft. This rotor fitted directly onto the end of a specially shortened crankshaft while the coil was mounted up under the tank so connected to the plug with a very short lead. The system was controlled by an ignition switch set in the centre of a lighting switch mounted in the back of the headlamp.

The Wipac generator also changed with a larger outer cover and the high tension lead being soldered directly to the internal ignition coil and emerging through a sleeve to curve round in a sweep to the plug. This gave a cleaner

look to the engine and easier access to the points and electrical connections.

In February 1950 *Motor Cycling* had a plunger framed model fitted with the Lucas electrics on test and reported very favourably on it. It was timed at 49 mph, returned well over 100 mpg and managed to stop in 22·5 ft from 30 mph, a figure that few other machines could approach. It behaved itself well in all aspects, comfort was aided by the plunger rear suspension and the model proved well able to cruise along all day at 40 mph without fuss. In fact, there were signs of overgearing and some riders were already finding that this led to condensation in the crankcase and ruined main bearings, a condition that the competition jobs avoided with their lower gearing and consequent higher engine speed.

The competition model was designed for trials or scrambles, fields in which BSA excelled, but Bantam owners were already beginning to race the 125 against the home tuned Villiers and cut-down pre-war 150s of the times. To meet a very apparent need, BSA, to their eternal credit, made a batch of close ratio gear sets which were to keep racing Bantams on the circuits for the best part of a decade.

Aside from a minor change to the horn button when fitted to conceal its wiring within the handlebars, the Bantam with its options continued unaltered through 1951 and for 1952 only required some very minor frame strengthening, minor mods to forks and hubs, and the removal of the cable control for the light switch, a normal one being fitted in the headlamp. The frame changes mainly concerned the size of the steering head gusset but included an increase in thickness of the rear stay tubes. The front forks gained synthetic rubber damping sleeves while the wheel spindle material was improved.

The big end bearing was made wider in 1953 by recessing the flywheels to accommodate the rod eye and the roller size changed from 7 ×

7 mm to $\frac{1}{4} \times \frac{3}{8}$ in. long. While this increased the load carrying area of the bearing, it also put up the weight of the rollers and, at speed, this was to prove detrimental. The cycle parts were also changed with the fitting of a conventional style front mudguard with separate number plate, pillion rest lugs on the rear frame tubes, chrome plated strips to conceal the tank joints and the option of a dualseat. The standard colour remained mist green but an all black finish was introduced as an option. In either case the wheel rims were chrome plated and no longer painted.

Early in the year a performance part for the Bantam appeared, the Hogan high-torque cylinder head developed by two very successful Bantam racing brothers. The head increased the

The first 175 cc Bantam, the D5 model of 1958 which was only built for the one year. Flange mounted Monobloc replaced clip fitting

Above **The D7 introduced in 1959 with new frame, forks, tank and centre panels**

Top **1958 model D5 with its deep tank**

compression ratio to 9:1 and gave about three times the cooling area of the standard item. It was cast in aluminium alloy, had a central sparking plug, and came with a timing strip and suitable size main jet. It proved to be popular on both road and track, although most had the ratio further increased and then the head would neatly crack in half along its centre line.

In May 1953 BSA announced a new flyweight engine for the cycle-motor market. This, the forerunner of the moped boom, had sprung up in the immediate postwar years when the clamour for simple local transport had led to a whole range of small clip-on engines being marketed for attachment to standard bicycles. These had proved exceptionally popular in Europe and

Above **The BSA-Sunbeam scooter fitted with the 175 cc two stroke single cylinder engine**

Below **Scooter engine and transmission unit**

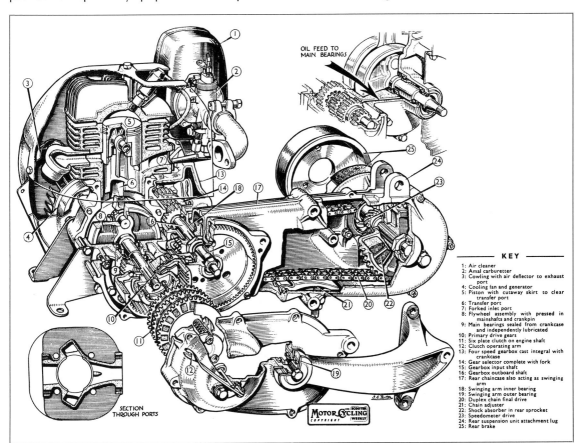

OIL FEED TO MAIN BEARINGS

SECTION THROUGH PORTS

MOTOR CYCLING WEEKLY

KEY

1: Air cleaner
2: Amal carburetter
3: Cowling with air deflector to exhaust port
4: Cooling fan and generator
5: Piston with cutaway skirt to clear transfer port
6: Transfer port
7: Forked inlet port
8: Flywheel assembly with pressed in mainshafts and crankpin
9: Main bearings sealed from crankcase and independently lubricated
10: Primary drive gears
11: Six plate clutch on engine shaft
12: Clutch operating arm
13: Four speed gearbox cast integral with crankcase
14: Gear selector complete with fork
15: Gearbox input shaft
16: Gearbox outboard shaft
17: Rear chaincase also acting as swinging arm
18: Swinging arm inner bearing
19: Swinging arm outer bearing
20: Duplex chain final drive
21: Chain adjuster
22: Shock absorber in rear sprocket
23: Speedometer drive
24: Rear suspension unit attachment lug
25: Rear brake

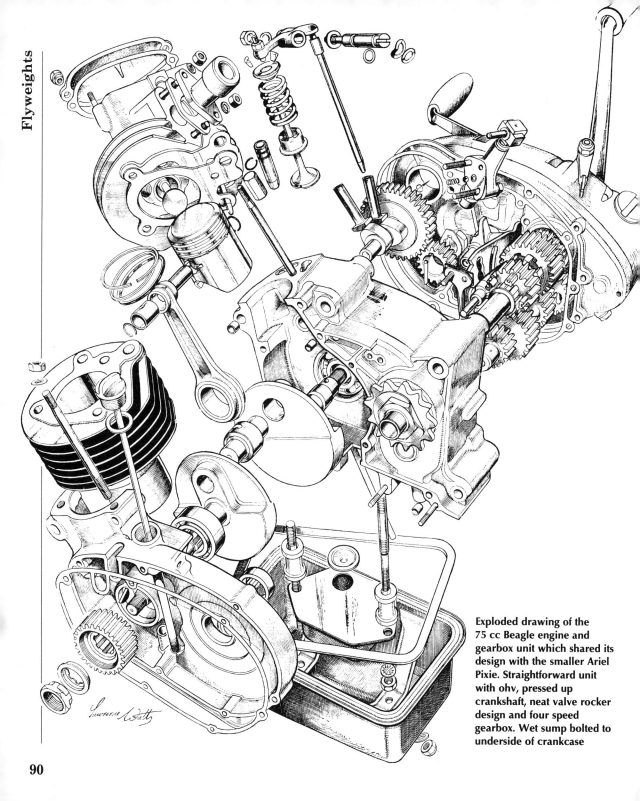

Exploded drawing of the
75 cc Beagle engine and
gearbox unit which shared its
design with the smaller Ariel
Pixie. Straightforward unit
with ohv, pressed up
crankshaft, neat valve rocker
design and four speed
gearbox. Wet sump bolted to
underside of crankcase

Complete Beagle as in 1964. Spine frame, leading link front forks and conventional cycle fittings did not attract enough sales

there were a dozen or more different makes available in England when BSA came onto the scene.

Many attachments drove front or rear wheel by a friction roller and had no clutch, but the BSA unit, called the Winged Wheel, had both a clutch and geared reduction, the entire unit forming a substitute rear wheel which fitted straight into the frame in place of the normal item. The only component not in the wheel assembly was the fuel tank which was formed as a flat carrier and mounted above the wheel.

The engine was a simple two stroke with forward facing horizontal cylinder on the left side of the wheel. Engine dimensions were 36 × 34 mm giving a capacity of 34·6 cc and construction was conventional with flywheel generator for ignition and 6 volt lights on the left, and reduction gears on the right. A two stage gear train was used with the engine driving the clutch drum and the output from this being geared to the main hub. The clutch had three driven plates with cork inserts and was clamped by ten small coil springs. The whole of the transmission was enclosed within a $9\frac{1}{2}$ in. diameter drum to

which the rim was spoked and whose inside surface was used for the two separately pivoted brake shoes to work against. The carburettor was a small Amal, the exhaust box and silencer could be dismantled for cleaning, and the whole assembly fitted quickly and easily to most standard bicycles, especially those made by BSA themselves.

Controls comprised the throttle, which also worked the choke, and clutch while the rear brake was connected to the bike's normal control lever. A machine fitted with a Winged Wheel was easy to start whether hot or cold and would cruise at 20 mph with a maximum of 25 mph. Lubrication was by petroil and fuel consumption was of the 200 mpg order, so the $\frac{1}{2}$ gallon tank kept most riders going for a week or more. Complete with controls, cables, tyre, tube, fuel tank and fittings, it sold for £25 0s 0d.

For 1954 an enlarged version of the Bantam appeared, the Bantam Major of 150 cc capacity fitted with the plunger spring frame as standard. At the same time the finning on the head and barrel of both the new and existing engines was greatly increased along with the size of the transfer ports. The increased capacity of the Major, coded the D3, was obtained by enlarging the bore to 57 mm while retaining the 58 mm stroke and the engine used the flywheels with thicker rims which were normally only fitted to the 125 with Lucas generator.

Externally the 150 was distinguished by the fitting of slightly heavier front forks, also fitted to the competition machines, with the headlamp cowled to them. It also had a slightly larger front brake and a tubular silencer with painted outlet. This silencer could be dismantled for cleaning and was used for all the road models while the competition ones retained the flat silencer. Two models of the 150 were available with either direct or battery lighting and the finish was in pastel grey with yellow tank panels.

There was little apparent change to the Bantam for 1955 with only minor amendments to

the rear number plate and toolbox mounting, while colours remained the same with the addition of a maroon option as well as the black for the 125. Less apparent was an increase in the spacing of the cylinder studs and the diameter of the barrel spigot. To accommodate this new crankcase castings were produced and among their features were two extra clamping screws making 13 in all.

The Winged Wheel continued to be available as a separate unit, built in the BSA Cycle works in Coventry Street, Birmingham, but was also made up into a complete machine. Both cross-bar and drop frames were listed and in both cases these were fitted with Webb girder-type spring forks and sold at £43 9s 6d. Unfortunately, it was really too late in the day to succeed and the trend was away from clip-on motors to the true moped. So the Winged Wheel was quietly grounded.

The Bantam continued to go from strength to strength, as highlighted by another *Motor Cycling* road test during 1955. This was of the 150 with battery lighting and the machine did all the things expected of it quietly and reliably.

For 1956 there was some simplification of the range and a new frame for the Major. The competition models were removed from the lists and the DI was fitted with the plunger frame as standard, the rigid no longer being available. The D3 received a new frame with swinging arm rear suspension and of built up construction, a new long, megaphone shaped silencer body, and a dualseat. Both models were available with either direct or battery lighting and the 125 continued to be sold with its saddle.

Also seen among the exhibits at the Earls Court show, held late in 1955, were two completely new models, one a 70 cc scooterette and the other a 200 cc scooter. Little more was heard of these for about a year and then the company decided that the scooter would be too expensive to produce so it was dropped. It had been called the 'Beeza' and used a lot of car practice in its design. Its main axis ran along the machine to drive the rear wheel by shaft and with the crankshaft in the same axis it was possible to lay the single cylinder down, across the machine. Thus the cylinder head lay on the left and the mainshaft on the right. The engine had side valves to keep the width down and these were positioned above the cylinder and at a considerable angle to it. This allowed the gear driven camshaft to move the valves via bell cranks which incorporated screw adjustors in one end. The front end of the camshaft carried the points cam and advance mechanism, while the equivalent crankshaft end had the alternator. A single cover enclosed the timing gear and carried the points mounting plate which had its own small cover. The camshaft drove the oil pump by skew gears, the pump itself being contained in the sump.

The crankshaft ran on ball and needle races and the connecting rod had a split big end with plain shells. The flywheel was mounted on the back of the crankshaft and gear cut for the electric starter. It carried the clutch and this drove straight back via a torsional damper to the all indirect four-speed gearbox. The output shaft lay above and further outboard of the input and its gears were all drilled for lightness. Gear selection was by a flat cam moving the two selectors and operated by two pedals linked to the positive stop mechanism. The rider pressed one pedal to change up and the other to go down.

A short shaft ran back from the gearbox to a pair of spiral bevel gears that turned the drive into the rear hub. The entire mechanism from engine to hub was carried in a series of alloy castings bolted into one unit. This was pivoted from a single point in the frame and controlled by a spring and separate damper units. Front suspension was by leading link forks controlled by a pair of special springs. Perforated 12 in. disc wheels were fitted and the mechanism was enclosed in a smooth body with footboards.

The scooterette, called the 'Dandy', was of

much lighter construction and had some unusual features. The frame followed moped lines with a step-through beam forming the main spine. At the front this carried forks with short leading links and a wire spoked front wheel whose mudguard was supplemented by a large rider-shield, or apron, that ran under the rider's feet. The rear of the frame beam carried the fuel tank and saddle while from its lowest point pivoted the swinging fork for the rear suspension carrying another spoked wheel. Both wheels had rather small drum brakes.

It was the fork that contained much that was unusual for it was based on the complete engine

Top left **The D7 ran for over seven years with minor changes. A 1962 example showing the 'Super' cover over the same old generator**

Left **The Silver Bantam in 1966, a final version of the D7 built down to a price**

Below **The de luxe D7 introduced in 1965 with a new tank shape, bright colour scheme and revised bars. Same engine well related to first D1**

unit. Brackets attached the crankcase to its pivot point on the frame and the single cylinder lay back to form part of the right fork arm. In fact the arm was completed by the addition of a steel pressing bolted to the cylinder head. Thus the crankshaft axis lay across the frame and the two-speed gearbox on the left with a further pressing forming the left fork arm.

The engine was a single cylinder two-stroke based on dimensions of 45 × 44 mm, which gave a capacity of 70 cc. Compression ratio was 7·25:1. It had an overhung crankshaft and the bulge over the end of the crankcase concealed the carburettor which was angled to feed back to a conventional inlet port. The exhaust lay beside it and was connected to a system bolted to the fork arm. Engine construction was straightforward with crowded roller big end and flywheel magneto ignition but this, with the points, was buried in the middle of the crankcase between engine and clutch. To reset the timing the engine had to come out of the frame. The drive went straight through the clutch to a gear drive back to the gearbox input shaft. This carried two gears which mated with two free running ones on the output shaft behind it. These were engaged by a sliding dog whose movement was controlled by springs and catches to give a pre-selector gearchange. Thus the rider could move the twist gear control on the handlebars but the gearbox would not change gear until the clutch was pulled in. For moving off the clutch was used in the normal manner.

Final drive to the rear wheel was by chain on the right side, covered with a guard. Starting was by a handlever, which replaced the original kickstarter but worked like one, on the gearbox and the entire assembly of engine unit and swinging fork was controlled by a pair of spring units. The machine was available in various colour schemes at a price of £74 8s 0d but its introduction onto the market was delayed until late in 1956 when it joined the model line up for 1957.

Before that was announced, the new Bantam Major with swinging fork frame was tested by *The Motor Cycle*, who found it comfortable to ride for long periods although they did criticise the high position of the foot controls.

There were no changes to the two Bantam models for 1957 but at the end of the year the D3 model was dropped to be replaced by a larger version, the 175 cc D5 Bantam Super. This followed exactly the same lines as the earlier models and used the same stroke. The bore was increased to 61·5 mm which gave a capacity of 172 cc and the compression ratio was 7·4:1. Internally the big end design was changed to use 4 × 8 mm rollers held in two half cages machined in aluminium alloy. These came together to surround the rollers and the assembly was lubricated by scollops on the outer faces of the rod eye, which also had radial oilholes to allow the oil to escape.

During 1957 the lubrication of the drive side mains had been altered with the oil seal moved inwards against the flywheel and both bearings then lubricated from a catchment filled by the primary chaincase oil. A drilled hole allowed the oil to drain away when it had done its job. This change had applied to both 125 and 150 cc engines and was continued on the new 175. At the same time the magneto side main was sealed off completely with an oil seal on the inboard side, in addition to the existing one, and its lubrication provided by a supply from the gearbox, again with a collection area and supply and drain holes. This arrangement was to continue on all Bantams.

The cycle parts of the D5 were similar to the D3 except that the brakes were the same size as

Top right **The D10 introduced in 1966 with points on right, alternator with improved output, more power and four plate clutch**

Right **The D10 Sports model with four speed gearbox, humped seat, special exhaust and flyscreen. This is a 1967 one with a Concentric Amal**

those fitted to the 125, but wider. Wheel size was down, tyre section increased, and a different and slightly larger petrol tank fitted. The area beneath the dualseat became partly enclosed with a toolbox in the rear frame loop on the right and battery cover on the left. As before, both direct and battery lighting versions were available but all were in maroon with ivory tank panels, as no colour options were offered.

The Dandy had earlier been the subject of a road test in which it reached 33 mph and returned 130 mpg. The brakes were fairly good and the machine was comfortable to ride, although the suspension was thought to be a trifle hard. The engine ran smoothly but its exhaust was rather noisy and there was gear whine as well. The pre-selector box worked fairly well but changed gear with a clonk and refused to go into neutral when the machine was at a standstill. As the clutch still had to be used to move off, some observers considered the gearbox over-complex for the novice rider whose main problems would centre on the clutch and moving off. This point, together with the general motorcycle appearance, were not to attract the buyers that BSA sought, and dealers were put off from selling the machine due to the buried ignition components. It continued into 1958 with some modifications to the gearchange and with a new centre stand and revised foot brake.

A D5 was out on test with *The Motor Cycle* early in 1958. It proved to be a little faster than the smaller models at 59 mph but was, of course, a good deal heavier than the rigid D1. Fuel consumption was around the 100 mpg mark and comfort and roadholding standards were high. The exhaust note was rather noisy, while the horn was subdued, but all told the D5 was well fitted out to continue the journeys the Bantam was so suited to.

Not for long, however, for although the D5 was listed along with the Dandy and D1, when the range for 1959 was announced it was to be replaced before the new year came in by a

The D10 Bushman of 1967 with its high level exhaust trail tyres, crankcase shield, single seat, increased ground clearance and lowered gearing. Note special air cleaner on angled hose

revised version, the D7, of the same capacity. While the Dandy and D1 were unchanged, the new Super Bantam had a new frame, hydraulically damped front forks, larger brakes, deeper mudguards and raised handlebars. An additional cover was fitted to the left side of the engine to enclose the magneto and clutch adjustment but underneath this the parts were unchanged. As always, it was available with direct or battery lighting.

After the motorcycle range had been announced, BSA held a formal press presentation of a new scooter range which held few secrets for the machines' existence had been well known for quite sometime. The range was launched under both the BSA and Triumph labels and under each brand name could be had the same scooter propelled either by a single cylinder, 175 cc two stroke engine, or a twin cylinder, 250 cc four stroke.

The single cylinder engine was based strongly

sion damper unit.

The engine unit was mounted in a duplex frame to which was bolted the steering head. The main frame supported the seat with the fuel tank beneath it and was enclosed by a body built up from steel pressings, easily removeable for servicing. The front forks were telescopic in action but with both legs on the same, left, side— one leg containing the fork spring and the other the hydraulic damper unit. Both were covered with a shroud and this design allowed the front wheel to be carried on a stub axle like the rear. Both wheels were pressed steel with 3·50 × 10 in. tyres and fitted to three studs on the brake drum, car fashion. Brakes were single leading shoe types of 5 in. diameter.

The electrics were straightforward with a 6-volt battery carried under a cover on the rear of the apron, and a large range of accessories were offered. Only the badges distinguished the BSA model, called a 'Sunbeam', from the Triumph Tigress apart from the colour, the first being in light polychromatic green and the second in shell blue sheen.

The 175 cc scooter was priced at £164 19s 8d which was competitive at the time. Unfortunately it had really come along too late in the day to be a success for the bulk of the market had been taken by the Italians leaving little for the various other makes then available. Although BSA were to keep the model in their lists for a number of years, with no significant changes, the day of the scooter was passing and sales dropped right off in the early 1960s. BSA kept trying but to no avail and in August 1965 the 175 scooter was withdrawn, the interesting 250 cc twin version having already gone the previous year.

Meanwhile the Dandy and two sizes of Bantam had continued through 1959 and into 1960 and 1961 with no changes except to the colours. There were only two mechanical changes for 1962, both affecting the D7, these being the fitting of a Torrington needle roller bearing to

on the D7 and used the same dimensions. It had smaller flywheels than the motorcycle engine and a more compact crankcase, while the mainshafts were changed to suit the fresh application. Piston and porting were common to the Bantam. The engine was cowled and cooled by a fan attached to the flywheel generator rotor on the right end of the crankshaft. On the left was the clutch which drove the gear primary drive. The four-speed gearbox was built in unit with the engine and gear changing was by a positive stop mechanism worked by a single pedal.

Pivoted on the main engine casting was a single swinging arm comprising two castings bolted together and braced by a third. The two enclosed the duplex chain final drive and contained a chain tensioner as the drive was on fixed centres. At the rear of the casting assembly was the rear hub and brake while movement of the assembly was controlled by a single suspen-

the small end and a slight lowering of the gearing by a change to the rear wheel sprocket. The D7 was also fitted with a new style of dualseat and the machine continued to serve its owners as always, smoothly and reliably. However, some owners were beginning to question whether the model was not moving away from its original light and simple layout. While enclosure gave a nice line, it also hindered battery maintenance, not really a desirable feature.

Although the Bantams and the 175 cc scooter continued on into 1963 without change, the Dandy was dropped during 1962. The much loved 125 cc Bantam was to go the same way in August 1963 and with its demise went one of the most successful British machines of all time that had been sold all over the world and used for countless chores in all manner of lands and seasons. One of the many such uses had been with the Post Office, and the telegram delivery boy on his red 150 plunger was a very familiar

sight. On the other side of the world the Bantam was used for sheep herding in Australia and its duties covered just about anything else in between. It had been the mainstay of the training scheme in Britain for many years and this alone must have helped its sales along. Although the 175 was to continue many felt that it was the smaller two stroke that represented all the best qualities of the Bantam.

In effect it was replaced with a completely new flyweight model of only 75 cc capacity announced in November 1962 while the D1 was still available. This was the BSA Beagle which was launched with the Ariel Pixie, a machine which used the same basic four stroke engine as the Beagle, but completely different cycle parts. The Pixie engine was of 50 cc and had dimensions of

The 1968 Bantam Sports model D14/4S with four speed gearbox. It was fitted with a larger diameter exhaust pipe and had a raised compression ratio

38·9 × 42 mm and the extra capacity of the Beagle was achieved by increasing the bore to 47·6 mm.

It was a straightforward engine with the single cylinder sloping forward a little and the four-speed gearbox built in unit. It had a wet sump with the main engine split-line passing vertically through the cylinder centre line but the gearbox was contained in the right crankcase half and its end cover extended forward to enclose the timing gear. The cylinder head was die cast in aluminium with the rocker boxes while the barrel was an iron casting spigotted into the crankcase. Flywheels were pressed together and ran on ball races including one outboard of the primary gear drive, but with the flywheel magneto outside it on the left. The timing gear was simply a camshaft driven by a pair of spur gears and moving tappets, solid alloy push rods and rockers laying across the head with adjustors at the valve end.

The sump was bolted to the bottom of the crankcase and a single plunger pump driven by the camshaft. Lubrication was extensive and covered the major bearings, the rocker gear, and the primary drive. The clutch and gearbox were conventional with the gearchange modelled on that used for other group unit construction gearboxes.

The Beagle frame was of the spine type built up from pressings with swinging fork rear suspension and leading link front. Aside from the lack of front down tube, the styling was normal motorcycle and the machine had drum brakes and wire spoke wheels, A dualseat, pillion rests and full electrical equipment were fitted.

While the new models may have been announced late in 1962, at that time production

Final Bantam, the D175 of 1969 with new crankcase castings, central plug and needle race clutch. It lasted to early 1971 with its 1948 origin still clear

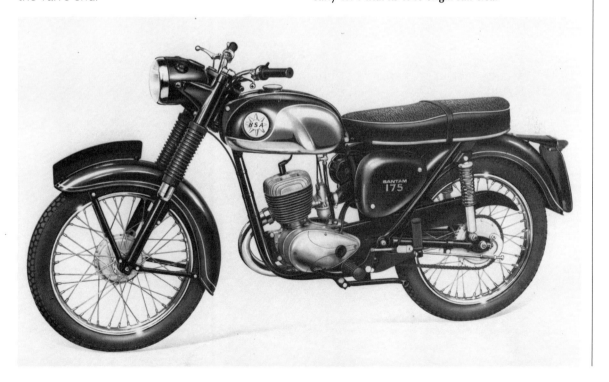

A flyweight with imported 50 cc engine unit introduced in 1979 for trail use. Another story

tools were still being made and it was to be late in 1963 before the production models began to come off the line. They received good reports, for the Beagle offered 40 mph cruising and 150 mpg consumption with a good town performance and handling. Comfort was quite acceptable, although the rear suspension was considered too stiff and there was confusion in the noise department with the horn too quiet and the induction too noisy.

All told it seemed to have possibilities but ran into some stiff competition from the small Honda stepthrough machines, which offered performance and weather protection. Rather sadly BSA's brave effort with the Beagle came to nought and, in August 1965, it was withdrawn with the scooter.

Meanwhile the D7 soldiered on with a modified silencer and a magnetic speedometer for 1964 and later that year there were changes

to the big end to improve lubrication and to the gear teeth to improve the box strength. This last change had the effect of closing the internal ratios up so there were no longer the large gaps between gears.

Also new for 1965 was a super de-luxe model with a revised tank finish and altered handlebars with ball ended control levers. During the year the Super model was replaced by the Silver Bantam, while the Super de-luxe was fitted with a modified carburettor. The Silver model was a low cost version with silver sheen finish applied to the tank side panels, mudguards, and mid-section panels. It and the de-luxe model ran on into 1966 but only up to July when a revised Bantam engine made its appearance.

This was the D10 which was very similar to the D7 it replaced but with several significant changes. The most obvious was the appearance of a small cover on the outside of the primary chaincase and this enclosed the contact breaker points. These had been moved as the old type Wipac flywheel magneto had finally been with-

drawn to be replaced by a modern six coil alternator with double the output. The engine was given a higher compression ratio and larger carburettor, which increased its power output, while the clutch had an extra plate fitted to deal with the added load.

The result was a top speed of 62 mph and much improved acceleration, better lighting, and the wellknown Bantam handling. The battery was hardly accessible under the seat and the assembly of panels and covers in the centre section was awkwardly contrived, but out on the road the machine continued to perform in the Bantam tradition.

The yawning gap in the gearbox was the next item to be dealt with for at last a four-speed assembly became available for the Bantam, still fitting in the same space as always but with a completely new set of gears and change mechanism. This new gearbox was fitted to two new D10 models while the Supreme was joined by a cheaper Silver version.

The first of the new models was the D10 Sports with special bars, humped back seat, flyscreen, separate headlamp, high level exhaust and full width hubs. The other was the Bushman and intended for cross-country or trail use so had lowered gearing, larger wheels with trail tyres, a crankcase shield, upswept exhaust and much increased ground clearance.

For 1967 there was a change to Concentric Amal carburettors but the D10 range only continued to the end of that year before being replaced by the D14 models. There were three of these, all fitted with the four-speed gearboxes, and they copied the earlier Supreme, Sports and Bushman in style and fittings.

Internally both the primary and secondary compression ratios were raised, the latter to 10:1, and a larger diameter exhaust pipe fitted which increased the power output to 13 bhp at 5750 rpm. On the outside the Bushman continued with its single seat but both it and the Sports model were fitted with heavier front forks,

these being hydraulically damped and equipped with gaiters.

The three models continued into the early part of 1969 but were then replaced by the final version of the Bantam, the D175, built in two forms, standard and Bushman.

The engine looked much as the Bantam always did but in fact had new crankcase and cylinder head castings, a stiffer crankshaft, central sparking plug, needle races in the clutch, and other minor detail changes which included the bolt threads which became unified.

The cycle parts were very similar to those of the D14 with the heavier pattern front forks fitted to both machines. The standard model was styled on the lines of the older Supreme model with low exhaust pipe and a normal road dualseat.

For 1970 the fork legs were hard chrome plated but otherwise the model was left alone and in fact was almost ignored in the last, final, massive trade and press launch held late that year. The Bushman had vanished but the Bantam was still there and went on unchanged into 1971 but sadly not for long.

In March 1971 the Bantam was dropped from the range and, after 60 years in the business of making motorcycles, BSA no longer had a lightweight machine for the commuter. No longer did countless trainees in the RAC scheme turn their first faltering wheels on an old D1, no longer could the Post Office buy its small capacity delivery machines. Of course, training and telegrams continued but the machines in use were Honda and Puch which encouraged users to continue with those makes.

Well over a half a million Bantams were built and sold in its 23 year history and there is still a market for such a machine. Sadly the BSA empire collapsed but from the ruins a few flyweights did emerge in the late 1970s but these were mainly mopeds and trail bikes built up using imported engine units. A sad ending for the cheeky little Beeza.

7 | Unit construction

In September 1958 BSA announced a new, unit construction, 250 cc four-stroke single that was, over the years, to become the basis of the whole of the single cylinder range.

The machine was introduced to replace the C12 but soon was asked to take on the work done by the B31 and its competition variants. It was a straightforward design and based on engine dimensions of 67 × 70 mm to give a capacity of 247 cc, had overhead valves, a compression ratio of 7·25:1 and a four-speed gearbox attached.

The unit was split vertically on the centre line of the iron barrel which spigoted into the crankcase. The two valve alloy head was spigoted to its top and fitted with a detachable casting carrying the rockers with adjustors at the valve ends. Valves were closed by duplex springs and opened by a pair of cams on a shaft directly above the crankshaft and driven from it by a pair of spur gears. The cams lifted tappets which sat side by side and ran directly in the case, and these in turn moved the alloy pushrods which lay at small angles to line up with the rockers, the outboard one moving the inlet side. The push rods were enclosed in a short tube between crankcase and cylinder head, otherwise they worked through cast-in holes.

The piston had one oil and two compression rings and its gudgeon pin was located by circlips and ran in a bronze small end bush. The big end was a plain bush running on a pin pressed into

The 250 cc C15 launched in September 1958 which became the basis for the entire unit construction range. Ignition points in housing distinguish the early models which remained unchanged in touring form for some years

the flywheels, one of which contained a sludge trap at the end of a drilled oilway blanked off by a screw. The crankshaft ran in a drive-side ballrace and timing-side bush. On the right it carried a skew gear inboard of the timing gears and this drove a shaft which ran nearly vertically down to the duplex gear oil pump and up to the ignition cam. This was contained in a unit with the points and condenser and driven via an advance mechanism. The complete unit with its cap was clamped in a hole in the crankcase so it sat behind the cylinder and could be rotated to set the coil ignition timing.

On the drive side the crankshaft carried a Lucas alternator and inboard of this a sprocket connected to the clutch with a duplex chain running without any tensioner. It drove a conventional, four-spring, four-plate clutch with vane type shock absorber contained in it and the primary drive was enclosed by an outer alloy cover. This attached to an inner section which was formed as part of the left crankcase half with a large hole in it to give access to the gearbox sprocket. This hole was blanked off by a plate which carried an oil seal to enclose the primary drive compartment.

The gearbox was completely conventional with layshaft below mainshaft, sleeve gear co-axial with mainshaft and on the left behind the clutch. Gear selection was by two forks moved by a quadrant plate turned by a simple positive stop mechanism. It gave an up-for-up movement to the pedal. The kickstarter worked on bottom gear and the clutch by a simple lever pulled by a cable running across behind the gearbox. The end cover which held this, and much of the change mechanism, extended forward to also enclose the timing gears although the two compartments were kept separate. A further simple casting, embellished with a star, covered the right side of the engine to enclose the gearbox. Beneath the oil pump was bolted a sump plate and the inlet and outlet pipes for the dry sump lubrication emerged just behind it.

Above **Launch time at Earls Court for the C15 with, from left, Brian Martin, Alan Jones, Bob Fearon and Bert Perrigo. Very typical BSA lines and styling used for range at that time**

Below **Left side of the C15 showing the clean lines of the whole machine which blend together well. A reliable model for work and play without frills or fancies**

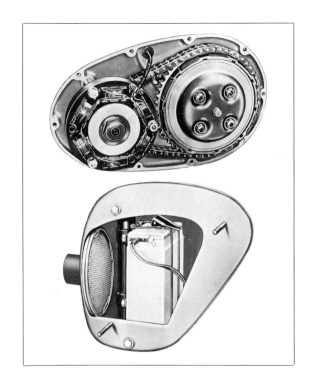

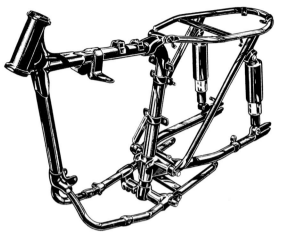

Above **The C15 cradle frame with bolted on rear section and right engine rail higher than left**

Left **C15 primary drive (above) showing alternator, duplex chain and clutch. Below are battery and air cleaner within central enclosure**

Below **Line drawing of the C15 engine and gearbox unit as first seen in 1958. Very simple drive for auxiliaries and plain bush big end**

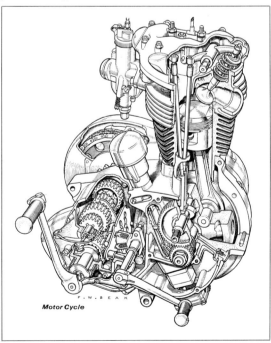

F.W.BEAK

Motor Cycle

Carburation was by an Amal Monobloc and the low level exhaust pipe was clamped to a stub in the head before running down along the right side of the machine to a tubular silencer.

The unit was mounted in a cradle frame with single top and down tubes, the latter splitting into a duplex cradle beneath the engine. The rear subframe was bolted on and supported the two units controlling the swinging fork at the rear. Front suspension was by BSA telescopic forks with progressive hydraulic damping and the fork ends were split with caps for the front wheel spindle. Both hubs were full width in cast-iron with the heads of the straight spokes concealed. Both brakes were the same size as were the rims and tyres sizes, a low riding position being assisted by the selection of the 17 in. size.

The cycle parts followed the general lines of the range with deeply valanced mudguards, dualseat, rubber mounted petrol tank, and the oil tank built into unit with the toolbox and air cleaner. Finish was red or blue and the tank carried pear-shaped badges.

Early in 1959 the basic road Star was joined by two competition models, labelled C15T and C15S for trials and scrambler. Internally the engines received different camshafts and altered compression ratios, while gearing and tyres were changed to suit the application. High level exhaust systems were fitted, without silencer on the scrambler, and the machines retained the standard frame, forks and hubs but with gaiters on the forks for protection and revised suspension springs. Fuel tanks were smaller, footrests moved, and a shorter dualseat and crankcase shield fitted. Energy transfer ignition was used and lights could be fitted if required for trials or enduro riding.

For 1960 there were a few minor engine modifications and the optional colour became almond green. In February, *Motor Cycling* road tested one which just about reached 70 mph but did return 100 mpg. The machine handled well, had good brakes and a nice gearchange, once bottom had been engaged for the first time each

day. The trick of freeing the clutch before starting the engine failed to help reduce the crash as it went in. That aside, the transmission worked well although the box whined in the gears.

Comfort was good, maintenance very easy to carry out, starting first kick, so all told the C15 carried on the tradition of the 250 cc BSA as offering cheap, reliable transport.

A short loan of a C15T indicated that, while this served its purpose, the energy transfer ignition had it limitations but there was no mention that the standard frame and hubs were far too heavy for serious trials work.

In the line up for 1961 was the first indication of how the basic C15 could be made to grow. The 250 became the 350 cc B40 by increasing the bore to 79 mm and, although the general construction of the complete machine was very similar to the C15, there were many changes to cope with the increased power and speed. In the engine the push rod tube went as these items were enclosed within the barrel casting, although the 250 remained unaltered. The cylinder head design was very similar but the valve angle was slightly smaller, a valve lifter was fitted, and the compression ratio 7:1.

The transmission followed the same lines but with raised gearing, and the frame and forks were modified to accommodate 18 in. wheels. The B40 retained the 6 in. rear brake but received a 7 in. one at the front, still in a full width, cast-iron hub with straight spokes. The petrol tank was a little larger and the other fittings copied the C15 in detail. Finish was royal red and black with chrome-plated tank panels carrying new round Star badges.

The three 250s continued with compression ratio and gearing changes for the two competition models. As the C15 was shown with an AA patrol box attached at the show, *Motor Cycling* tested one with a sidecar fitted. Geared down it acquitted itself well enough, although the braking and consumption figures changed by quite a large amount.

Scrambles model C15S built from 1959 to 1962 with open pipe

The B40 introduced for 1961. Very similar to C15 but no separate pushrod tube, 18 in. wheels and 7 in. front brake. On show in France

The C15T trials model in 1962. It is minus lights but has suitable wheels and tyres, an upswept exhaust pipe and small silencer, small tank, single seat and folding kickstart lever curled round the footrest

In January 1961 *The Motor Cycle* road tested a B40 and, naturally, the added capacity moved what was essentially a C15 along well with a top speed in the middle seventies, good acceleration and an overall fuel consumption of 86 mpg. Braking was still up to scratch, thanks to the larger front unit, but comfort would have been improved if the rear damper units had had spring rate adjustors. Not difficult to arrange, even for a private owner. The horn was rather weak and the toolbox lid awkward to replace but aside from these details the B40 proved a satisfactory machine.

April brought news of a more sporting 250 with increased power output and to indicate the performance it was typed the SS80 and called the Sports Star. The additional power was gained by increasing the compression ratio, carburettor, and valve size, fitting high duty valve springs and a sports camshaft. At first a piston giving 10:1 went in but very quickly this was reduced to 8·75:1. To deal with the higher ratio the big end was changed to a double row caged roller assembly and the flywheels from the standard cast-iron to steel forgings. The mains remained unaltered as was the lubricating system. The fins of the cylinder head were polished, which may have helped to distinguish it from the standard item, but cannot have helped heat dissipation.

On the transmission side a slipper tensioner appeared in the primary chaincase and a set of close ratio gears was fitted. The cycle parts were nearly all from the C15 with only the slightly larger petrol tank and flat handlebars differing. Frame, forks, hubs and mudguards all remained as on the standard 250. A road test by *The Motor Cycle* showed that it performed much as the B40 but with the power produced at higher engine speeds and the cam effect more noticeable.

The brake proved to be up to the mark for the machine's speed, although only just, and other testers were to suggest that the B40 unit would match the performance better. The handling was good, although the machine did weave a little on high speed bends with ripples in the road surface. The exhaust note was too loud to allow full performance to be used in town, while the horn was too quiet.

Part of the reason for the appearance of the sports 250 was the legislation which had then been recently introduced restricting learner riders to under 250 cc solos. This was to remain in force and produce a trend of super sporting machines. Often the performance was better than that of the larger variant but at the expense of a restricted power band and more peaky output. Thus the learner was restricted to machines which became less suitable for his or her knowledge and experience. Commercially it was to become pointless offering a low performance but easy-to-ride 250, as few riders would buy one.

For 1962 BSA introduced a number of changes to their range of unit singles with the compression ratio of the C15 rising a little to 7·5:1 and a new horn, improved ignition switch, and 60 watt

A C15 on show at Earls Court fitted with many of the Motoplas accessories available from this BSA owned company. A profitable line that often could make more than the machine they were fitted to

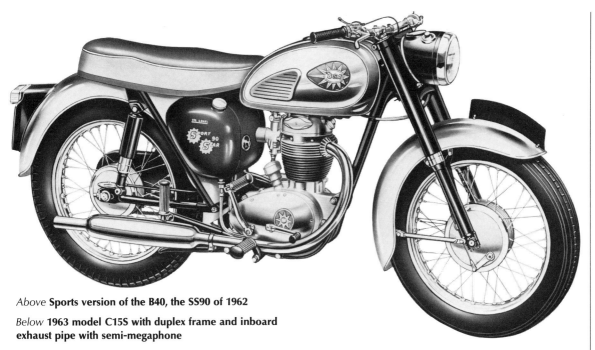

Above **Sports version of the B40, the SS90 of 1962**

Below **1963 model C15S with duplex frame and inboard exhaust pipe with semi-megaphone**

Above **The B44 Victor Grand Prix scrambler for 1965 based on the machines used by world champion Jeff Smith**

Left **1963 model C15T in the new duplex frame and fitted with lights**

alternator being fitted. Its standard colour remained red but the optional became sapphire blue with blue and ivory tank panels. The two competition machines were fitted with the camshaft from the SS80, together with that model's roller big end and primary chain tensioner along with the 7 in. front brake from the B40. In addition the rear rim section was increased and the gearing altered with a change to the engine sprocket as well as the final drive ones. The B40 received the same electrical changes as the C15, together with the roller big end and primary chain tensioner, while its front brake shoes changed to a floating design.

During the year, in May, some further changes to the competition models were announced. They both were fitted with 2 gallon light-alloy petrol tanks with quick action filler caps, alloy guards, adjustable rear suspension units, 7 in. diameter non-full width front brakes and some measures to improve starting. The energy transfer ignition had not proved to be too successful and one of the factors was the advance range. This was such that, if the engine had enough spark to start, it would be caught short on full advance and fail to rev. Conversely, if set to rev, it would not start unless run down a steep hill. There were stories of works machines being lifted over hedges in six-day events, started in this fashion, and then lifted back to the rider! To help improve matters the advance range was cut down, another ignition coil fitted, and the kickstarter to engine ratio raised. On the scrambler only, strutted bars and an exhaust pipe with integral expansion chamber and reverse cone megaphone were fitted.

The next move in the range came just a week later with the appearance of the SS90, a sports version of the B40 on the lines of the 250. It incorporated most of the features of the smaller machine and the performance was gained by raising the compression ratio to 8·75 to 1, fitting a sports camshaft and bigger inlet valve and carburettor.

The cycle parts were from the B40 but a close ratio gearbox from the 250 scrambler was fitted and the finish was in flamboyant red with chrome-plated tank panels and mudguards. The tank carried the pear-shaped badges.

On test the model number was not too optimistic as *Motor Cycle* managed 85 mph with a heavy rider in poor conditions of wind and rain. The machine reached close to 80 in third and returned between 60 and 85 mpg depending on how rapidly it was driven. Handling and braking also received high praise but comfort a little less as the rear units were thought to be too hard. The engine rattled a little with its sporting components but the exhaust was well muffled.

All six singles carried on into 1963 with no changes for the road models, but the two competition ones received a new frame based on the works ones. At the same time a central oil tank of slightly larger size was adopted along with a new air cleaner, stronger swinging fork, exhaust system which passed inside the frame above the fork pivot, and a kick-start lever that folded at its lower end. The compression ratio of the trials model was put back to 7·5:1 and it adopted the C15 camshaft, while the scrambles machine rear tyre became a full sized 4·00 × 18 mounted on a WM3 rim.

The C15 finally joined the other models in 1964 with the adoption of the roller big end and primary chain tensioner. It also received a rise in compression ratio to 8·0:1, the three-gallon petrol tank, and a change of colour shade to royal red. Both sports models were fitted with blade mudguards in place of the valanced ones but otherwise were not altered except for the gearing on the SS80. On the competition machines light alloy shrouds were fitted to the tops of the fork legs and gaiters added for protection. The optional lighting was no longer listed for the trials bike, which also went up to an 8:1 compression ratio, while the gearing of both machines was altered a little. All the road models were fitted with a magnetic speedometer.

Left **The C15 as built from 1965 to 1967 with points in timing cover, external clutch lever and improved gearbox**

Below left **The 1965 B40 which had the same changes as the C15 that year. A neat if unspectacular model with adequate performance**

Below **The British Army version B40 which made use of company scrambling experience to produce what was wanted**

The B44GP Victor production scambler built from 1965 to 1967

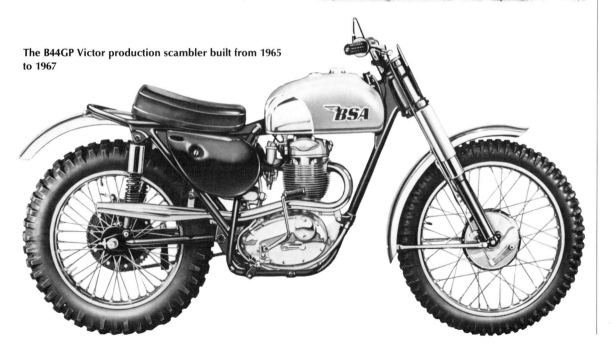

There were quite a few changes for 1965, the most obvious being the move of the points into the timing chest. The cam and the advance mechanism were driven from the end of the camshaft and the points plate mounted in a recess in the timing cover with a small chrome-plated lid over it. Also noticeable was a change in clutch operation with the cable connected to an external lever on top of the gearbox and pivoted in the new timing cover. Its lower end carried a small pinion which pushed a rack bearing directly onto the clutch push rod. This made it much easier to connect up. Internally the gearbox teeth were changed to a stub-tooth form, the gearchange improved by altering the profile of the selector quadrant plunger, and the kickstarter mechanism was changed to a face ratchet mounted on the end of the mainshaft and turned by a quadrant. This replaced the earlier arrangement which had driven the layshaft bottom gear with pawl and internal ratchet. The SS80 was fitted with chrome-plated mudguards as standard and otherwise the road single range continued as before.

To supplement it came the Victor Grand Prix, a larger, full-blooded scrambler based on the works model ridden so successfully by Jeff Smith. The new machine had evolved over the years from the C15S, via the B40 and into a 420 cc capacity using a longer stroke and a connecting rod left over from another un-related earlier experiment. Development led on to the final engine dimensions of 79 × 90 mm to give 441 cc and a redesigned and much more robust crankcase with roller drive and ball timing main bearings. Onto this went a light alloy cylinder with chrome-plated bore and this allowed a compression ratio of 11·4:1 to be used. It breathed through an air-box fitted with two filters and this sat square in the frame as the normal oil tank was dispensed with. In its place was a system using the top and front down frame tubes as supply tanks feeding a header tank below the air-box of usual construction.

The 1966 C15 still little changed from its first form and still doing the same job of providing reliable transport in the BSA tradition

The 1966 model C15 Sportsman with humped seat, swept back bars and separate headlamp shell. Internally the gears became standard not close ratio

This engine was coupled with the stub-tooth form gearbox which was more able to withstand the loads put on it and installed in the oil tank frame. This looked much like those used for the competition 250s apart from the oil pipe connections and the filler plug just behind the steering column. It was, however, made in Reynolds 531 tubing and carried a new design of front fork, developed by Jeff Smith and also used by all the twins.

The new fork used external springs enclosed and protected by gaiters which also kept the dirt off the stanchions and seals. Inside each leg a damper rod was suspended from the top nut with a clack valve and scalloped restrictor at its lower end. This assembly moved in a damper tube secured to the fork leg and this had an external taper which varied the damping rate. Hydraulic bump and rebound stops were employed and the fork ends were designed for the non-full width type of front hub with its pull-out spindle which had a left-hand thread. In keeping with this was the old pattern crinkle rear hub offering quickly detachable facilities, really an essential for a scrambles machine.

While this new model was welcomed by the competition rider there were also some machines removed from the range, with both 250 competition models and the two 350s disappearing during the year. There were further changes for 1966, with the C15 being fitted with chrome tank panels as standard and the SS80 changing its name to the C15 Sportsman. It also changed its dualseat for one with a racing hump, its bars for a pair that swept back more, its headlamp for a separate chrome-plated one, and its gears from close to standard ratios.

New was the Victor Enduro, a trail bike based on the scrambler but with a detuned engine using a linered barrel. It used the C15T frame with

The 1967 C25 Barracuda presented a new image for the unit single. High compression ratio, fierce cams and big valves matched the new style tank, seat and barrel fins

Above **A B44 Victor Roadster on test in 1967 ridden by Bob Currie. Very similar performance to that of Barracuda but less tiring to ride thanks to low down pull of engine**

Left **The Victor Roadster in its 1966 livery with Grand Prix tank. Much of the equipment is trail orientated including the well tucked in exhaust pipe. Humped seat is pure roadster**

Right **The 1968 Starfire of 250 cc. Virtually identical with 440 apart from side cover flashes. Fast on the road if driven hard, also handled well**

the new, shuttle valve forks, the normal oil tank and was equipped with trail tyres, exhaust system and seat. Because it was also intended for enduro use it had direct lights, a stop lamp, and a bulb horn fitted. Finish was black with the petrol tank deep ivory.

Motor Cycle road tested a 250 cc Sportsman in the middle of the year and reported little change from the older SS80 model. It went, it stopped, it handled and was more comfortable. The horn was rather useless even before it failed, and as usual the toolbox lid was easy to remove and nearly impossible to replace.

In July 1966 both the 250s had the lower half changed to the Victor design with ball and roller main bearings. With this came a stronger crankcase, bigger oil pump and revised oil feed into the crankshaft with an oil seal running on the crankshaft end. The new pump rotated the opposite way to the old so the oil pipes had to be crossed over. There were also transmission changes as the Victor gears were adopted with

needle roller layshaft bearings and the rear chain was lubricated from the primary chaincase under the control of a metering needle. A welcome set of improvements which assisted the production department.

In fact the C15 Sportsman had a short life with its sturdier bottom end for it was replaced in the 1967 model line up by the C25 Barracuda. This was a super sports 250, still with the same basic layout as the C15 but with a new, square fin alloy barrel on the Victor crankcase. The compression ratio was up to 9·5:1, while a completely new crankshaft ran on the ball and roller mains. The shaft was a one-piece forging with separate flywheels pressed onto each web and retained by four radial bolts. The light alloy connecting rod had a split big end with shell bearings, a most unusual arrangement for a high performance single. The remainder of the specification was geared to that image with fierce cams and a big inlet valve. Like the old Gold Star, the rockers worked on eccentric spindles which were

rotated to adjust the valve clearance. The frame was similar to that of the Victor trail machine with the same forks and hubs. Both petrol and oil tanks were in fibreglass, as was the left side cover, and the electrics were 12 volt with zener diode control. A small cover in the primary chaincase gave access to a pointer and a mark on the rotor which were used to strobe check the ignition timing. Two further changes away from the C15 image were the fitting of a heavier rear chain and a larger rear brake to match the 7 in. front.

Finish was in bushfire orange and white with black frame, chromed mudguards and humped dualseat. At the same time a second machine was listed as the B25 and called the Starfire. It was destined for the USA market and had the same specification as the Barracuda but was finished in sapphire blue and ivory.

Also added into the range was a larger version of the Barracuda using the Victor Enduro engine to make a Victor Roadster. Like the 250, it had the heavier rear chain and bigger rear brake, as did the Enduro model. The scrambler also gained the brake but not the chain, while its front rim size went down to WM1.

The gradual drift away from commuter machines to high power sports models received a further nudge in June when the tried and tested C15 was dropped from the range after nearly a decade of service. This was not to everyone's liking and one sign of another direction to go in was the reappearance of the B40 in battledress. This came about to meet a Ministry of Defence order for 2000 machines which was based on a need to cover road or track in a great variety of conditions in reasonable speed and complete reliability.

The B40WD was developed from the road model by reducing the compression ratio, refitting the valve lifter, improving air and oil filtration and fitting a carburettor with butterfly throttle. The frame was from the C15 trials model and was fitted with forks with two-way damping.

The rear chain was fully enclosed and both wheels were quickly detachable and fitted with sealed bearings. It was finished in the one colour of khaki green with some dull chrome plating and was fitted with panniers. It performed well and in time some of these models reached the home market and proved to be very nice to ride indeed. Like the rest of the range in 1967 they had 12 volt electrics.

In fact, the Victor Roadster and the smaller Barracuda represented two ways of achieving the same end with similar top speeds at about 90 mph, although the larger machine accelerated better and pulled from low down. The 250 needed to be ridden using the gears and revs to their maximum advantage so for easy riding the

Victor was to be preferred. Both models handled and braked about the same for they had the same equipment and virtually the same weight to stop or throw about in the corners. The short wheelbase and high ground clearance made balancing the machine at the lights awkward except for those with long legs; these features also made for a light front end, but the machines steered well enough even over poor surfaces.

Before the end of the year the Victor scrambler had been dropped and the Enduro was an export only machine. For 1968 the Barracuda continued under its American B25 Starfire name and the Victor Roadster was renamed the Shooting Star, an old twin title from the 1950s. The two road models were built for all markets in full export trim so came with high-rise bars, side reflectors on the tail light unit, and also beneath the tank. The larger machine was further altered with an 8 in. front brake in a full width hub, fork leg caps to hold the hub spindle, and improved rocker box lubrication. It also received a toggle light switch in the headlamp, gaitered forks, and an anodised light-alloy tank badge.

1969 saw the Starfire continued with its compression ratio raised to 10 : 1 and fitted with a 7 in. diameter twin leading shoe front brake. The petrol tank was changed to a steel one of $3\frac{1}{4}$ gallons and a second version of the same model introduced. This was the Fleet Star with lower compression ratio, lowered gearing, and black or white finish, and was designed for customers

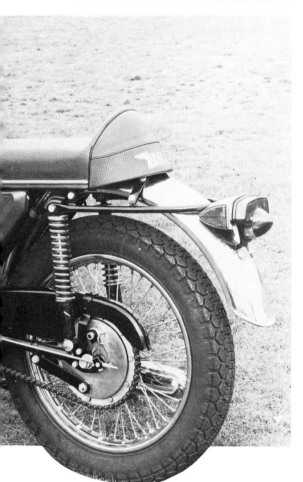

Above **Engine unit of the 1968 B44VR model fitted with Concentric and air filter**

Left **Drive side of B44VR with its high seat, sports guards and American specification side reflectors**

who would use machines in bulk, such as delivery firms, police, the forces, and large organizations.

The Shooting Star also received the twin leading shoe brake and steel petrol tank along with other detail improvements, while the Enduro model became the Victor Special. This was an export only machine, very similar to its predecessor, but fitted with an 8 in. front brake, coil ignition and full lighting equipment.

In addition the Starfire could also be bought in this semi-trail format in which case the exhaust was taken along the left side above the chaincase and carried a wire shield. The machine was also fitted with wide bars and fat tyres along with a small tank, while the centre stand was removed. The only problems were the rather sharp bark of the exhaust and the vibration due to engine speed, a trouble the larger machine escaped.

There were few changes for 1970, the main ones being the adoption of a new oil pump, an oil pressure switch and warning light, and hard chromed fork legs. For the rest, detail improvements kept the models going until October when they were replaced in total by the new range shown at the massive trade and press launch.

Among the extensive new range were five push rod singles, two of 250 cc based on the B25 and three, based on the B44, stretched out to a full 500 cc. All had many parts in common starting with a new frame which housed the oil in the single top and front down tubes. The remainder of the frame was of duplex construction and carried the swinging fork on needle roller bearings with the pivot point moveable for chain adjustment. To assist this a slot was cut in each mounting plate and a peg and cam fitted to each side of the pivot.

The front forks turned on taper roller bearings and were of the slimline type with alloy legs which had each cap secured by four bolts. No gaiters were fitted and the fork internals were

based on the existing designs to give two-way hydraulic damping.

All models had new style conical hubs with an 8 in. twin leading shoe brake offered at the front end of both 250 and 500 cc road machines, and a 6 in. single leading shoe for the other models. All machines had a 7 in. rear brake in a hub that was no longer quickly detachable and all brakes were adjusted by turning cams with click stops. Access for this was through holes drilled in the back of the hub cone. The 8 in. brake had an air scoop and was operated by a balanced cable working two short lever arms.

The two engines looked very similar and the 250 continued much as before with plain big end and crankshaft supported on single races each side. The larger engine was stretched out to 500 cc with dimensions of 84 × 90 mm and, like the 250, had a 10:1 compression ratio. Its crankshaft was totally different as it was built up with a needle roller big end assembly and ran on three main bearings. Two of these were on the drive side with the inboard one a roller and the other a ball, while a second roller was used on the timing side.

The primary drives were very similar and all based on the earlier machines, although the ratios for the 250 and the 500 differed. Lubrication also varied with the smaller machine having a conventional, separate, arrangement while the 500 received its chain oil via the mains up to a level controlled by a weir which returned excess oil to the crankcase. The main lubrication system itself was slightly different as the 250, with its plain big end, had a full flow oil filter and an oil pressure warning light.

The electrics were mainly housed in a single box mounted up under the petrol tank. In it were the zener, condenser, flasher control, capacitor for emergency ignition, ignition switch, rectifier, ignition coil and connector for the headlamp. The whole unit could be removed as one for servicing and was controlled by Lucas switches on the headlamp and handlebars. These lacked

1970 Shooting Star ready to go into its plastic packing bag

The 1971 Victor 500 with new frame, forks and hubs.
Trail models had the small front brake, sprung mudguard
and braced bars

any indication as to their function and were not to be too successful.

For the rest, the machines were kitted out to suit their designated name and purpose. In both engine sizes there was an SS model, this being a Street Scrambler which resurrected the Gold Star name to the annoyance of many enthusiasts. Like all the models, it had a sinuous black exhaust pipe which curled back alongside the cylinder barrel above the timing case to sweep inside the frame and join an odd upswept silencer. This was of box shape and followed the line of the subframe to terminate in a high level outlet. It carried a perforated heat shield to protect the passenger.

Petrol tanks on the SS models were in steel and of either 2 or 3 gallon capacity and the machines were fully equipped with lights, indicators, road mudguards and studded road tyres.

Each of the trail models was named the Victor and was remarkably similar to the Street Scramblers. Differences concerned the front

brake size, the size and type of tyres fitted, the gearing, the petrol tank which was 2 gallons without the option, and the front mudguard which was sprung and so sat well clear of the wheel. The trail machines carried the full complement of equipment as the road ones and all four, 250 and 500 cc of each type, were fitted with a crankcase shield.

This made it all the more unusual that the B50MX lacked this normal form of protection for its underside as it was built and sold as a full-blooded moto-cross machine. It looked like the Victor model minus lights and silencer but internally it used a different camshaft and closer ratio bottom gear. The overall gearing was lowered, scrambles tyres fitted and a small one-gallon fuel tank used. Ignition was by the energy transfer system and the dry weight was a very respectable 240 lb.

The new range of singles was only part of the massive BSA and Triumph launch when some 13 new machines appeared, all to be fed into the production lines at Small Heath and Meriden. If the production headaches this could cause were not enough there were also very considerable technical problems with many of the new machines. At the same time the company was in

Last of the line, the B50MX as proposed for 1973. In 1974 it was sold in America as the Triumph TR5MX. A strong runner in the BSA tradition

1971 Gold Star 250 cc in the final format. Big front brake with air scoop and road bars

serious financial trouble and it really was inevitable that the range would have to be drastically cut back so that some machines could be built.

Of the singles, the two 250s were the first to disappear in August 1971 when the 500 Victor became an export only model. Shades of 1946 all over again. The three 500s ran on into 1972 with minor changes but the last days of the once great BSA company were fast approaching. The final BSA catalogue showed just four machines on a twice folded sheet and only one of those was a single, the 500 cc Gold Star, but to many not a real Goldie just a spurious imitation. It could not last, of course, and production ground to a halt in 1972. A year later documents were signed and BSA ceased to exist as a separate company, becoming part of the NVT combine that was to later sink beneath the financial waves.

It was the end but although the company had gone the machines had not vanished entirely and showed up on two fronts. One of these was in the guise of a scrambler, as described in a later chapter, and the other was NVT Project 92. This was an experimental one-off that was conceived from available parts and ideas in the group. The idea was to create a single using the Commando Isolastic principle of engine, gearbox and swinging fork in one unit suspended from the frame and front forks.

The frame chosen was from the ill-fated 350 cc BSA Fury and Triumph Bandit twin which never reached production but for which a batch of frames had been made. Into this on Norton mountings went a B50 engine tipped forward a little in the same style as the Atlas engine was when it went into the Commando frame. A swinging fork was mounted in plates bolted to the rear of the engine unit which had a barrel and head with interrupted finning fitted at a later date. Otherwise it was the standard B50.

The cycle parts were a collection of NVT items with the front forks the type introduced for the 1971 BSA and Triumph ranges, the front brake the 8 in. twin leading shoe in the conical hub from the same source and a rear hub with drum brake cobbled up from pieces. The Commando image was fostered by using a one-into-two exhaust system which used two Commando type black cap or mute type silencers together with seat and tank from the same machine.

A left gearchange and right brake were fitted, neither of which worked very well from the cross-over, and the machine had a number of raw edges, an inevitable result with a prototype. However, the idea did work and the result was a very smooth single, light in weight and with very adequate performance. It could have been a success but really came too early in 1973–74 as the public were still then preoccupied with multis. It was not until the late 1970s that enough riders craved the charm of the single for it to reappear on the market. By then NVT were long gone.

And Gold Stars, real or not, were fast becoming a memory of what the English big single was with its high gearing and massive flywheels which gave it that effortless high speed cruising. It had a charm hard to match.

8 | Road racing

The Gold Star BSA will always be associated with one race in particular, the Clubmans TT which it came to dominate until it was the only real machine to choose for the event. It was held to be responsible for the ending of the series but this is unfair for they were dropped when crowded out of a busy race week. It was alleged that the BSA made for a boring race as there were so few other competitive makes and, although this became true for the 350, it did not really apply to the 500 until the final year. It was hardly BSA's fault that one of their range of models, looked on as commuting machines, should prove to be better than the products from their more sporting contemporaries. Much of the success came from starting with a good, reliable basic design which could produce what was needed when fitted with the right internals. There was no mystique about the cams or combustion chamber, just the correct balance of ingredients.

The first Clubmans TT races were held in 1947 at the first postwar meeting and were for Senior machines up to 1000cc, Juniors of 350 cc, and 250 cc Lightweight, all three races being run concurrently. The regulations were designed to bar genuine racing models, such as the Manx or KTT, by stipulating that only catalogue machines produced with lighting equipment and kick-starters were eligible. In fact it was compulsory for riders to remove all the lighting equipment and wheel stands and allowable for them to take off batteries and dynamos. Machines had to be

Right **Outstanding contemporary photo from doyen Tom March of Peter Davey and Gold Star at Cadwell Park. Clubmans racing at its best**

kickstarted in the race and after a compulsory pit-stop, but during it could be bump-started.

There were BSAs in that first event even if not among the leaders at the end but a little later that year the prototype Gold Star ran in the Manx Grand Prix. This used the B29 engine as a basis with a magnesium alloy crankcase and light alloy cylinder head fitted with hairpin valve springs. In the race it ran out of fuel but showed promise, especially as a high speed roadster.

For the 1948 Clubmans races the rules remained much as they were and a BSA finished last in the 350 cc event. For 1949 open exhausts without megaphones were still allowed and the Gold Star was available. In sharp contrast to the previous year the Goldie held the first two places for most of the race with the second machine retiring with a broken chain on the last lap but Harold Clark coming home the winner.

This was the start of the domination by the 350 cc Goldie for year by year it tightened its grip on the event until in 1956, the last year of the Clubmans on the TT circuit, all but two of the starters were Gold Star mounted and only a 3rd place Norton interrupted the long line of BSAs which ran down to 22nd place. They then continued on from 24th to 50th and last, but by then that was a position hard for them to avoid.

It was not quite so easy in the 500 cc class where the Norton International and Triumph

Left **350 cc Gold Star in racing trim with an experimental leading link front fork. Pictured in the Isle of Man with rider Charlie Salt**

Below left **Eddie Dow at speed on his BSA**

Right **Frantic work in the pits on the Goldie ridden by D. P. Hewaitson and P. Manning in the Bemsee 1000 production race at Oulton Park**

Below **Gold Star at speed on a real road circuit. The felt on the left engine rail for collecting chain oil looks as if it will not make it to the finish**

twin held the Goldie at bay until 1954. Eddie Dow nearly upset the opposition the year before but crashed when lying second. Then the big single won its first Clubmans and in 1955 it was Dow's turn when nearly half of the small field on the Clypse circuit were on BSAs.

1956 saw the final Clubmans races on the Mountain course and three-quarters of the senior starters were Gold Star mounted. Bernard Codd, having already won the 350, took the 500 as well to become the only rider to do the double and the big BSA occupied the first six places.

In all BSA won the Junior eight times in a row coupled with the Senior for the last three years so

it was only too apparent what a rider had to be on to have a chance in the event. Then in 1957 the TT Jubilee was held and the Clubmans was squeezed out of the crowded programme to become a national mainland race and, in doing so, it lost its magic as a race for the boys on the TT circuit using a road machine. A decade was to go by before such an event was to reappear.

Away from the TT the BSA was also in use in national road races, more usually in the non-experts events where the first-year men took their early tentative racing steps. Among them were riders such as Bob McIntyre, Derek Minter and Phil Read, who were to rapidly move on to

other machines and events on which they became famous but who rode the Goldie in their early days.

While the Gold Star was no mean performer, its weight told against it when ridden in competition with the Manx or the 7R. Despite this it was an easy starter and, for a racing machine, very docile to ride so could often make a final by dint of disappearing down the road in the heat while the field was still pushing.

One rider who tired of the BSA weight was my friend, Fred Launchbury, who had a season of quick starts followed by being badly outbraked at the corners. The solution was to fit a 350 cc

Gold Star engine into the G45 Matchless, retaining all the AMC cycle parts. Naturally the lower right frame tube had to be kinked to clear the oil pump but that aside the engine went in nicely. The result was a machine that weighed less than a 7R, steered and braked with the best, pulled a very high gear, and was cheap and easy to maintain. It was geared to run to 7000 rpm as it pulled so well and, while it could be turned over at 8000, this would break the crankshaft. A valve cost £1 4s 0d, when the 7R one was £6 0s 0d and a Norton one a tenner.

During the 1950s the factory built some special rigid, racing Gold Stars, first for Daytona

Above **Five foot trophy for the US East Coast championship won by Tom Clark on his Gold Star in 1960 at Fayettville, North Carolina. It carries the Confederate flag dropped in 1863**

Above left **Gold Star in use in American TT race, similar to flat track but with brakes allowed**

Left **Gold Star at the unique Daytona race held on combined road and beach course. Note double bars, clip-ons for 4 miles of straight and uprights for 0·2 miles of corners**

and later for US flat track racing. The Daytona event at the time was unique as the course comprised two miles of beach, a hairpin turn onto the road and then two miles of rather narrow road to another hairpin back onto the beach. The 200-mile event was hard on machines and riders but BSA were successful in 1954 with their twins winning and Gold Stars in the placings. In later years they ran DB-type machines fitted with massive air cleaners and two sets of handlebars, clip-ons for the straights and normal for the turns.

During the same period a very special racing 250 was built up at BSA and very nearly became a genuine works entry. It began in 1949 when Bert Hopwood produced a concept drawing of a machine with a horizontal single cylinder engine and separate gearbox in a neat duplex cradle frame with swinging fork rear and leading link front suspension. The engine had four valves, radially disposed and opened by rockers and two camshafts running in an inverted vee from front to rear of the cylinder head and coupled by a pair of bevels. This gear junction was driven by a shaft that ran across the engine to the right and was chain driven from the crankshaft.

This was the basis of the scheme that was passed to Doug Hele in 1950 with instructions to revamp it as he thought fit to produce an exciting machine far removed from the solid, reliable but mundane range of models. The new bike had to become a new Gold Star but with a more radical approach than the simple push rod engine. The new rules were to shun the Goldie approach of tuning a basic touring engine and to build a machine that was fast, exotic, complex if necessary, and above all competitive and practical. The new rules called for an imaginative approach and allowed for the pushing forward of technical frontiers. Behind this lay Hopwood's basic plan that would allow the technical novelty to capture the press headlines and a detuned racer to still retain the usual BSA reliability without the stolid reputation.

The first machine was to be a 250 cc racer from which other capacities could be developed. At that time Guzzi were winning most 250 cc races with their horizontal single and were to go on to take the 350 cc title five times in a row with a stretched version. Their 500 single was not exactly unsuccessful either.

The first thing Hele did was to turn the camshafts round so they ran across the head and could be driven by a vertical shaft on the right with Oldhams couplings and two further pairs of bevels. This was geared directly to the one-piece crankshaft which meant a split big end eye and plain bearing. The rod was very special with the cap studs integral with it and the first design was lightened down by Hele until it could take prolonged running at 10,500 rpm, short blasts at 11,500, and a blip to 12,000.

The rod carried a conventional piston of 70 mm diameter which was coupled with a

Geoff Monty on his BSA based GMS ridden by himself and Tommy Robb to many successes. The oil pump housing was known to touch ground

64·5 mm stroke to give the 248 cc capacity. This was again a change from the original design which had been drawn as 68 × 68 mm and was adopted to allow the use of larger valves. Compression ratio was 10·0:1 but the rather large valve angles would have prohibited anything greater. Works development could easily have led on to the later style parallel, narrow angle, valve layout with flat top piston.

The piston ran in a cylinder with horizontal fins matched by the head and various covers bolted to it. This was not the firm's first four-valve head for as far back as 1913 they had made a one-off with twin overhead camshafts. That one was for a 500 with the traditional 85 × 88 mm dimensions and the head was completely bare of fins.

Right **John Cooper with the works MC1 single of 250 cc with four valves. Very unusual construction, monoshock but never raced**

Below **GMS rear frame, very light, very strong and very good. Norton hub**

Each camshaft opened two valves via finger followers and the inlet one was driven from the crankshaft by chain with a further chain connecting its left end to the exhaust camshaft. Separate ports were provided for both inlet and exhaust and the barrel made up for the lack of head fins. It was machined from a 56 lb billet of mild steel with many thin, closely spaced fins and when finished weighed $3\frac{1}{2}$ lb.

The MC1 also had twin inlets which were placed parallel to allow the carburettor bodies to clear the frame but not before flow tests had been made using a rig on which the inlet ports could be moved. On the exhaust side a pipe ran back low down on each side to a shallow taper megaphone with a small reverse cone.

The engine was very compact with an outside flywheel on the left inboard of the chain primary drive. This ran in an electron oil bath, well finned on the outside and drove a four-speed racing

Burman gearbox with the clutch outside the case in the air. In the original Hopwood drawing the machine is shown with a BSA gearbox. Initial chain lubrication problems caused by the high running speed were overcome by increasing the case capacity and providing a weir system to feed oil onto the top chain run.

The frame into which this engine and gearbox assembly was fitted was very different to the original concept. It was duplex with cross-over at the headstock rather like the featherbed Norton but much lower for the top rails ran back from the bottom of the headstock to just above the gearbox. They curved tightly round this, ran forward under the crankcase before turning upwards to pass either side of the cylinder on their way to the top of the headstock. From that point a single tube ran back to a cross tube between the top rails above the gearbox. In front of this a second cross tube was braced to the

single tube with a substantial bracket which also acted as the mount for a single Girling suspension strut which sat horizontal beneath the seat. This strut was connected to a swinging fork with upper triangle to give a monoshock suspension system similar to the Vincent or Yamaha.

This alone was unusual for the time, but the front forks were equally different from the normal telescopic. First of all the head bearings were turned inside out with the stem clamped to the frame tubes top and bottom. The fork itself rotated round this stem and was built up from pressings as a leading link type controlled by two spring units. It passed between the main frame tubes and the pressing carried a short cross tube just behind the pivot stem onto which the handlebars clamped.

The brakes were both single leading shoe drum, the front fully floating in a full width hub. The rear was cable operated from a cross-shaft and link so no outer cable was needed. Rims were light alloy, spoked to the hubs and racing tyres were fitted.

Ignition was at first by magneto but later changed to coil, and the oil was carried under the seat in a tank which surrounded the suspension strut. The fuel tank now seen on the bike is a rather crude but massive 7 gallon item intended to allow a non-stop ride in the TT, but for short circuit events a smaller tank would have been used. The large one is beautifully purposeful even if ugly.

The result was a machine that weighed 248 lb dry with a power output of 32 bhp at 10,000 rpm. Initial tests at MIRA were encouraging with the machine lapping at 104 to 105 mph without a fairing, and, once a few teething problems had been ironed out, the machine was ridden at Oulton Park by Geoff Duke. He found it capable of competitive times even with brakes that could have been better, but the handling was good and the engine ran smoothly up to its five figure ceiling.

Unfortunately the media heard of Duke's

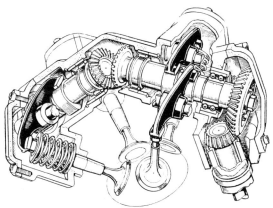

Above **The ingenious fully 4-valve head and twin camshafts of the racing 250 cc single**

Top **A C15 on Hangar Straight at Silverstone with a 250 cc Ducati single and Ariel Arrow twin whose rider is really well down to it**

Right **Clive Brown on the Mead and Tomkinson endurance BSA single**

involvement and he entered the machine as a GDS in the 250 cc TT so pressure came onto BSA to run the machine in Grand Prix races. At that time it was still a prototype and the company had not set up for a full scale attempt in that field, although no doubt the competition department could have made a good showing. The memories of the 1921 TT must have reappeared and BSA decided that they would not be pressured into going racing in a half prepared state. Either they ran a full works team or not. In the end the appearance of the new 250 cc NSU racing twins in 1954 must have influenced the decision for they were so much quicker than the previous year and had more power than the MC1 single could hope to attain.

In 1955 the last attempt to race the BSA was made with an entry at Silverstone but management demanded a guaranteed win, this was not possible, so the entry was scratched. Nearly 20 years later the machine was sold off with other prototypes and went to Stanford Hall on show.

While the complex BSA machine was never to race in anger the man behind much of the Gold Star development, Roland Pike, was also working on a simpler idea. Pike had many years of experience with Rudge engines and around the middle 1950s passed much of this, together with his Gold Star knowhow, on to Geoff Monty. Geoff had been racing for some years with specials, one of the earlier ones being a 7R in a lightweight frame followed by a cut-down Velocette KTT which did well in 250 cc races.

Geoff sought low weight and a simple engine which would be easy to maintain in the hectic rush of the English short circuit season. The basis of the engine was a 350 cc Gold Star into which a one-piece crankshaft with outside flywheel was fitted. The bore was 71 mm and combined with a 63 mm stroke. Much of the timing gear was Gold Star, modified to suit the very short barrel, while the head had a new inlet port made by boring into it on the centre line and welding a tube into the resulting hole.

Above **Fred Launchbury with his Bantam. Down tube is bent to pull engine further forward**

Above left **1980 CCM road racer derived from the BSA**

Left **Fred Launchbury at Snetterton in front**

The gearbox was an old type Manx Norton, although a Swedish five-speed unit was tried later on, and the primary chain was open with an alloy guard. The exhaust system swept back to a megaphone in Gold Star style.

The frame was based on a large diameter single tube which ran from the headstock back to curve down above the fork pivot. This was supported in a pair of alloy plates which hung from a cross-tube welded to the main one. At the front two down-tubes supported the front of the engine and the rear was bolted to massive plates surrounding the gearbox. The result was an open frame that became very rigid when the easily removed engine and gearbox unit was installed.

The swinging fork was built up from sheet steel, while the front forks were Norton. Hubs were also Norton, well lightened, and the oil tank a most complex shape in order to get it between the engine plates, behind the engine, in front of the gearbox, beneath the float chamber and completely out of the way. The left front down-tube was used as a reservoir for the chain oiler and the right one reserved for an oil cooler if required.

The machine was called the GMS and was very successful on the short circuits at first with a full dustbin and later a dolphin. The screen was moulded, with difficulty, in Geoff's bath! Two machines were built and at one memorable Blandford meeting they ran first and second until Geoff hit a snag but his rider, Tommy Robb, won. In the Isle of Man its best year was 1959 when Tommy was fourth to the works MVs and he followed this up with a fourth in the Ulster.

The same principle of keeping it simple and light led to some tuned C15s being raced during the 1960s and later to some quick racers based

on the Victor. Perhaps the best known of these was one entered by Mike Tomkinson who first became involved at the 1966 Earls Court show. There he decided that a modified roadster Victor would be suitable for the 24-hour Barcelona race and other long distance production machine events. In 1967 it proved to be fast enough to lead the unlimited class at one stage before some troubles struck. The same machine was run, less lights, in the Manx that year and in the 500-miler at Brands in 1968 before going on to a 6th in Spain, despite some engine problems.

The works themselves followed the same ideas and built up a full 500 cc racing single by 1970. This was based on the successful scramblers but with many internal modifications and, while the cycle parts look standard, they too had their share of changes. The machine was quite successful but despite the existence of a market for such a model at that time, BSA knew that the machine was far too removed from standard for them to contemplate this. In time, of course, BSA were to be no more and the TZ Yamaha made all such ideas obsolete.

The one area where the BSA single refuses to give up is with the Bantam. The machine had scarcely been launched when two-stroke enthusiasts, recognising the potential, seized upon it for the newly introduced 125 cc class. The first to do so was Bunny Armstrong, who ran his machine at Silverstone in 1949 and then talked fellow local club members, George Todd and Fred Launchbury, into entering the class.

During those early years the Hogan brothers quickly came to the forefront with John usually finishing ahead of Peter. Peter, however, later went on to build a Bantam twin which ran quickly enough for the time but had handling problems. In those days Bantams appeared with rotory drum type inlet valves, while in Australia some very fast speeds were recorded using drainpipe carburettors and alcohol fuel.

The mainstay of Bantam racing in the 1950s was the machine's cheapness, availability of spares, and the one hundred or so sets of close gears John Hogan talked BSA into making around 1950. Wipac also came up with a strengthened magneto, as the standard one burst at speed as one rider showed when his went through his director's windscreen in a car park demonstration!

Development was slow but also went on at BSA, and George Todd liased with the factory during this period on expansion boxes and a revised gearbox design. He also did a great deal of work on engines using smaller flywheels and a caged big end which took many trials to perfect.

Late in 1960 Bantam racing received a decided lift when the Bantam Racing Club was formed. They ran their first meeting the following year and celebrated their 21st anniversary in August 1981. In between hundreds of races were run, mainly for Bantams but other classes were also included.

In 1962 Fred Launchbury began his domination of BRC racing, having been using the George Todd Bantam since 1957 without being headed by a similar model. That year I decided it was time a Bantam ran in a TT again and managed to finish 16th in the 125 event. Fred also took to the Isle of Man from 1963 and over the next decade was followed by many other club riders who put up some extraordinary performances even though still stuck with the three-speed gearbox.

Even this obstacle was tackled by one or two riders using a two-speed gearbox bolted to the side of the existing unit and made from an old Bantam engine with the crankcase cut away. In England the owner used a left twistgrip change while an Australian coupled the two together. The result only gave five speeds due to the internal ratios available but if the factory had got in on the act they could have built a six-speed unit on the same lines by changing some gear sizes.

So in the 1980s the BSA single still races on, even if in the form of a 125 cc two-stroke.

9 | Off-road competition

To many people the Gold Star is best known for its performance in the Clubmans TT and the epitome of the Goldie is a late model DBD in Clubmans trim with clip-ons, rear sets and swept back exhaust. The road racing was, however, a very small part of the BSA competition activity and really one that had little to do with the works. BSA themselves were not entrants, even in the background, in the TT and their involvement was small. No doubt they were happy that the machines won and they went so far as to send a van full of spares and some works knowhow to the Island but no way were they going to be directly drawn into road racing.

Off road the story was completely different for the BSA competition department was extremely active in trials and scrambles. They were also very successful, even with machines that were not really the best suited for the events, and achieved much of this by employing a veritable army of aces. In the BSA line-up were a whole range of riders whom any factory would be pleased to sign, but leading them were the BSA super-aces, men who dominated their field, many to serve BSA faithfully and well for many years.

This powerful team stemmed from the background history of spectacular tests conducted in

Jeff Smith on the Gold Star winning a scramble, a sight that was so common. Twice world champion and a brilliant trials rider

Left **The works 250 in 1962 based on the C15 but somewhat modified. It has the 1963 type frame, a very works oil tank and the exhaust on the left**

Right **John Harris at speed on the 350 in 1962 at Hawkstone**

Far right **Eric Cheney (in cap) with special based on the BSA single as seen in 1966**

Below right **Vic Eastwood cornering hard on the unit construction single**

Below **Derek Rickman in 1957 on the 500 cc Gold Star. Later famous with his brother for their Metisse machines**

the 1920s to prove and promote the products. As described, these had more than made their point and culminated in the successful Maudes Trophy attempt in 1938. Backing up these highlights were a host of successes in weekend sporting events beginning with the reliability trials of the twenties.

BSA were fortunate then to gain the services of Bert Perrigo, an outstanding rider who took over the competition department before later moving on to other senior roles in the company. His ability is perhaps highlighted by his winning the solo class of the first British Experts trials held in 1929 and in 1932 he was a member of the English team which won the ISDT Trophy. During his career he was to take the solo experts title once again and to represent his country six times in the ISDT. He won virtually every major trial at one time or another and retained his enthusiasm for motorcycles to the end.

He brought in Harold Flook to deal with the sidecar class and, with Fred Povey on a solo, the three of them formed a powerful team in the trials world of the early 1930s. Flook won the sidecar experts three times in a row and Povey took the 1934 solo class. In 1937 Bert retired from the continuous round of trials, although he still rode in six days events. Flook left BSA and in his place appeared Harold Tozer to continue the BSA dominance of the sidecar trials class.

Just before the war a new name was seen in the Army team on their BSAs, that of Fred Rist. Corporal in 1938, he was a Sergeant the following year in the aborted ISDT. After the war he was soon on the BSA squad with newcomer Bill Nicholson and, still with his sidecar, Harold Tozer who always stuck to the pre-war M-type engine which pulled like a dray horse. Bert Perrigo himself rode again in trials just after the war but was soon back to running the team and talking Nicholson into riding in scrambles.

For this field Nicholson used a 1940 B29 with a McCandless swinging fork conversion which made some of the opposition envious. Factory

Above **A Gold Star in ISDT trim with some spares on board and some changes to help speed maintenance**

Top **Final BSA development project was this speedway machine using the B50 as a basis. This is the Mark 2 with Rob North frame which went well**

policy soon had him back on plungers but, although these looked like the standard units as sold to the public, he cleverly introduced hydraulic damping under the covers.

In 1947 another name destined for fame was seen in the BSA team, Geoff Duke, who won his first major event with them before moving on to Nortons. At that time Nicholson and Rist dominated the solo events while Tozer seldom failed to capture the sidecar award in every trial he ran in. Behind them were several other riders, all capable of winning national events and ready

to step into the breach if one of the leaders struck trouble.

For 1950 they were joined by John Draper and Basil Hall with John Avery in mid-season, to concentrate on 250 cc races. The competition shop also began to run a 'tweaked-up' Bantam in a few suitable events. All the works machines were well modified of course and as far back as 1946 had been using alloy heads and barrels to help cut the weight down. Internally the scrambles motors used all the go-faster pieces developed for racing and Nicholson had his own cams to supplement the official ones. Among these were cams for wet and dry circuits and he was known to change them if the weather conditions altered. The trials jobs were equally modified as even those that bore the Gold Star engine numbers often contained detuned B31 parts and used road cams and low compression pistons.

Lampkin leads Banks is all that was written on this picture and it summed up the strength of the BSA team. This existed right to the end just as it had for so many decades

Nicholson had a great year in 1951 winning the trials star, the tough Scott for the second year in succession, and tying for the solo experts title. By that time he had another swing-arm frame and spent much time sorting out the Girling units. In the end he replaced the damping system with his own design and then moved on to sort out the gearbox on the singles.

He was joined in the shop by Brian Martin in 1952 who went on the successful Maudes trophy run on the twins with Rist and Norman Vanhouse, while in 1953 BSA managed to sign Jeff Smith, the man who at 17 had tied in the experts with Nicholson. Jeff was to stay at Small Heath

nearly to the end and stood at the top of the tree in both trials and scrambles for two decades. In the same year Harold Tozer retired to the cheers of the other sidecar men and his place was taken by Frank Darrieulat both in the team and in the results sheets.

Bert Perrigo finally left the competition shop that year for a short spell at Ariel before returning to the Small Heath works as chief development engineer. The team continued its successful ways, even pressing the Bantam into use on occasions and one of the two-stroke riders was Brian Stonebridge who forced the little machines along at a fine pace.

Jeff Smith, Brian Martin, John Draper, Terry Cheshire, Geoff Ward, Frank Darrieulat, Arthur Lampkin, Brian Stonebridge and Derek Rickman were all in the BSA squad in the late 1950 period and in 1958 Brian Martin became competition manager while still a very active rider. By the end of the decade the big Goldie had gone and the

Above **Brian Martin with the prototype C15 trials model at the 1958 Mitcham Vase trial in which he was 250 cc class winner**

Left **Trials sidecars have their snags discovered John Harris when his BSA outfit got stuck. Helping to pull it clear is the great Sammy Miller**

Left **A unit construction BSA set up for ISDT work with very small headlight, spares and large apron over the carburettor**

Right **A very neatly tucked in exhaust system and useful kickstart grace this competition Bantam**

Below **Jeff Smith under electric power on a show trials course set up by Filtrate. BSA cycle parts—of course**

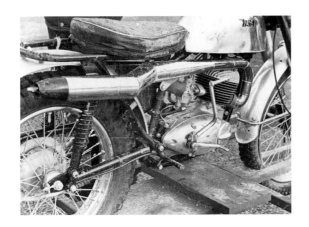

team was on the newer C15 models but it made little difference to the results. In 1959 Smith won the Scott, Lampkin the scrambles star, and the team many, many prizes. Their only real problem was Sammy Miller with his Ariel on his way to becoming the greatest trials rider of all time, and in the process beating the BSA men with their own subsidiary. Sam would have won on anything, of course.

Jeff Smith continued to be the number one rider and won the experts again in 1963. At the same time he was scrambling the unit single which was gradually stretched out until it reached 420 cc. It was further developed into the Victor range and it was on the works development model that Smith took the world title in 1964 and 1965, a tremendous feat for a rider who went round Europe with limited support to take on and beat the world's best. An effort to reduce the weight of his machine even further led to the titanium frame that could not be mended in the field so proved to be more successful in theory than in practice. With the frame came a rear disc brake, most unusual for moto-cross, and the chain adjuster cam at the rear fork pivot, as used on the 1971 road models.

BSA stuck to their four-stroke singles right to the end in a world that became dominated by two-strokes and they still continued to have plenty of successes. A good few were in televised scrambles and one rider who became well known that way was John Banks, who took up the world title trail for BSA in 1968 and 1969. Unfortunately the ring-dings were going rather quicker and he was unable to emulate Smith's victories but he did the next best thing by finishing second in both years.

And then, suddenly, it was 1971, the accountants were looking for a means to reduce the overheads so the competition shop was axed. Jeff Smith took his vast experience to Canada, Brian Martin moved to fresh fields, and John Banks had to ride two-strokes but not for long.

Alongside the BSA there had been one or two other four-strokes and one of the most successful was that built by Eric Cheney using a B40 as a starting point. In the process of becoming a Cheney-BSA it grew to 441 cc, received extensive internal changes, and was fitted into a very nice duplex frame that featured many special parts to reduce weight and improve performance. By 1973 John Banks had become its rider.

Another machine which started from the same base was the CCM run by Alan Clews. At first these were Victors with modifications but over the years the BSA content decreased as the machines became more and more special. They also built road racing versions and ultimately moved into this field with other engines.

It was sad that such a successful competition department which had won so many victories and contributed so much to the development of the firm's products should go at the stroke of an accountant's pen. Perhaps it was symbolic of why the company as a whole failed for the competition riders wanted to build better motorcycles and the money was made for that purpose. The accountants wanted to make money by building motorcycles and could not see how a Gold Star scrambler hurtling over the crest of a hill was raw excitement.

They killed the department but the record and the legends of the singles and the men who rode them live on.

Appendix | *Postwar Gold Star* Specifications in full

These are presented in their own section along with notes on colour and machine recognition to separate them from the other BSA singles. The data on the 1938–39 models is not included here but remains in the general data section. The specifications are in the form of notes on each section of the machine with a table of a typical range of builds taken from one year to show how versatile the Gold Star was.

Engine

The engines used the standard bore and stroke so were 71 × 88 mm for 348 cc, and 85 × 88 mm for 499 cc. A range of camshafts, carburettors and compression ratios were available so the power output depended on the build state.

The flywheels of the 350 were 8 in. diameter with a 55 per cent balance factor in 1949, this changing to $7\frac{1}{4}$ in. and 58 per cent in 1955. The 1954 500 cc engine had oval wheels with 65 per cent but a year later these had become round and the factor was 58 per cent, the same as the 350. Both engines continued with this to the end of production.

All engines had magneto ignition and a 60 watt dynamo when a generator was fitted. The electric system was 6 volt.

Power output

This varied very much according to the specification of the engine and depended on the piston, valves, cams and carburettor fitted. Most

published figures refer to the racing and Clubman engines.

The first 350s produced 25 bhp at 6000 rpm in ZB form with an open pipe. BB units gave 27 at 7000, while the CB was up to 30. The DB series produced this figure at 7500 rpm when fitted with a silencer, while exchanging this for an open pipe and megaphone brought the power up to 32·5 bhp. Figures for the 500 were ZB—28 at 5500 rising with the BB to 34·5 at 6400 on an open pipe. The CB pushed the figure up to 38 at 6500, while the DBD with silencer managed 40 at 7000, and with megaphone went to 42. Development engines would produce up to 5 bhp more in either size.

Connecting rod lengths

Three lengths, all used in 350 but only longest and shortest in 500.

Long rod: $7\frac{3}{8}$ in. centres

used	ZB32	1949 to 1951
	ZB34	1950 to 1952
	BB34	1953 to 1955

Medium rod: $6\frac{7}{8}$ in. centres

used	ZB32	1952 only
	BB32	1953 to 1955

Short rod: $6\frac{15}{32}$ in. centres

used	CB32	1954 to 1955
	DB32	1955 to 1962
	CB34	1954 to 1955
	DB34	1955 to 1957
	DBD34	1956 to 1963

Gearbox

The gearbox used from 1949 to 1952 was available with a choice of three sets of internal ratios. That used for the swinging fork frame from 1953 onwards had more choice with six sets of internals and could be had with needle roller bearings fitted to the layshaft, when the suffix 'T' was stamped after the type letters, and to the sleeve gear also when the figure '2' was added, thus—'T2'.

The numbers of teeth on each gear and the resulting ratios are given in the tables—

1949–1952

	Mainshaft				Layshaft			
Type	Sleeve	3rd	2nd	1st	Sleeve	3rd	2nd	1st
Standard	28	25	20	16	17	20	25	29
Scrambles	28	25	22	18	17	20	23	27
Racing	26	25	23	19	19	20	22	26

Ratios	Top	3rd	2nd	1st
Standard	1	1·318	2·059	2·985
Scrambles	1	1·318	1·722	2·471
Racing	1	1·095	1·309	1·873

1953 onwards

	Mainshaft				Layshaft			
Type	Sleeve	2nd	3rd	1st	Sleeve	2nd	3rd	1st
RRT2	25	22	24	19	18	21	19	24
RR	25	22	24	18	18	21	19	25
DAY	26	22	25	18	17	21	18	25
SC	25	19	22	16	18	24	21	27
STD	26	20	24	16	17	23	19	27
TR1	26	17	22	14	17	26	21	29

Ratios

Type	Marking	Top	3rd	2nd	1st
Extra close	RRT2	1	1·100	1·326	1·754
Extra close	RR	1	1·100	1·326	1·929
Close	DAY	1	1·101	1·460	2·124
Scrambles	SC	1	1·326	1·754	2·344
Standard	STD	1	1·211	1·759	2·581
Trials or Wide	TR1	1	1·460	2·339	3·168

All Gold Stars were fitted with 43-tooth clutch and 42- or 46-tooth rear wheel sprockets. A 44-tooth clutch was available as an option. Engine sprockets with from 16 to 23 teeth were available at various times and either 16 or 19-tooth gearbox sprockets were used. Some top gear ratios which were therefore available are set out in the table and intermediate ratios can be calculated by combining these with the correct gearbox internal figures—

Top Gear Ratios (clutch—43T, rear wheel—42T)

Engine	16	17	18	19	20	21
16T gearbox	7·055	6·640	6·271	5·941	5·644	5·375
19T gearbox	5·941	5·591	5·281	5·003	4·753	4·526

Transmission chains

Lengths were to suit the frame and sprockets

used but all models had $\frac{1}{2} \times \frac{5}{16}$ primary and $\frac{5}{8} \times \frac{1}{4}$ rear chains until 1958 when $\frac{5}{8} \times \frac{3}{8}$ was adopted.

Suspension

At the front, BSA telescopic forks common to the A, B and M ranges, were fitted. Shrouds and mudguard fittings varied to suit the application but the basic forks remained the same. Late type A and B forks have separate ends to clamp the wheel spindle but all Gold Stars have a pull-out spindle. Thus the forks remained with the right leg threaded (with a left-hand thread) and the left leg split and clamped with a single bolt. Fork travel was 5·75 in.

Original rear suspension was by undamped plungers with 2·25 in. movement. From 1953 the swinging fork frame was used with Girling units to give 3.5 in. wheel movement. For 1953 only, fat Girlings were fitted to all models and continued on scrambles machines in 1954. Spring rates available were 107 lb/in. for light touring and Clubman, 120 lb/in. for standard riders of these models, and 155 lb/in. for scrambles.

In 1954 slimline Girlings were adopted except for scrambles, and these fell into line in 1955. Spring rates were 90 lb/in. for Clubman, 110 lb/in. for touring, with 130 lb/in. available to special order. The scrambler was fitted with 110 lb/in. springs but had dampers with a stronger action.

Brakes

The 1949 350 was fitted with a 7 in. diameter brake, 1·12 in. wide. In 1950 this was increased to 8 in. diameter and 1·38 in. wide and this size was also fitted to the 500. It remained the standard fitment for both machines for the rest of their model life when built for racing, Clubmans, or touring use. All scramblers retained the 7 in. front brake except for late Catalina scrambles which used the 8 in. one. From 1956 the 190 mm diameter full-width front brake was available as an option, this had 2 in. wide shoes.

All Gold Stars built from 1949 to 1963 were fitted with 7 in. diameter rear brake with shoes 1·12 in. wide.

Tyres

These were selected to suit the purpose for which the machine was built so could be ribbed, triple studded racing, trials universal or sports scrambles to choice. Rim sections were to suit the tyre size and diameters ranged from 19 to 21 in. for the front, and 18 to 19 in. for the rear. For racing and road use light alloy rims were available and commonly fitted in place of the standard steel items.

Petrol tanks

The 1949 B32 was fitted with a 3 gallon tank as standard with a 2 gallon option being available. By 1952 tanks of 2, 3 or 4 gallons were in use and the fitment depended on the machine specification, but there was always a choice, either of 2 or 3 gallons, or of 3 or 4 gallons.

From 1956 the tanks were available in 2 or 4 gallon capacity in steel and in 2 or 5 gallon in aluminium alloy. In 1960 the scramblers were fitted with the 2 gallon alloy tank as standard with the Clubman available with a steel tank of 2 or 4 gallons, or either of the alloy ones.

Oil tank

On the rigid and plunger frames used up to 1952 the standard oil tank of 5-pints capacity was fitted to the saddle tube. From 1953, on the swinging fork frame, the oil tank was fixed in the right rear frame loop and was of 6-pints capacity. It was mounted with special swivel bolts so that it was not stressed by frame movement when ridden. At the same time the old type rigid metal pipes with rubber connections were changed to the armoured flexible type. From 1959 the scrambles models had the option of a central oil tank.

Machine dimensions

These varied according to the specification but

the plunger frame wheelbase was 54·75 in., and that of the swinging fork one 56 in. Ground clearance was 5 in. with the scramblers claiming 6·25 while the seat height was 30·5 in., the scrambles machines being one inch up on this.

Dry weight was given as 374 lb up to 1952 and 380 lb after. Again, it was very dependent on specification but even in racing form the Goldie weighed a good deal more than a Manx or 7R.

Typical machine specifications—B32—1952

Note this applies to B32 after ZB32GS6001 only – other models differ.

Electrics—Lucas standard or special magdyno, Lucas magneto or BTH magneto

Specification	Touring	Trials	International Trials	Scrambles 1	Scrambles 2	Racing 1	Racing 2	Clubmans
Piston part no.	65–1681	65–1681	65–1616	65–1616	65–1674	65–1674	65–1687	65–1616
Compression ratio	6·5	6·5	8·0	8·0	9·0	9·0	13·0	8·0
Compression plate (in.)	—	—	$\frac{1}{32}$	—	—	0·012	—	0·012
To give ratio	—	—	7·5	—	—	8·8	—	7·8
Fuel	Pool	Pool	80 octane	Pool	50/50	50/50	Alcohol	Pool
Carb Type	Std or TT	Std	Std	TT	TT	TT or RN	TT	TT
Carb. Choke (in.)	1 or $1\frac{3}{32}$	1	1	$1\frac{3}{32}$	$1\frac{3}{32}$	$1\frac{3}{32}$	$1\frac{3}{32}$	$1\frac{3}{32}$
Inlet Cam	65·2448	65·2420	65·2420	65·2448	65·2448	65·2444	65·2448	65·2444
Exhaust Cam	65·2452	65·2420	65·2420	65·2450	65·2450	65·2446	65·2450	65·2446
In.Clear (in.)	0·008	0·003	0·003	0·008	0·008	0·008	0·008	0·008
Ex. Clear (in.)	0·010	0·003	0·003	0·010	0·010	0·010	0·010	0·010
Valve Timing at. 0·018 in.								
Inlet opens	43	25	25	43	43	60	43	60
Inlet closes	73	65	65	73	73	85	73	85
Exhaust opens	64	65	65	70	70	80	70	80
Exhaust closes	34	25	25	45	45	55	45	55
Ignition (in.)	0·437	0·437	0·437	0·437	0·437	0·469	0·375	0·469
Ignition (degree)	36	36	36	36	36	39	34	39
Sprockets								
Engine	17	16	16	16	16	18	18	19
Gearbox	19	16	16	16	16	19	19	19
Box type	Std	Std	Std	Scramble	Scramble	Racing	Racing	Racing
Top gear ratio	5·591	7·055	7·055	7·055	7·055	5·281	5·281	5·003
Tank capacity	3 or 4	2 or 3	2 or 3	2 or 3	2 or 3	3 or 4	3 or 4	3 or 4
Brakes—front	8	7	7	7	7	8	8	8
Front tyre	3·00 × 21	3·00 × 21	3·00 × 21	2·75 × 21	2·75 × 21	3·00 × 21	3·00 × 21	3·00 × 21
Front tyre type	Rib	Trials	Trials	Sports	Sports	Rib	Rib	Rib
Rear Tyre	3·25 × 19	4·00 × 19	4·00 × 19	4·00 × 19	4·00 × 19	3·25 × 19	3·25 × 19	3·25 × 19
Rear tyre type	Racing	Trials	Trials	Sports	Sports	Racing	Racing	Racing

Gold Star colours

1949

B32: black frame, forks, oil tank, headlamp shell, engine plates, rear plunger upper covers, toolbox. Oil tank has level transfer and toolbox piled arms transfer. Chrome-plated exhaust system, mudguards, mudguard stays, fork spring covers, plunger lower covers, chaincase, chainguard, brake back plates, headlamp rim, handlebars, other bright parts. Petrol tank chrome-plated with matt silver panels lined in maroon with Gold Star transfers on each side. Wheel rims chrome-plated with matt silver centres, lined in maroon.

1950

B34: as **B32**, both as in 1949.

1951

no change

1952

no change until affected by nickel shortage. Finish then changed for mudguards, stays, chaincase, chainguard, brake back plates and handlebars, which were painted matt silver. Petrol tank matt silver with maroon lining and Gold Star badges. Rims matt silver, lined in maroon, unless in light alloy. Remainder unchanged in black or chrome.

1953

finish adopted much as in 1949 and to remain unchanged to end of production. Black frame, forks, swinging fork, headlamp shell, upper and lower damper covers, oil tank, toolbox, fork yokes, most small brackets in frame centre section. Chrome-plated mudguards, chainguard, wheel rims (unless light alloy), damper lower covers, fork spring covers, headlamp rim, exhaust system, bars, mudguard stays, kickstart and gear levers. Transfers: Oil level and piled arms on oil tank. Petrol tank matt silver with chrome-plated side panels lined in maroon. Fitted with round Gold Star badges with red background.

Model recognition

1949

B32: new model with all alloy engine with no separate push rod tunnel. ZB type.

1950

B32: 8 in. front brake

B34: as B32 including new front brake. **ZB** type.

1951

Late in year **B34** changed to die-cast head and barrel with separate rocker box.

1952

B32: from engine number ZB32GS–6001, die-cast head and barrel with separate rocker box, shorter rod, shorter barrel with one less fin, increased downdraught, modified timing cover for oil breather, eccentric brake pedal pin.

1953

BB models still with small fins. Swinging fork frame, fat Girlings, new oil tank, dualseat, new gearbox.

1954

BB continued, **CB** introduced with big finned engine, eccentric rocker spindles, five through-bolts for head fixing, swept-back exhaust, short rod, oval flywheels on 500 only, mechanical breather, GP carburettor, slim Girlings, needle bearings for layshaft.

1955

BB and **CB** continued, **DB** introduced with four through-bolt head, thicker cylinder liner, vertical float mount, clip-ons standard, tubular silencer, vented brakes, alloy muff on rear drum, fitted with speedo and rev-counter, smaller non-oval flywheels.

1956

350 in **DB** form only, **500** in **DB** and introduced in **DBD** with $1\frac{1}{2}$ in. GP. Megaphone shape silencers, sleeve gear needle roller bearings, 190 mm front brake option, 5 gallon alloy tank option.

1957

No tourers, **DB** and **DBD** models in Clubmans, Scrambles and racing trim only.

1958

350 models and **500** racer dropped leaving **DBD 500** only in Clubmans and Scrambles form.

1959

As 1958 but with **500** available with 350 engine fitted. Centre oil tank option for Scrambler.

1960

As 1959. 2 gallon tank standard on Scrambler.

1961

As 1960.

1962

As 1960, very few 350s built, 350 dropped during year.

1963

As 1960 in 500 cc capacity only for Clubmans or Scrambles use, fitted with DBD engine. Production stopped during year.

Gold Star prices

After the war the 350 cc B32 appeared late in 1948 priced at £166 10s 0d plus £44 19s 1d purchase tax, making a total of £211 9s 1d to which had to be added £5 1s 8d for a speedometer.

Machine prices as listed over the years had to assume a catalogue build although many machines were supplied in different forms or with extras. The listed prices were:

Date	B32			B34		
	£	s.	d.	£	s.	d.
18.11.48	211	9	1	—		
6.10.49	216	10	9	229	4	9
9.10.50	216	10	9	229	4	9
1.11.51	242	15	7	253	0	0
2.10.52	245	0	4	255	4	9
23. 4.53	231	14	0	241	7	4
22.10.53	230	2	0	239	14	0
14.10.54	238	16	0	250	16	0
23. 6.55	—			260	8	0

	Clubman	Scrambler
2.10.58	310 12 7	282 11 2
3. 9.59	307 11 11	273 4 4
8. 9.60	312 14 5	278 6 11
31. 8.61	325 2 6	285 2 0
6. 9.62	350 11 0	307 10 0

Gold Star extras

There were many of these and often the listed price only applied when the item was ordered with a new machine as it was substituted for the standard item and fitted during manufacture.

A few of the items and their prices are listed below—

		£	s.	d.
1952	dualseat	3	16	8
1954	alloy rims	9	12	0
1959	for Clubmans:			
	rev-counter	7	16	10
	5-gallon alloy tank	23	14	5
	alloy rims	10	12	4
	190 mm front brake	5	6	2
	racing seat	1	19	10
	for Scrambler:			
	central oil tank	5	13	5
	air filter	4	16	6
	2-gallon tank	8	5	11
	rev-counter	7	16	10
	shortened dualseat	1	5	4
	GP carburettor	13	17	6

Most of the 1959 items continued to be listed up to the end and, although the prices increased, it was not by any great amount with the rev-counter becoming £8 5s. 8d. and the central oil tank £6 8s. 5d.

Gold Star engine and frame numbers

Note that all postwar Gold Star engines have the letters GS in the number after the type and size letters.

Year	Model	Engine	Frame
1938	500	JM24-101	JM24-101
1939	500	KM24-101	KM24-101
1949	350	ZB32GS-101 ⎫	⎰ ZB31-101 rigid and
	500	ZB34GS-101 ⎭	⎱ ZB32S-101 plunger
1950	350	ZB32GS-2001 ⎫	⎰ ZB31-9001 rigid and
	500	ZB34GS-2001 ⎭	⎱ ZB32S-2001 plunger
1951	350	ZB32GS-3001 ⎫	⎰ ZB31-14001 rigid and
	500	ZB34GS-3001 ⎭	⎱ ZB32S-3001 plunger

Year	Model	Engine	Frame
1952	350	ZB32GS-4001	ZB31-19001 rigid and ZB32S-4001 plunger
	350 Clubman	ZB32GS-6001	
	500 sandcast	ZB34GS-4001	
	500 die cast	ZB34GS-5001	
1953	350	BB32GS-101	BB31-101 rigid or BB32S-101 plunger or BB32A-101 s/a
	500	BB34GS-101	
1954	350	BB32GS-1001	CB32-101
	350 new Clubman	CB32GS-101	
	500	BB34GS-1001	
	500 new Clubman	CB34GS-101	
	500 Daytona	BB34GSD-101	CB32D-101 rigid (very few made)
1955	350	BB32GS-2001	
	350 Clubman	CB32GS-501	
	500	BB34GS-2001	CB32-1501
	500 Clubman	CB34GS-501	
	350 new	DB32GS-101	CB32-4001 1956 models produced in 1955
	500 new	DB34GS-101	
1956–57	350	DB32GS-501	
	500	DB34GS-501	CB32-4001
	500 new head	DBD34GS-2001	
	500 USA	DB34GS-501	BB32R-301 rigid
1958	500	DBD34GS-3001	CB32-7001
1959	350	DB32GS-1501	CB32-7873
	500	DBD34GS-3753	
	500 Catalina	DBD34GS-3753	CB32C-101
1960	350	DB32GS-1601	CB32-8701
	500	DBD34GS-4601	
	500 Catalina	DBD34GS-4601	CB32C-351
1961	350	DB32GS-1741	CB32-10101
	500	DBD34GS-5684	
	500 Catalina	DBD34GS-5684	CB32C-601
1962	350	DB32GS-1794	CB32-11001
	500	DBD34GS-6504	
	500 Catalina	DBD34GS-6504	CB32C-741
1963	500	DBD34GS-6881	CB32-11451
	500 Catalina	DBD34GS-6881	CB32C-857

Other Singles Specifications

Model	B20	B21	B22	B23
Year from	**1937**	**1937**	**1937**	**1937**
Year to	**1938**	**1939**	**1938**	**1939**
Bore (mm)	63	63	63	71
Stroke (mm)	80	80	80	88
Capacity (cc)	249	249	249	348
Compression ratio (to 1)	5·0 **1**	6·7 **2**	7·5 **3**	5·0 **4**
Valve position	SV	ohv	ohv	SV
inlet opens BTDC	10	16·5	35	10
inlet closes ABDC	55	48·5	75	55
exhaust opens BBDC	60	53·5	70	60
exhaust closes ATDC	15	21·5	40	15
Valve clearance (cold) inlet (in.)	0·004	0·003 **5**	0·003	0·004 **6**
Valve clearance (cold) exhaust (in.)	0·006	0·003 **5**	0·003	0·010 **6**
Ignition timing (in.)	0·312	0·437	0·437	0·312
Points gap (in.)	0·012	0·012	0·012	0·012
Primary drive chain	$\frac{1}{2} \times \frac{5}{16}$	$\frac{1}{2} \times \frac{5}{16}$	$\frac{1}{2} \times \frac{5}{16}$	$\frac{1}{2} \times \frac{5}{16}$
Rear chain	$\frac{1}{2} \times \frac{5}{16}$	$\frac{1}{2} \times \frac{5}{16}$	$\frac{1}{2} \times \frac{5}{16}$	$\frac{1}{2} \times \frac{5}{16}$
Sprockets: engine (T)	17	18 **7**	17 **8**	18
O/A ratio: top	6·6	6·2 **9**	6·6 **10**	6·2
O/A ratio: 3rd	8·6	8·1	8·6	8·1
O/A ratio: 2nd	13·2	12·4	13·2	12·4 **11**
O/A ratio: 1st	19·4	18·2	19·4	18·2 **12**
Front tyre (in.)	3·00 × 19	3·00 × 19 **13**	3·00 × 20	3·25 × 19
Rear tyre (in.)	3·00 × 19	3·00 × 19 **13**	3·25 × 19	3·25 × 19
Brake front dia. (in.)	5·5	5·5	5·5	5·5
Brake rear dia. (in.)	5·5	5·5	5·5	5·5
Front suspension	girder	girder	girder	girder
Rear type	rigid	rigid	rigid	rigid
Petrol tank (Imp. Gal)	2·75	2·75 **14**	2·75	2·75 **14**
Oil tank (Imp. pint)	4·0	4·0 **15**	4·0	4·0 **15**
Ignition system	magneto	magneto	magneto	magneto
Generator type	dynamo	dynamo	dynamo	dynamo
Battery (volt)	6	6	6	6
Wheelbase (in.)	52	52	52	52
Ground clear. (in.)	4·9 **16**	4·9 **16**	4·9 **16**	4·9 **16**
Seat height (in.)	28·5	28·5	28·5	28·5

1 1938—5·5 **2** 1938—6·2, 1939—6·5 **3** 1938—6·8 **4** 1939—5·25 **5** 1939 de-luxe—0·006, 0·006 **6** 1939 de-luxe—0·008, 0·012 **7** 1939—17 **8** 1938—18 **9** 1939 de-luxe—6·5 **10** 1938—6·2 **11** 1939 de-luxe—12·3 **12** 1939 de-luxe—17·6 **13** 1939 de-luxe—3·25 **14** 1939 de-luxe—3·0 **15** 1939 de-luxe—5·0 **16** 1938—5·4

Model	B24	B25	B26	B29
Year from	**1937**	**1937**	**1937**	**1940**
Year to	**1939**	**1939**	**1939**	
Bore (mm)	71	71	71	71
Stroke (mm)	88	88	88	88
Capacity (cc)	348	348	348	348

Model	B24	B25	B26	B29
Year from	**1937**	**1937**	**1937**	**1940**
Year to	**1939**	**1939**	**1939**	
Compression ratio (to 1)	6·7 **1**	7·5 **1**	6·7 **9**	7·2
Valve position ohv				
inlet opens BTDC	35	35	35	35
inlet closes ABDC	75	75	75	
exhaust opens BBDC	70	70	70	
exhaust closes ATDC	40	40	40	
Valve clearance (cold) inlet (in.)	0·003 **2**	0·003 **2**	0.003 **2**	0·003
Valve clearance (cold) exhaust (in.)	0.003 **2**	0·003 **2**	0·003 **2**	0·003
Ignition timing (in.)	0·437	0·437	0·437	0·437
Points gap (in.)	0·012	0·012	0·012	0·012
Primary drive chain	$\frac{1}{2} \times \frac{5}{16}$	$\frac{1}{2} \times \frac{5}{16}$	$\frac{1}{2} \times \frac{5}{16}$	
Rear chain	$\frac{5}{8} \times \frac{1}{4}$	$\frac{5}{8} \times \frac{1}{4}$	$\frac{5}{8} \times \frac{1}{4}$	
Sprockets: engine (T)	21	19	20	17
O/A ratio: top	5·5 **3**	6·0	5·7 **7**	
O/A ratio: 3rd	7·1	7·8	7·3	
O/A ratio: 2nd	10·9	12·0	11·4	
O/A ratio: 1st	15·5	17·0	16·2	
Front tyre (in.)	3·00 × 20	2·75 × 21	3·25 × 19	
Rear tyre (in.)	3·25 × 19	4·00 × 18	3·25 × 19	
Brake front dia. (in.)	5·5 **4**	5·5 **4**	5·5 **4**	7·0
Brake rear dia. (in.)	7·0	7·0	7·0	7·0
Front suspension	girder	girder	girder	girder
Rear type	rigid	rigid	rigid	rigid
Petrol tank (Imp. gal)	2·75 **5**	2·75 **5**	2·75 **5**	3·0
Oil tank (Imp. pint)	4·0 **6**	4·0 **6**	4·0 **6**	5·0
Ignition system	magneto	magneto	magneto	magneto
Generator type	dynamo	dynamo	dynamo	dynamo
Battery (volt)	6	6	6	6
Wheelbase (in.)	52	52	52	
Ground clear (in.)	4·9 **8**	4·9 **8**	4·9 **8**	
Seat height (in.)	28·5	28·5	28·5	

1 1938—6·8, 1939—7·25 **2** 1939—0·006 **3** 1939—5·6 **4** 1939—7.0 **5** 1939—3.0 **6** 1939—5·0
7 1939 single port—5·6, 7·3, 11·1, 15·9, twin port as 1938 **8** 1938 on—5·4 **9** 1938—6·2, 1939—6·75

Model	M19	M22	M23	M24
Year from	**1937**	**1937**	**1937**	**1938**
Year to	**1938**	**1939**	**1940**	**1939**
Bore (mm)	68·8	82	82	82
Stroke (mm)	94	94	94	94
Capacity (cc)	349	496	496	496
Compression ratio (to 1)	7·25	6·8 **1**	7·5 **2**	7·75
Compression opt. high				12·5
Valve position	ohv	ohv	ohv	ohv
inlet opens BTDC	35	35	45	
inlet closes ABDC	75	75	70	
exhaust opens BBDC	75	75	65	
exhaust closes ATDC	35	35	35	
Valve clearance (cold) inlet (in.)	0·003	0·003	0·003 **3**	0·003

Model	M19	M22	M23	M24
Year from	**1937**	**1937**	**1937**	**1938**
Year to	**1938**	**1939**	**1940**	**1939**
Valve clearance (cold) exhaust (in.)	0·003	0·003	0·003 **3**	0·003
Ignition timing (in.)	0·437	0·375	0·375 **4**	0·500 **6**
Points gap (in.)	0·012	0·012	0·012	0·012
Primary drive chain	$\frac{1}{2} \times \frac{5}{16}$	$\frac{1}{2} \times \frac{5}{16}$	$\frac{1}{2} \times \frac{5}{16}$	$\frac{1}{2} \times \frac{5}{16}$
Rear chain	$\frac{5}{8} \times \frac{1}{4}$	$\frac{5}{8} \times \frac{1}{4}$	$\frac{5}{8} \times \frac{3}{8}$ **5**	$\frac{5}{8} \times \frac{1}{4}$
Sprockets: engine (T)	18	21	21	21

1 1938—6·2, 1939—6·5   **2** 1938—6·8, 1939—7·1   **3** 1939 on—0·006   **4** 1940—0·437   **5** 1938 on — $\frac{5}{8} \times \frac{1}{4}$ **6** 1939—0·437

	M19	M22	M23	M24
O/A ratio: top	5·7 **1**	4·8 **3**	4·8 **4**	4·8 **8**
O/A ratio: 3rd	7·5	6·3	6·3	6·3
O/A ratio: 2nd	11·8	9·9	9·9	9·9
O/A ratio: 1st	17·0	14·3	14·3	14·3
Front tyre (in.)	3·25 × 19	3·25 × 19	3·00 × 20	3·00 × 20
Rear tyre (in.)	3·25 × 19	3·25 × 19	3·25 × 19 **5**	3·25 × 19 **5**
Brake front dia. (in.)	7·0	7·0	7·0	7·0
Brake front width (in.)	1·38	1·38	1·38	1·38
Brake rear dia. (in.)	7·0	7·0	7·0	7·0
Brake rear width (in.)	1·38	1·38	1·38	1·38
Front suspension	girder	girder	girder	girder
Rear type	rigid	rigid	rigid	rigid
Petrol tank (Imp.) pint	3·0	3·0	3·0 **6**	3·0 **6**
Oil tank (Imp.) pint	6·0 **2**	6·0 **2**	6·0 **2 7**	4·0 **7**
Ignition system	magneto	magneto	magneto	magneto
Generator type	dynamo	dynamo	dynamo	dynamo
Battery (volt)	6	6	6	6
Wheelbase (in.)	54	54	54	54
Ground clear. (in.)	4·6	4·6	4·6	4·6
Seat height (in.)	28·5	28·5	28·5	28·5
Power: bhp				28 **9**
@ rpm				5250

1 s/c—6·7   **2** 1938—4·0   **3** s/c 5·6   **4** s/c 5·6, 1939—close ratio option available   **5** 1939—3·50 × 19
6 1939—3·5   **7** 1939—5·0   **8** 1939—4·8, 5·2, 8·15, 11·8; wide ratio option available   **9** 36 on dope

Model	M20	M21	M33
Year from	**1937**	**1937**	**1947**
Year to	**1955**	**1963**	**1957**
Bore (mm)	82	85 **6**	85
Stroke (mm)	94	105 **6**	88
Capacity (cc)	496	596 **7**	499
Compression ratio (to 1)	5·0 **1**	5·0	6·8 **12**
Valve position	side	side	ohv
inlet opens BTDC	10 **2**	10 **8**	25
inlet closes ABDC	55	55	65
exhaust opens BBDC	60	60	65
exhaust closes ATDC	15	15	25
Valve clearance (cold) inlet (in.)	0·004 **3 9**	0·004 **3 9**	0·003
Valve clearance (cold) exhaust (in.)	0·006 **4**	0·006 **10**	0·003

Model	M20	M21	M33
Year from	**1937**	**1937**	**1947**
Year to	**1955**	**1963**	**1957**
Ignition timing (in.)	0·312 **5**	0·312 **11**	0·375
Points gap (in.)	0·012	0·012	0·012
Primary drive chain	$\frac{1}{2} \times \frac{5}{16}$	$\frac{1}{2} \times \frac{5}{16}$	$\frac{1}{2} \times \frac{5}{16}$
Rear chain	$\frac{5}{8} \times \frac{1}{4}$	$\frac{5}{8} \times \frac{1}{4}$	$\frac{5}{8} \times \frac{1}{4}$
Sprockets: engine (T)	18	20	20
Sprockets: clutch (T)	43	43	43
Sprockets: gearbox (T)	19	19	19
Sprockets: rear wheel (T)	42	42	42
O/A ratio: top	5·3 **13**	4·8 **21**	4·8 **25**
O/A ratio: 3rd	7·0	6·3	6·3
O/A ratio: 2nd	10·9	9·9	9·9
O/A ratio: 1st	15·8	14·3	14·3
Front tyre (in.)	3·25 × 19 **14**	3·50 × 19 **22**	3·25 × 19
Rear tyre (in.)	3·25 × 19	3·50 × 19	3·50 × 19
Rim front	WM2	WM2	WM2
Rim rear	WM2 **15**	WM2 **15**	WM2 **15**
Brake front dia. (in.)	7·0	7·0 **24**	7·0 **24**
Brake front width (in.)	1·38 **16**	1·38 **24 23**	1·12 **24**
Brake rear dia. (in.)	7·0	7·0	7·0
Brake rear width (in.)	1·38	1·38	1·38
Front suspension	girder **17**	girder **17**	girder **17**
Rear type	rigid **18**	rigid **18**	rigid **18**
Petrol tank (Imp. gal)	3·0 **19**	3·0 **19**	3·0
Oil tank (Imp. pint)	6·0 **20**	6·0 **20**	5·0

1 1945—4·9 **2** 1945—25/65/65/25 **3** 1939—0·008 **4** 1937–8, also shown as 0·012, 1939—0·012
5 1938—0.375, 1939—0.437 **6** 1938 on—82 × 112 **7** 1938 on—591 cc **8** 1946—25/65/65/25 **9** 1949—0·010
10 1937–8, also shown as 0·010, 1939—0·012 **11** 1938—0.375, 1939—0.437 **12** 1955 on 6·5
13 s/c 5·9 **14** 1939 std—3·00 × 20 **15** 1952—WM3 **16** 1945—1.12 **17** 1948—teles **18** 1951—plunger option
19 1939 only—3·5 **20** 1938—4·0, 1939—5·0 **21** s/c 5·6, 1939—5·9 **22** 1946—3·25 × 19 **23** 1946—1·12
24 1956—8 × 1·38 **25** s/c—5·6

	M20	M21	M33
Ignition system	magneto	magneto	magneto
Generator type	dynamo	dynamo **4**	dynamo
Output (watts)	60 **1**	60 **1**	60 **1**
Battery (volt)	6	6	6
Wheelbase (in)	54	54	54
Ground clear. (in)	4·6 **2**	4·6 **2**	5·5
Seat height (in)	28·5 **3**	28·5 **3**	28·5 **3**
Width (bars) in.)	27·25	27·25	27·25
Length (in.)	85	85	85
Dry weight (lb.)	369	370	372
Power: bhp	13	15	23
@ rpm	4200	4000	5500

1 from 1949 **2** 1949—5·5 **3** 1949—30·5 **4** 1961—alternator version also

Model	B31	B32	B33	B34
Year from	1945	1946	1947	1947
Year to	1959	1957	1960	1957
Bore (mm)	71	71	85	85
Stroke (mm)	88	88	88	88
Capacity (cc)	348	348	499	499
Compression ratio (to 1)	6·5	6·5	6·8 **2**	6·8
Valve position	ohv	ohv	ohv	ohv
inlet opens BTDC	25	25	25	25
inlet closes ABDC	65	65	65	65
exhaust opens BBDC	65	65	65	65
exhaust closes ATDC	25	25	25	25
Valve clearance (cold) inlet (in.)	0·003	0·003	0·003	0·003
Valve clearance (cold) exhaust (in.)	0·003	0·003	0·003	0·003
Ignition timing degree	38	38	38 **3**	38
Points gap (in.)	0·012	0·012	0·012	0·012
Primary drive chain	$\frac{1}{2} \times \frac{5}{16}$	$\frac{1}{2} \times \frac{5}{16}$	$\frac{1}{2} \times \frac{5}{16}$	$\frac{1}{2} \times \frac{5}{16}$
Rear chain	$\frac{5}{8} \times \frac{1}{4}$ **1**	$\frac{5}{8} \times \frac{1}{4}$	$\frac{5}{8} \times \frac{1}{4}$ **1**	$\frac{5}{8} \times \frac{1}{4}$
Sprockets: engine (T)	17	16	19	17 **4**
Sprockets: clutch (T)	43	43	43	43
Sprockets: gearbox (T)	19	16	19	19 **4**
Sprockets: rear wheel (T)	42	42	42	42
Box ratio: top	1·0 **5 6**	1·0 **5**	1·0 **5 6**	1·0 **5**
Box ratio: 3rd	1·3	1·3	1·3	1·3
Box ratio: 2nd	2·0	2·0	2·0	2·0
Box ratio: 1st	2·8	2·8	2·8	2·8
O/A ratio: top	5·6	7·1	5·0	5·6 **14**
O/A ratio: 3rd	7·3	9·2	6·5	7·3
O/A ratio: 2nd	11·1	14·2	10·0	11·1
O/A ratio: 1st	15·9	20·1	14·2	15·9
Front tyre (in.)	3·25 × 19	2·75 × 21	3·25 × 19	2·75 × 21
Rear tyre (in.)	3·25 × 19	4·00 × 19	3·50 × 19	4·00 × 19
Rim front	WM2	WM1	WM2	WM1
Rim rear	WM2	WM3	WM2	WM3
Brake front dia. (in.)	7	7	7 **16 17**	7
Brake front width (in.)	1·12 **8 9**	1·12 **8**	1·12 **8 9 17**	1·12 **8**
Brake rear dia. (in.)	7	7	7	7
Brake rear width (in.)	1·12 **8 9**	1·12 **8**	1·12 **8 9**	1·12 **8**
Front suspension	Teles	Teles	Teles	Teles
Front movement (in.)	5·75	5·75	5·75	5·75
Rear type	rigid **7 10**	rigid **7 10 13**	rigid **7 10**	rigid **7 10 13**
Petrol tank (Imp. gal)	3·0 **11**	3·0 **15**	3·0 **11**	3·0 **15**
Oil tank (Imp. pint)	5·0 **12**	5·0 **12**	5·0 **12**	5·0 **12**
Box capacity (Imp. pint)	1·0	1·0	1·0	1·0
Ignition system	magneto **18**	magneto	magneto **18**	magneto
Generator type	dynamo **19**	dynamo **24**	dynamo **19**	dynamo **24**
Output (watts)	40 **20**	40 **20**	40 **20**	40 **20**
Battery (volt)	6	6	6	6
Wheelbase (in.)	52·5 **21**	54	52·5 **21**	54·0
Ground clear. (in.)	5·75 **21**	6·00	5·75 **21**	6·5
Seat height (in.)	28·75	31·5	28·75	29·5
Width (bars) (in.)	28	27·2	28	27·2

Appendix

Model	B31	B32	B33	B34
Year from	1945	1946	1947	1947
Year to	1959	1957	1960	1957
Length (in.)	81·5 **21**	83·5	81·5 **21**	83·5
Dry weight (lb)	324 **22 23**	308	340 **25 26**	318
Wet weight (lb)				338
Power: bhp	17	17	23	23
@ rpm	5500	5500	5500	5500

1 1958 on—$\frac{5}{8} \times \frac{3}{8}$ **2** 1955 on—6·5 **3** 1958 on—35 **4** 1949—20/16 **5** 1949—1, 1·32, 2·06, 2·98 **6** S/A frame—1, 1·211, 1·759, 2·581 **7** 1949 on—plunger option **8** 1956—1·5 **9** 1958 on—1·12 **10** 1954—S/A **11** 1956—4·0 **12** s/a—6 **13** 1955 on—rigid **14** 1949—5·64 **15** 1952—2 gal option **16** 1958 on—7 **17** 1953—8 × 1·38 **18** 1958 on—coil **19** 1958 on—alternator **20** 1949—60 **21** S/A—56, 85, 5 **22** S/A—410 **23** 1958—396 **24** 1954 on—not fitted **25** S/A—421 **26** 1958—404

Model	C10	C11	C12	C10L
Year from	1938	1939	1940	1953
Year to	1953	1953	1940	1957
Bore (mm)	63	63	71	63
Stroke (mm)	80	80	88	80
Capacity (cc)	249	249	348	249
Compression ratio (to 1)	5·0	6·5	5·0	5·0
Valve position	side	ohv	side	side
inlet opens BTDC	30 **1**	25	25	34 **2**
inlet closes ABDC	60	70	70	78
exhaust opens BBDC	50	70	70	74
exhaust closes ATDC	25	25	25	38
Valve clearance (cold) inlet (in.)	0.004	0·003	0·004	0·012 **2**
Valve clearance (cold) exhaust (in.)	0·006	0·003	0·006	0·015 **2**
Ignition timing (in.)	0.031	0·031	0·031	tdc **2**
Points gap (in.)	0·012	0·012	0·012	0.015 **2**
Primary drive chain	$\frac{1}{2} \times \frac{5}{16}$	$\frac{1}{2} \times \frac{5}{16}$	$\frac{1}{2} \times \frac{5}{16}$	$\frac{1}{2} \times \frac{5}{16}$
Rear chain	$\frac{1}{2} \times \frac{5}{16}$	$\frac{1}{2} \times \frac{5}{16}$	$\frac{1}{2} \times \frac{5}{16}$	$\frac{1}{2} \times \frac{5}{16}$
Sprockets: engine (T)	16	16	17	16
Sprockets: clutch (T)	43	43	43	43
Sprockets: gearbox (T)	17	17	17	19
Sprockets: rear wheel (T)	42	42	42	47
Box ratio: top	1·0	1·0	1·0	1·0 **14**
Box ratio: 2nd	1·5	1·5	1·5	1·5
Box ratio: 1st	2·2	2·2	2·2	2·2
O/A ratio: top	6·6 **3**	6·6 **3**	6·25	6·6 **15**
O/A ratio: 2nd	9·8	9·8	9·4	9·8
O/A ratio: 1st	14·5	14·5	13·8	14·5
Front tyre (in.)	3·00 × 19	3·00 × 20 **4**	3·00 × 20	2·75 × 19
Rear tyre (in.)	3·00 × 19	3·00 × 20 **4**	3·00 × 20	2·75 × 19
Rim front	WM1	WM1	WM1	WM1
Rim rear	WM1	WM1	WM1	WM1
Brake front dia. (in.)	5·5	5·5	5·5	5·5
Brake front width (in.)	1	1	1	1
Brake rear dia. (in.)	5·5	5·5	5·5	5·0
Brake rear width (in.)	1	1	1	0·62

Model	C10	C11	C12	C10L
Year from	**1938**	**1939**	**1940**	**1953**
Year to	**1953**	**1953**	**1940**	**1957**
Front suspension	girder **5**	girder **5**	girder	teles
Front movement (in.)	6 (teles)	6 (teles)		3·75 **16**
Rear type	rigid **6**	rigid **6**	rigid	plunger
Rear movement (in.)	2 (plunger)	2 (plunger)		2
Petrol tank (Imp. gal)	2·0 **7**	2·0 **7**	2·0	2·75
Oil tank (Imp. pint)	4·0	4·0	4·0	4·5
Box capacity (Imp. pint)	0·50 **8**	0·50 **8**	0·50	0·50
Ignition system	coil	coil	coil	coil
Generator type	dynamo	dynamo	dynamo	alternator
Output (watts)	35 **9**	35 **9**	35	48
Battery (volt)	6	6	6	6
Wheelbase (in.)	51·0 **10**	51·0 **10**	51·0	52·5
Ground clear. (in.)	4·0 **11**	4·0 **11**	4·0	5
Seat height (in.)	26·0 **12**	26·0 **12**	26·0	29·5
Width (bars) (in.)	29 **13**	29 **13**		26·5
Length (in.)	80·5 **13**	80·5 **13**		81
Dry weight (lb.)	246	248 **13**	280	256
Power: bhp	8	11	10	8
@ rpm	5000	5400	4800	5000

1 1940—as C11 **2** 1953—4 as 1953 C10 **3** 1951—4-speed option 6·65, 8·06, 11·7, 17·15 **4** 1953—3·00 × 19 **5** 1946—teles **6** 1951—plunger option **7** 1945—2·5 **8** 1945—3-speed box, 1951—4-speed—1·0 **9** 1949—60 **10** 1946—52 **11** 1946—5·62 **12** 1946—28·25 **13** in 1946 **14** 1956—4-speed **15** 1956—6·6, 8·0, 11·7, 17·1 **16** 1956—6

Model	C11G	C12
Year from	**1954**	**1956**
Year to	**1955**	**1958**
Bore (mm)	63	63
Stroke (mm)	80	80
Capacity (cc)	249	249
Compression ratio (to 1)	6·5	6·5
Valve position	ohv	ohv
inlet opens BTDC	34 **1**	34
inlet closes ABDC	78	78
exhaust opens BBDC	74	74
exhaust closes ATDC	38	38
Valve clearance (cold) inlet (in.)	0·010 **1**	0·010
Valve clearance (cold) exhaust (in.)	0·012 **1**	0·012
Ignition timing degree	tdc **1**	tdc
Points gap (in.)	0·015 **1**	0·015
Primary drive chain	$\frac{1}{2} \times \frac{5}{16}$	$\frac{1}{2} \times \frac{5}{16}$
Rear chain	$\frac{1}{2} \times \frac{5}{16}$	$\frac{1}{2} \times \frac{5}{16}$
Sprockets: engine (T)	17	17
Sprockets: clutch (T)	43	43
Sprockets: gearbox (T)	17	19
Sprockets: rear wheel (T)	42	47
Box ratio: top	1·0	1·0
Box ratio: 3rd		1·22

Model	C11G	C12
Year from	**1954**	**1956**
Year to	**1955**	**1958**
Box ratio: 2nd	1·48	1·77
Box ratio: 1st	2·25	2·58
O/A ratio: top	6·25 **2**	6·26
O/A ratio: 3rd		7·64
O/A ratio: 2nd	9·25	11–1
O/A ratio: 1st	14·1	16·15
Front tyre (in.)	3·00 × 19	3·00 × 19
Rear tyre (in.)	3·00 × 19	3·00 × 19 **6**
Rim front	WM1	WM1
Rim rear	WM1	WM1
Brake front dia. (in.)	7 **3**	7
Brake front width (in.)	1·12 **3**	1·12
Brake rear dia. (in.)	5·5	5·5
Brake rear width (in.)	1	1
Front suspension	teles	teles
Front movement (in.)	6	6
Rear type	plunger **4**	s/a
Rear movement (in.)	2	2·38
Petrol tank (Imp. gal)	2·75	2·75
Oil tank (Imp. pint)	4·5	4·0
Box capacity (Imp. pint)	0·5 **5**	0·5
Ignition system	coil	coil
Generator type	alternator	alternator
Output (watts)	48	50
Battery (volt)	6	6
Wheelbase (in.)	53·5	54
Ground clear. (in.)	4·5	4·0
Seat height (in.)	29·5	29·5
Width (bars) (in.)	26·5	26·5
Length (in.)	82	82
Dry weight (lb)	301 **7**	312
Power: bhp	11	11
@ rpm	5400	5200

1 1954 as 1953 C11   **2** 4-speed option: 6·25, 7·6, 11·0, 16·13   **3** 1954—5·5 × 1   **4** 1954—rigid option
5 4-speed—1·0   **6** 3·25 × 19 to special order   **7** 308 with 4 speeds & plungers

Model	D1	D3	D5	D7
Year from	**1948**	**1954**	**1958**	**1959**
Year to	**1963**	**1957**	**1958**	**1966**
Bore (mm)	52	57	61·5	61·5
Stroke (mm)	58	58	58	58
Capacity (cc)	123	148	172	172
Compression ratio (to 1)	6·5	6·4	7·4	7·4
Valve position	two-stroke	two-stroke	two-stroke	two-stroke
Ignition timing degrees	26·5	26·5	26·5	17
Points gap (in.)	0·015	0·015	0·015	0·015
Primary drive chain	$\frac{3}{8} \times \frac{1}{4}$	$\frac{3}{8} \times \frac{1}{4}$	$\frac{3}{8} \times \frac{1}{4}$	$\frac{3}{8} \times \frac{1}{4}$
Rear chain	$\frac{1}{2} \times \frac{5}{16}$	$\frac{1}{2} \times \frac{5}{16}$	$\frac{1}{2} \times \frac{5}{16}$	$\frac{1}{2} \times \frac{5}{16}$

Model	D1	D3	D5	D7
Year from	**1948**	**1954**	**1958**	**1959**
Year to	**1963**	**1957**	**1958**	**1966**
Sprockets: engine (T)	17	17	17	17
Sprockets: clutch (T)	38	38	38	38
Sprockets: gearbox (T)	15	15	16	16
Sprockets: rear wheel (T)	47 **1**	47 **1**	46	46 **2**
Box ratio: top	1·0	1·0	1·0	1·0
Box ratio: 2nd	1·675	1·675	1·675	1·675 **8**
Box ratio: 1st	3·144	3·144	3·144	3·144 **8**
O/A ratio: top	7·0 **3**	7·0 **3**	6·426	6·426 **9**
O/A ratio: 2nd	11·7	11·7	10·76	10·76 **10**
O/A ratio: 1st	22·1	22·1	20·2	20·2 **10**
Front tyre (in.)	2·75 × 19	2·75 × 19	3·00 × 18	3·00 × 18
Rear tyre (in.)	2·75 × 19 **4**	2·75 × 19 **4**	3·00 × 18	3·00 × 18
Rim front	WM1	WM1	WM1	WM1
Rim rear	WM1	WM1	WM1	WM1
Brake front dia. (in.)	5	5·5	5	5·5
Brake front width (in.)	0·62	1	0·87	1
Brake rear dia. (in.)	5	5	5	5·5
Brake rear width (in.)	0·62	0·62	0·87	1
Front suspension	teles	teles	teles	teles
Front movement (in.)	3·75	3·75	3·75	3·0
Rear type	rigid **5**	plunger **6 7**	s/a	s/a
Rear movement (in.)	plunger—2·0	2·0 **7**	2·4	2·4
Petrol tank (Imp. gal)	1·75	1·75	2·0	2·0 **11**
Oil tank	petroil	petroil	petroil	petroil
Box capacity (Imp. pint)	0·75	0·75	0·75	0·75
Ignition system	flywheel-mag **12**	flywheel-mag	flywheel-mag	flywheel-mag **17**
Generator type	alternator	alternator	alternator	alternator
Output (watts)	30 **13**	30	30	30
Battery (volt)	3 **13**	6	6	6
Wheelbase (in.)	50	50	52	51·1 **18**
Ground clear. (in.)	4·25 **14**	4·75 **14**	5·5	5·5 **19**
Seat height (in.)	27·25 **15**	27 **15**	31	31 **20**
Width overall (in.)	26·5	26·5	26·5	27·75 **21**
Length (in.)	77	77	81	79·4 **22**
Dry weight (lb)	153 **16**	183	216	224 **23**
Power: bhp	4·5	5·3	7·4	7·4
@ rpm	5000	5000	4750	4750

1 Comp—58   **2** 1962—47   **3** Comp—8·64   **4** Comp 3·25 × 19   **5** 1950—plunger   **6** Comp rigid opt
7 1956—s/a—2·4   **8** 1965—1·41, 2·64   **9** 1962—6·566   **10** 1965—9·24, 17·34   **11** 1966—1·9
12 1950—Lucas option—coil   **13** Lucas—45 watt, 6 volt battery   **14** Comp 7·0   **15** Comp 29
16 1952—167 to 194 depending on spec   **17** 1966—coil   **18** 1966—50·5   **19** 1966—6·5   **20** 1966—30·5
21 1966—27   **22** 1966—78   **23** 1966—214

Model	D10	D10–4 Sports	D10–B Bushman	D14/4 & D175
Year from	**1966**	**1966**	**1966**	**1968**
Year to	**1967**	**1967**	**1967**	**1971**
Bore (mm)	61·5	61·5	61·5	61·5
Stroke (mm)	58	58	58	58
Capacity (cc)	172	172	172	172
Compression ratio (to 1)	8·65	8·65	8·65	10 **1**
Valve position	two-stroke	two-stroke	two-stroke	two-stroke
Ignition timing degrees	19	19	19	16·5
Points gap (in.)	0·012	0·012	0·012	0·012
Primary drive chain	$\frac{3}{8} \times \frac{1}{4}$	$\frac{3}{8} \times \frac{1}{4}$	$\frac{3}{8} \times \frac{1}{4}$	$\frac{3}{8} \times \frac{1}{4}$
Rear chain	$\frac{1}{2} \times \frac{5}{16}$	$\frac{1}{2} \times \frac{5}{16}$	$\frac{1}{2} \times \frac{5}{16}$	$\frac{1}{2} \times \frac{5}{16}$
Sprockets: engine (T)	17	17	17	17
Sprockets: clutch (T)	38	38	38	38
Sprockets: gearbox (T)	16	16	16	16
Sprockets: rear wheel (T)	47	47	58	47 **2**
Box ratio: top	1·0	1·0	1·0	
Box ratio: 3rd		1·30	1·30	1·30
Box ratio: 2nd	1·41	1·83	1·83	1·83
Box ratio: 1st	2·64	2·84	2·84	2·84
O/A ratio: top	6·566	6·566	8·1	6·566 **3**
O/A ratio: 3rd		8·55	10·5	8·55
O/A ratio: 2nd	9·24	12·04	14·8	12·04
O/A ratio: 1st	17·34	18·68	23·0	18·68
Front tyre (in.)	3·00 × 18	3·00 × 18	3·00 × 19	3·00 × 18 **4**
Rear tyre (in.)	3·00 × 18	3·00 × 18	3·00 × 19	3·00 × 18 **4**
Rim front	WM1	WM1	WM1	WM1
Rim rear	WM1	WM1	WM2	WM1
Brake front dia. (in.)	5·5	5·5	5·5	5·5
Brake front width (in.)	1	1	1	1
Brake rear dia. (in.)	5·5	5·5	5·5	5·5
Brake rear width (in.)	1	1	1	1
Front suspension	Teles	Teles	Teles	Teles
Front movement (in.)	3	3	3	5 **5**
Rear type	s/a	s/a	s/a	s/a
Rear movement (in.)	2·4	2·4	2·4	2·4
Petrol tank (Imp. gal)	1·9	1·9	1·9	1·9
Oil tank	petroil	petroil	petroil	petroil
Box capacity (Imp. pint)	0·75	0·75	0·75	0·75 **6**
Ignition system	coil	coil	energy transfer	coil **3**
Generator type	alternator	alternator	alternator	alternator
Output (watts)	60	60	60	60
Battery (volt)	6	6		6
Wheelbase (in.)	50	50	50	50
Ground clear. (in.)	6·75	6·75	10	6·75 **3**
Seat height (in.)	31	30·25	30·5	31 **3**
Width (in.)	27·75	23	27·75	27·75
Length (in.)	77·5	77·5	78	77·5 **3**
Dry weight (lb.)	215	221	222	215 **3**
Power: bhp	10	10	10	12·6
@ rpm	6000	6000	6000	5750

1 1969—9·5   **2** Bushman—58   **3** Bushman as—D10-B   **4** Bushman—3·00 × 19 and 3·25 × 18
5 D14/4 only—3   **6** 1969—1·0

Appendix

Model	Winged Wheel	Dandy	Scooter	Beagle
Year from	**1953**	**1956**	**1959**	**1963**
Year to	**1955**	**1962**	**1965**	**1965**
Bore (mm)	36	45	61·5	47·6
Stroke (mm)	34	44	58	42
Capacity (cc)	34·6	70	172	74·7
Compression ratio (to 1)		7·25	7·4	9·0
Valve position	two-stroke	two-stroke	two-stroke	ohv
inlet opens BTDC				23 **2**
inlet closes ABDC				46
exhaust opens BBDC				42
exhaust closes ATDC				27
Valve clearance (cold) inlet (in.)				0·003
Valve clearance (cold) exhaust (in.)				0·003
Ignition timing (in.)		0·156	0·156	0·135
Points gap (in.)		0·015	0·020	0·012
Primary drive	gears	gears	gears	gears
Rear drive	gears	$\frac{1}{2} \times \frac{3}{16}$	$\frac{3}{8}$ duplex	$\frac{1}{2} \times \frac{5}{16}$
gears: engine (T)	17		45	27
gears: clutch (T)	66		102	90
gears: gearbox (T)	17	13 **1**		13
gears: rear wheel (T)	82	27 **1**		45
O/A ratio: top	18·727	9·7	4·93	11·54
O/A ratio: 3rd			6·29	15·1
O/A ratio: 2nd			10·08	23·8
O/A ratio: 1st		21·2	14·75	34·4
Front tyre (in.)		2·50 × 15	3·50 × 10	2·25 × 19
Rear tyre (in.)	26 × 1·75	2·50 × 15	3·50 × 10	2·25 × 19
Rim front				WMO
Rim rear				WMO
Brake front dia. (in.)		4	5	4·5
Brake front width (in.)		0·87	1	0·87
Brake rear dia. (in.)	9·5	4	5	5
Brake rear width (in.)	0·62	0·87	1	0·62
Front suspension		leading link	teles	leading link
Front movement (in.)		2·5	4·4	2·4
Rear type		s/a	s/a	s/a
Rear movement (in.)		2·5	2·6	1·5
Petrol tank (Imp. gal)	0·5	0·75	1·5	2·0
Oil tank (Imp. pint)				1·5
Box capacity (Imp. pint)	0·125	0·33		0·33
Ignition system	flywheel-mag	flywheel-mag	flywheel-mag	flywheel-mag
Generator type	alternator	alternator	alternator	alternator
Output (watts)	9			23
Battery (volt)		dry 4·5	6	
Wheelbase (in.)			48	46
Ground clear. (in.)			5	7·5
Seat height (in.)			28	29
Width (in.)			24	23·5
Length (in.)			72	72·5
Dry weight (lb)	unit 27		236	140
Power: bhp	1·0			
@ rpm	6000			

1 Sprockets   **2** 1964—35/53/60/32

Model	C15	C15T	C15S	SS80 **5**
Year from	**1958**	**1959**	**1959**	**1961**
Year to	**1967**	**1965**	**1965**	**1966**
Bore (mm)	67	67	67	67
Stroke (mm)	70	70	70	70
Capacity (cc)	247	247	247	247
Compression ratio (to 1)	7·25 **1**	7·5 **2**	9·0 **3**	8·75 **4**
Valve position	ohv	ohv	ohv	ohv
inlet opens BTDC	26	41·5 **6 7**	41·5 **6**	51
inlet closes ABDC	70	62·5	62·5	68
exhaust opens BBDC	61·5	62·5	62·5	78
exhaust closes ATDC	34·5	41·5	41·5	37
Valve clearance (cold) inlet (in.)	0·008	0·004 **8**	0·004 **8**	0·008
Valve clearance (cold) exhaust (in.)	0·010	0·004 **8**	0·004 **8**	0·010
Ignition timing degrees	37 **9**	34 **9**	34 **9**	15·5 retard **9**
Points gap (in.)	0·012 **10**	0·015	0·015	0·015
Primary drive chain	$\frac{3}{8}$ duplex	$\frac{3}{8}$ duplex	$\frac{3}{8}$ duplex	$\frac{3}{8}$ duplex
Rear chain	$\frac{1}{2} \times \frac{5}{16}$	$\frac{1}{2} \times \frac{5}{16}$	$\frac{1}{2} \times \frac{5}{16}$	$\frac{1}{2} \times \frac{5}{16}$
Sprockets: engine (T)	23	23 **11**	23 **11**	23
Sprockets: clutch (T)	52	52	52	52
Sprockets: gearbox (T)	17	16 **12**	16 **12**	17 **14**
Sprockets: rear wheel (T)	45	56 **12 13**	56 **12**	45
Box ratio: top	1·0	1·0	1·0	1·0
Box ratio: 3rd	1·278	1·632	1·278 **15**	1·202 **16**
Box ratio: 2nd	1·761	2·447	1·761 **15**	1·657 **16**
Box ratio: 1st	2·667	3·167	2·667 **15**	2·112 **16**
O/A ratio: top	5·985	7·913 **17**	7·913 **18**	5·985 **19**
O/A ratio: 3rd	7·649	12·91 **17**	10·11 **18**	7·194 **19**
O/A ratio: 2nd	10·54	19·36 **17**	13·93 **18**	9·917 **19**
O/A ratio: 1st	15·96	25·06 **17**	21·10 **18**	12·64 **19**
Front tyre (in.)	3·25 × 17	3·00 × 20	3·00 × 20	3·25 × 17
Rear tyre (in.)	3·25 × 17	4·00 × 18	3·50 × 19 **20**	3·25 × 17
Rim front	WM2	WM1	WM1	WM2
Rim rear	WM2	WM2 **21**	WM1 **22**	WM2
Brake front dia. (in.)	6	6 **23**	6 **23**	6
Brake front width (in.)	0.87	0.87 **23**	0·87 **23**	0·87
Brake rear dia. (in.)	6	6	6	6
Brake rear width (in.)	0·87	0·87	0·87	0·87
Front suspension	teles	teles	teles	teles
Front movement (in.)	4·5 **24**	5	5	5
Rear type	s/a	s/a	s/a	s/a
Rear movement (in.)	2·4	2·4	2·4	2·4
Petrol tank (Imp. gal)	2·5 **25**	2·0	2·0	3 **25**
Oil tank (Imp. pints)	4·0	4·0 **26**	4·0 **26**	4
Box capacity (Imp. pint)	0·5 **27**	0·5 **27**	0·5 **27**	0·75 **28**
Chaincase (Imp. pint)	0·25	0·25	0·25	0·25
Ignition system	Coil	Energy transfer	Energy transfer	coil
Generator type	alternator	alternator	alternator	alternator
Output (watts)	50 **29**	60	60	60
Battery (volt)	6			6
Wheelbase (in.)	51·2 **30**	51·7 **31**	51·2 **32**	51·2 **30**
Ground clear. (in.)	5 **33**	6·25 **34**	6·5 **35**	5

Model	C15	C15T	C15S	SS80 5
Year from	**1958**	**1959**	**1959**	**1961**
Year to	**1967**	**1965**	**1965**	**1966**
Seat height (in.)	30 **36**	32·5 **37**	32·5 **38**	30 **36**
Width (bars) (in.)	26	31·1	31·1	28 **39**
Length (in.)	78	81 **40**	81·5 **40**	78
Dry weight (lb.)	280 **41**	275 **42**	265 **43**	275
Power: bhp	15			20
@ rpm	7000			7250

1 1962—7·5, 1964—8·0 **2** 1961–62—6·4, 1964—8·0 **3** 1961—10.0 **4** 10·0 first few only **5** 1966—C15S **6** 1961 figures, 1962—51/68/78/37 **7** 1963—as C15 **8** 1962—0·008/0·010 **9** 1962—15.5 retard, 1963—5 retard, 1965—33·5 **10** 1962—0·015 **11** 1962–63 only—18 **12** 1962–63—18/56, 1964—15/60 **13** 1961—60 **14** 1964—16 **15** 1961—1·202, 1·657, 2·112 **16** 1966—1·278, 1·761, 2·667 **17** 1961—8·478, 13·84, 20·75, 26·85; 1962—8·99, 14·67, 22·0, 28·5; 1964—9·04, 14·8, 22·1, 28·64 **18** 1961—7·913, 9·51, 13·11, 16·71; 1962—8·99, 10·80, 14·9, 19·0; 1964—9·04, 10·87, 14·98, 19·1 **19** 1964—6·36, 7·64, 10·54, 13·43, 1966—6·359, 8·126, 11·20, 16·96 **20** 1963—4·00 × 18 **21** 1962—WM3 **22** 1962—WM2, 1963—WM3 **23** 1962—7 × 1·12 **24** 1962—5·0 **25** 1964—3·0, 1966—2·6 **26** 1963–5.0 **27** 1962 only—0·75 **28** 1963—0·5 **29** 1962—60 **30** 1966—51·5 **31** 1961–62—50·5 **32** 1961—51, 1963—51·7 **33** 1966—5·5 **34** 1961—6·5, 1962—8, 1963—7·2 **35** 1962—7·75, 1963—7 **36** 1966—30.5 **37** 1961—33 **38** 1963—32 **39** 1963—27, 1966—26·5 **40** 1963—80·5 **41** 1962—275, 1965—280 **42** 1962—280, 1963—265, 1965—270 **43** 1962 only—270, 1965—270

Model	B40	SS90	B44GP	B44VE 3
Year from	**1960**	**1962**	**1965**	**1966**
Year to	**1965**	**1965**	**1967**	**1970**
Bore (mm)	79	79	79	79
Stroke (mm)	70	70	90	90
Capacity (cc)	343	343	441	441
Compression ratio (to 1)	7·0	8·75	11·4	9·4
Valve position	ohv	ohv	ohv	ohv
inlet opens BTDC	26	51	63	51
inlet closes ABDC	70	68	72	68
exhaust opens BBDC	61·5	78	80	78
exhaust closes ATDC	34·5	37	55	37
Valve clearance (cold) inlet (in.)	0·008	0·008	0·015	0·008
Valve clearance (cold) exhaust (in.)	0·010	0·010	0·015	0·010
Ignition timing degree	8·5 retard **1**	5 retard **2**	28	28 **4**
Points gap (in.)	0·015	0·015	0·015	0·015
Primary drive chain	$\frac{3}{8}$ duplex	$\frac{3}{8}$ duplex	$\frac{3}{8}$ duplex	$\frac{3}{8}$ duplex
Rear chain	$\frac{1}{2} \times \frac{5}{16}$	$\frac{1}{2} \times \frac{5}{16}$	$\frac{1}{2} \times \frac{5}{16}$	$\frac{1}{2} \times \frac{5}{16}$ **5**
Sprockets: engine (T)	23	23	28	28
Sprockets: clutch (T)	52	52	52	52
Sprockets: gearbox (T)	19	18	16	18 **6**
Sprockets: rear wheel (T)	46	46	60	52 **6**
Box ratio: top	1·0	1·0	1·0	1·0
Box ratio: 3rd	1·278	1·202	1·244	1·244
Box ratio: 2nd	1·761	1·657	1·646	1·646
Box ratio: 1st	2·667	2·112	2·183	2·652
O/A ratio: top	5·474	5·778	6·964	5·365 **11**

Model	B40	SS90	B44GP	B44VE 3
Year from	1960	1962	1965	1966
Year to	1965	1965	1967	1970
O/A ratio: 3rd	7·00	6·945	8·664	6·674 **11**
O/A ratio: 2nd	9·64	9·574	11·46	8·831 **11**
O/A ratio: 1st	14·60	12·20	15·20	14·23 **11**
Front tyre (in.)	3·25 × 18	3·25 × 18	3·00 × 20	3·25 × 19
Rear tyre (in.)	3·50 × 18	3·50 × 18	4·00 × 18	4·00 × 18
Rim front	WM2	WM2	WM2 **8**	WM2
Rim rear	WM2	WM2	WM3	WM3
Brake front dia. (in.)	7	7	7	7 **10**
Brake front width (in.)	1·12	1·12	1·12	1·12 **10**
Brake rear dia. (in.)	6	6	6 **9**	6 **9**
Brake rear width (in.)	0·87	0·87	0·87 **9**	0·87 **9**
Front suspension	teles	teles	teles	teles
Front movement (in.)	5	5	5·75	5·75 **12**
Rear type	s/a	s/a	s/a	s/a
Rear movement (in.)	2·4	2·4	3·3	2·75 **13**
Petrol tank (Imp. gal)	3·0	3·0	1·38	1·75
Oil tank (Imp. pint)	4	4	4·25	5
Box capacity (Imp. pint)	0·5 **7**	0·5	0·5	0·5
Chaincase (Imp. pint)	0·25	0·25	0·25	0·25
Ignition system	coil	coil	energy transfer	energy transfer **14**
Generator type	alternator	alternator	alternator	alternator
Output (watts)	60	60	60	60 **15**
Battery (volt)	6	6		12 **16**
Wheelbase (in.)	54 **17**	52	52	53 **18**
Ground clear. (in.)	7	7	8·5	8·5 **19**
Seat height (in.)	32	32	32	32
Width (bars) (in.)	26	27	32	32 **19**
Length (in.)	80	80	82	82 **19**
Dry weight (lb)	300 **20**	295 **21**	255	288 **19**
Power: bhp	21	24		28 **22**
@ rpm	7000	7000		6500 **22**

1 1962—15.5 retard, 1963—5 retard, 1965—33.5 **2** 1965—33.5 **3** 1969—B44VS **4** 1969—29/31 **5** 1967—$\frac{5}{8}$ × $\frac{1}{4}$ **6** 1967—17/49 **7** 1962 only—0·75 **8** 1967—WM1 **9** 1967—7 × 1·12 **10** 1969—8 × 1·62 **11** 1967—5·353, 6·659, 8·811, 14·20 **12** 1969—5·25 **13** 1969—2·56 **14** 1969—coil **15** 1969—115 **16** 1969 on **17** 1963—52 **18** 1967—52 **19** 1969—8.0, 28·2, 83·2, 306 **20** 1963-64—295 **21** 1965—300 **22** in 1969

Model	C25 **1**	B25SS	B25T
Year from	1967	1971	1971
Year to	1970	1971	1971
Bore (mm)	67	67	67
Stroke (mm)	70	70	70
Capacity (cc)	247	247	247
Compression ratio (to 1)	9·5 **2**	10	10
Valve position	ohv	ohv	ohv
inlet opens BTDC	51	51	51
inlet closes ABDC	68	68	68

Model	C25 1	B25SS	B25T
Year from	1967	1971	1971
Year to	1970	1971	1971
exhaust opens BBDC	78	78	78
exhaust closes ATDC	37	37	37
Valve clearance (cold) inlet (in.)	0·008	0·008	0·008
Valve clearance (cold) exhaust (in.)	0·010	0·010	0·010
Ignition timing degree	35 3	37	37
Points gap (in.)	0·015	0·015	0·015
Primary drive chain	$\frac{3}{8}$ duplex	$\frac{3}{8}$ duplex	$\frac{3}{8}$ duplex
Rear chain	$\frac{5}{8} \times \frac{1}{4}$	$\frac{5}{8} \times \frac{1}{4}$	$\frac{5}{8} \times \frac{1}{4}$
Sprockets: engine (T)	23	23	23
Sprockets: clutch (T)	52	52	52
Sprockets: gearbox (T)	16	17	16
Sprockets: rear wheel (T)	49 4	52	52
Box ratio: top	1·0	1·0	1·0
Box ratio: 3rd	1·244	1·244	1·244
Box ratio: 2nd	1·646	1·646	1·646
Box ratio: 1st	2·652	2·652	2·652
O/A ratio: top	6·924 5	6·916	7·348
O/A ratio: 3rd	8·613	8·603	9·141
O/A ratio: 2nd	11·40	11·38	12·09
O/A ratio: 1st	18·36	18·34	19·49
Front tyre (in.)	3·25 × 18	3·25 × 18	3·00 × 20
Rear tyre (in.)	3·50 × 18	3·50 × 18	4·00 × 18
Rim front	WM2	WM2	WM1
Rim rear	WM2	WM2	WM3
Brake front dia. (in.)	7 6	6 or 8	6
Brake front width (in.)	1·12 6		0·87
Brake rear dia. (in.)	7	7	7
Brake rear width (in.)	1·12	1·12	1·12
Front suspension	teles	teles	teles
Front movement (in.)	5·75 7	6·75	6·75
Rear type	s/a	s/a	s/a
Rear movement (in.)	2·75 8	2·56	2·56
Petrol tank (Imp. gal)	1·75 9	2 or 3	2
Oil tank (Imp. pint)	4	4	4
Box capacity (Imp. pint)	0·5	0·5	0·5
Chaincase (Imp. pint)	0·25	0·25	0·25
Ignition system	coil	coil	coil
Generator type	alternator	alternator	alternator
Output (watts)	115	108	108
Battery (volt)	12	12	12
Wheelbase (in.)	52 10	54	54
Ground clear. (in.)	7·5 11	7	7·5
Seat height (in.)	31	32	32
Width (bars) (in.)	28	29	29
Length (in.)	82 12	85	85
Dry weight (lb)	315 13	290	287
Power: bhp	25 14		
@ rpm	8000 14		

1 1968—B25 & in 1969 as Fleet Star also   2 1969—B25-10: 1, Fleet Star 8·5   3 1969—37   4 1969 Fleet Star—52   5 1969 Fleet Star 7·35   6 1969—7(2LS) × 1·56   7 1969—5·25   8 1969—2·56   9 1969—3·25   10 1969—53   11 1969—7   12 1969—83   13 1969—302   14 1969—24/8250, Fleet Star—21

Model	B44VR [1]	B50SS	B50T	B50MX
Year from	1966	1971	1971	1971
Year to	1970	1972	1972	1972
Bore (mm)	79	84	84	84
Stroke (mm)	90	90	90	90
Capacity (cc)	441	499	499	499
Compression ratio (to 1)	9·4	10	10	10
Valve position	ohv	ohv	ohv	ohv
inlet opens BTDC	51	51	51	63
inlet closes ABDC	68	68	68	72
exhaust opens BBDC	78	78	78	80
exhaust closes ATDC	37	37	37	55
Valve clearance (cold) inlet (in.)	0·008	0·008	0·008	0·008
Valve clearance (cold) exhaust (in.)	0·010	0·010	0·010	0·010
Ignition timing degree	28 [2]	30 [5]	30 [5]	30 [5]
Points gap (in.)	0·015	0·015	0·015	0·015
Primary drive chain	$\frac{3}{8}$ duplex	$\frac{3}{8}$ duplex	$\frac{3}{8}$ duplex	$\frac{3}{8}$ duplex
Rear chain	$\frac{5}{8} \times \frac{1}{4}$	$\frac{5}{8} \times \frac{1}{4}$	$\frac{5}{8} \times \frac{1}{4}$	$\frac{5}{8} \times \frac{1}{4}$
Sprockets: engine (T)	28	28	28	28
Sprockets: clutch (T)	52	52	52	52
Sprockets: gearbox (T)	17 [3,4]	16 [6]	15	14
Sprockets: rear wheel (T)	49 [3]	52 [6]	52	52
Box ratio: top	1·0	1·0	1·0	1·0
Box ratio: 3rd	1·244	1·244	1·244	1·244
Box ratio: 2nd	1·646	1·646	1·646	1·646
Box ratio: 1st	2·652	2·652	2·652	2·183
O/A ratio: top	5·353 [7] [8]	6·036 [14]	6·438	6·898
O/A ratio: 3rd	6·659 [7] [8]	7·508 [14]	8·009	8·581
O/A ratio: 2nd	8·811 [7] [8]	9·935 [14]	10·60	11·35
O/A ratio: 1st	14·20 [7] [8]	16·01 [14]	17·07	15·06
Front tyre (in.)	3·25 × 18	3·25 × 18	3·00 × 20	3·00 × 20
Rear tyre (in.)	3·50 × 18	3·50 × 18	4·00 × 18	4·00 × 18
Rim front	WM2	WM2	WM1	WM1
Rim rear	WM2	WM2	WM3	WM3
Brake front dia. (in.)	7 [9] [10]	8	6	6
Brake front width (in.)	1·12 [9] [10]		0·87	0·87
Brake rear dia. (in.)	7	7	7	7
Brake rear width (in.)	1·12	1·12	1·12	1·12
Front suspension	Teles	Teles	Teles	Teles
Front movement (in.)	5·75 [11]	6·75	6·75	6·75
Rear type	s/a	s/a	s/a	s/a
Rear movement (in.)	2·75 [12]	2·56	2·56	2·94
Petrol tank (Imp. gal)	1·75 [13]	2 or 3	2	1
Oil tank (Imp. pint)	4	4	4	4
Box capacity (Imp. pint)	0·5	0·5	0·5	0·5
Chaincase (Imp. pint)	0·25	0·25	0·25	0·25
Ignition system	coil	coil	coil	energy transfer
Generator type	alternator	alternator	alternator	
Output (watts)	115	108	108	
Battery (volt)	12	12	12	
Wheelbase (in.)	52 [15]	54 [20]	54 [20]	54 [20]
Ground clear. (in.)	7·5 [16]	7 [21]	7·5	7·5

Model	B44VR 1	B50SS	B50T	B50MX
Year from	1966	1971	1971	1971
Year to	1970	1972	1972	1972
Seat height (in.)	31	32	32	32
Width (bars) (in.)	28 17	29	29	33·5
Length (in.)	82 18	85 22	85	82·5 23
Dry weight (lb)	320	310	298	240 24
Power: bhp	29 19	34	34	38
@ rpm	5750 19	6200	6200	6200
Torque (ft. lb)				
@ rpm				

1 1968—B44SS **2** 1969—29/31 **3** 1969—17/47 **4** 1967—18 **5** 1972—34 **6** 1972—17/47
7 1969—5·134, 6·387, 8·451, 13·62 **8** 1967—5·056, 6·289, 8·321,13·41 **9** 1969—7 × 1·56(2LS) **10** 1968—8 × 1·62
11 1969—5·25 **12** 1969—2·56 **13** 1969—3·25 **14** 1972—5·134, 6·387, 8·451, 13·62 **15** 1969—53
16 1969—7 **17** 1969—28·2 **18** 1969—83·2 **19** 1969—28/6500 **20** 1972—55·5 **21** 1972—7·5 **22** 1972—84·3
23 1972—81·5 **24** 1972—256

Photograph overleaf **BSA blow-up. A certain Neville de Gruchy's engine succumbed to too much abuse, in Jersey on 21 August, 1958**

Colours

1937

All models had a general finish of black for the frame, forks, headlamp shell, mudguards, oil tank, toolbox, chaincase and chainguard. The exhaust system, headlamp rim, handlebars and some minor parts were chrome-plated. Various finishes were employed for the petrol tank and wheel rims, as set out below, together with any changes from the general finish as above.

B20, B23, M20, M21

Green tank with gold lining and oval tank transfer, option of chrome-plated tank with green panels; black rims.

B21, B26, M19, M22

Chrome-plated tank with BSA green panels and oval tank transfer, black rims.

B22

Chrome-plated tank with Empire Star green panels and BSA star tank transfer, black rims.

B24, M23

As B22, but chrome-plated rims.

B25

As B22, but chrome-plated rims, chaincase, mudguards, and parts of hubs and brakes.

1938

General notes as for 1937, variations to tank and rim finish as detailed below.

B20, B21, B23, B26

Unchanged.

B22, B24, M23

Chrome-plated tank with Empire Star green or red panels and BSA star tank transfer. Chrome-plated rims with green or red centres. Chrome-plated oil tank with black panels.

B25

Tank and rims as B22, remainder as in 1937 plus chrome-plated oil tank.

M19, M22

As 1937 except for chrome-plated rims with black centres.

M20, M21

As 1938 M19.

M24

Chrome-plated tank with matt silver panels and BSA Gold Star badges. Chrome-plated rims with black centres, chrome-plated oil tank with black panels. Show model had silver rim centres and oil tank panels.

C10

Green tank with gold lining and oval tank transfer, black wheel rims.

1939

General notes as for 1937, variations to tank and rim finish, as detailed below.

B21 standard

Chrome-plated tank with matt silver panels, round BSA tank badge, black rims.

B21 de-luxe

As B21 standard except for matt silver rims

B23 standard and de-luxe

Matt silver tank with maroon lining, round BSA tank badge, black rims.

B24

Chrome-plated tank with matt silver panels and BSA star tank transfer. Chrome-plated rims with matt silver centres.

B25

As B24 except wheel rims with silver centres and chrome-plated mudguards.

B26

As B21 standard.

B26 twin port

As standard except rims matt silver with black lines.

M20 standard

As B26 twin port.

M20 de-luxe

Tank as B21, rims as B24.

M21

As M20 de-luxe.

M22

Tank as B21, chrome-plated rims with black centres.

M23

As B24.

M24

As B24.

C10 de-luxe

As B23.

C11

As B23.

1940

Generally as 1937. All models were shown as having chrome-plated rims with silver centres.

C10 and C12

Matt silver tank with black outer and red inner lining, BSA oval badges.

C11

Chrome-plated tank with matt silver panels, BSA oval badges.

M20, M21, B29

As C11.

M23

As C11 except tank badge was BSA star.

1945

General finish of black for frame, forks, headlamp shell, mudguards, oil tank, toolbox, chaincase and chainguard. The exhaust system, headlamp rim, handlebars and minor fittings were chrome plated. Details of tanks and wheel rims are set out next, together with other variations.

C10, C11, B31

Chrome-plated tank with matt silver panels lined in black. Winged BSA badge on tank side. Rims matt silver with black lining, brake back plates chrome-plated.

M20

Matt silver tank lined in black, black rims and brake back plates.

1946
C10, C11, B31, M20

As in 1945.

M21

As M20.

B32

Generally as B31 but with chrome-plating applied to mudguards, stays, front stand and rear chainguard.

1947
C10, C11, B31, M20, M21

As in 1946.

B33

As B31, from July a matt silver stripe was added to the mudguards.

B32

Wheel rims chrome-plated with matt silver centres lined black.

B34

As B32.

1948
C10, C11 standard, B31, B33, M20, M21

As in 1947.

C11 de-luxe

Chrome-plated tank with blue panels, rims chrome-plated with lined blue centres.

B32

As before except tank panels and rim centres in Brunswick green, gold lined; optional chrome-plated chaincase.

B34

As B32 except colour in Devon red.

B31 option

Tank and rims as B32.

B33 option

Tank and rims as B34.

M33

General finish as range, tank chrome-plated with matt silver panels lined in black, rims chrome-plated with matt silver centres lined black. Black brake back plates.

M20 and M21 option

Tank and rims as M33.

All models with telescopic forks except C10 and C11 standard had the front fork lower spring covers chrome-plated.

1949

C10, C11, B31, B32, B33, B34, M20, M21, M33

As in 1948 with same options.

D1

Mist green for all cycle parts including frame, forks, mudguards, headlamp shell and rim, toolbox, rear carrier, chainguard, stand, wheel rims. Piled arms transfer on toolbox, gear indicator transfer on chainguard. Petrol tank Mist green with yellow side panels carrying BSA transfer. Chrome-plated exhaust pipe, silencer, handle-bars and minor controls.

1950

Range as in 1949, competition and plunger-framed Bantams as rigid model.

1951

No changes but during the year the nickel supply position began to restrict chrome-plating. C model tanks were finished in blue and beige in place of blue and chrome.

1952

No changes were announced but during the year nickel was in short supply so tanks and wheel rims were painted. Chrome-plating was restricted to the exhaust pipes, silencers and minor fittings.

Tanks carried small round BSA badges with a wing pattern

that ran back to the kneegrips, in yellow and chrome-plate. The **B31** was in green and the **B33** in red with their wheel rims in silver with green or red centres to match. The **B32** and **B34** were not altered from the 1948 finish.

1953

Chrome-plated wheel rims on all models.

D1

Continued as before in Mist green, option of black also available.

C range

All painted items maroon, chrome tank panels, option of black for all painted parts except tank which remained maroon.

B31 and B33

As C range, B31 front brake back plate polished and chrome-plated; black option available as for C range.

B32 and B34

As in 1948 except for matt silver tank panels. Finish thus very similar to Gold Star.

M range

Maroon tank with chrome side panels, all other painted parts in black.

Winged Wheel

Black drum, polished alloy main casting.

1954
D1

As in 1953.

D3

Similar to D1 in Pastel grey with yellow tank panels, silencer fishtail painted.

C10L

Dark green frame, lower fork yoke, hubs, stand, brake back plates, engine plates, plunger spring upper covers and chainguard. Light green forks, mudguards, headlamp shell, oil tank and toolbox. Petrol tank dark green with light green side panels lined in gold. Round BSA badge, chrome-plated strips on tank. Chrome-plated wheel rims, headlamp rim, exhaust system and detail parts.

C11G
As C11 in 1953 in maroon only, tank badge changed to round type with BSA piled arms insignia.

B31 and B33
As 1953 in maroon with chrome tank panels and round BSA badges with piled arms insignia.

B32 and B34
As 1953 in black and chrome-plating, petrol tank in natural aluminium with small black winged BSA transfer.

M range
As 1953 with maroon tank and badges as B31, remainder in black.

1955
D1
As before plus further option of maroon.

D3, 'C', 'B' and 'M' ranges
As 1954.

1956
D1
Green

D3
Grey, as before.

C10L
As 1954.

C12
All painted parts maroon, petrol tank with cream panels.

'B' and 'M' ranges
As 1954.

1957
'D' range
Standard colours as 1956, options of black or maroon.

C10L
As 1954.

C12
As 1956, option of chrome-plated tank panels, option of black in place of maroon.

B31 and B33
As 1954, option of all black.

B32 and B34
As 1954.

'M' range
As 1954 but with cream tank panels as standard, chrome-plated panels an option.

Dandy
Chrome-plated wheel rims, colour schemes in light green, honey beige, dark lavender and grey.

1958
D1
As 1957.

D5
Maroon with ivory tank panels.

C12
As 1957.

B31 and B33
Black frame and forks, chrome tank panels; mudguards, oil and petrol tanks in Almond green for B31 and Gunmetal grey for B33.

M21
As 1957.

Dandy
Lavender grey or honey beige, option of ivory for frame and forks with maroon mudguards, tank, carrier and apron.

C15
Black frame, forks, headlamp shell, chainguard. Red or blue option for petrol and oil tanks, mudguards and centre section. Pear-shaped tank badges. Chrome plated handlebars, exhaust system, headlamp rim, tank strips, wheel rims and edges of brake back plates.

1959
D1
As 1957 in green, black or maroon with cream tank panel.

D7

Black with ivory tank panel.

B31, B33, M21, Dandy and C15

As 1958.

175 Scooter

Light polychromatic green.

C15T and C15S

Black frame, forks, oil tank. Blue tank with chrome-plated side panels. Chrome-plated mudguards as option.

1960
D1

Black frame, forks, headlamp and toolbox. Tank and mudguards in Mist green, Fuchsia red, or black; tank panels in ivory.

D7

Black frame, forks and headlamp shell. Tank, mudguards, toolbox, battery lid and centre panel in Sapphire blue, Fuchsia red or black; tank panels in ivory. Chrome-plated wheel rims, headlamp rim, exhaust system, handlebars and minor parts.

B33

Black frame, forks, headlamp shell. Petrol tank, oil tank and mudguards Princess grey, pear-shaped tank badges.

M21

As 1957.

C15

As 1958, except option colour Almond green.

C15T, C15S, 175 Scooter, Dandy

As 1959.

1961
'D' range

As 1960 except D7 Fuchsia red changed to Royal red.

M21, C15T, C15S

As 1959.

C15

As 1960.

B40

As 1960 C15 but in Royal red and black. Chrome-plated tank panels, round BSA star badge.

SS80

Black frame, forks, mudguards, oil tank, centre panel. Petrol tank in black with round BSA star badge, chrome-plated panels, gold lined. Silver sheen hubs and hub cover plates. Two stars on side of oil tank and toolbox, option of chrome-plated mudguards.

175 Scooter

As 1959 plus options of Fuchsia red or Sapphire blue. Two-tone option of any colour with cream apron.

Dandy

Options of maroon and ivory or blue and ivory.

1962
'D' range

As 1961, **D7** with pear-shaped tank badges.

C15

As 1960 except option colour Sapphire blue with blue and ivory tank panels.

C15T and C15S

As 1959 but during year adopted light-alloy tank and mudguards leaving frame, forks, oil tank and hubs black with front brake back plate chrome-plated.

M21, B40, 175 Scooter and Dandy

As 1961.

SS80

As 1961 except petrol tank, oil tank, toolbox, centre panel and mudguards in Polychromatic blue. Chrome-plated tank panels.

SS90

Similar to SS80 with black frame, forks and headlamp shell. Flamboyant red petrol tank, oil tank, toolbox and centre panel, chrome-plated tank panels and mudguards. Pear-shaped tank badges. Option of all black and chrome.

1963
'D' range, C15, C15T, C15S, SS90, 175 Scooter and M21

As 1962.

B40

As 1961, black option available.

SS80

As 1961, black option available, pear-shaped tank badges.

1964
D7, C15T, C15S, SS90 and 175 Scooter

As 1962.

B40 and SS80

As 1963.

C15

As 1962 but colour listed as Royal red not Fuchsia red.

Beagle

Green frame and major part of petrol tank; ivory tank panels, forks, mudguards and swinging fork; chrome-plated wheel rims, handlebars, exhaust system and headlamp rim.

1965
D7

Super model as 1962. Super de-luxe with Ruby red tank, mudguards and centre panels with white lines on tank and guards. Chrome-plated tank panels, round badges, black frame and forks.

C15T, C15S, SS90 and 175 Scooter

As 1962.

B40

As 1963.

C15

As 1964.

SS80

As 1963 except chrome-plated mudguards standard.

Beagle

Royal red and ivory in 1964 pattern.

B44GP

Black frame, forks and hubs, petrol tank yellow.

1966
D7

De-luxe as 1965. Silver Bantam with blue tank, round badges, silver sheen for tank side panels, centre panels and mudguards, remainder as de-luxe.

D10 Supreme

Electric blue tank upper rear, mudguards and centre panels; white lining for tank and mudguards; petrol tank lower front chrome-plated with round badges and white top between seams. Black frame, forks, and chainguard; silver hubs.

D10 Silver

As D7 Silver.

D10 Sports

As Supreme but in red with chrome-plated mudguards, cylinder barrel silver and chequered stripe on tank top between seams.

D10 Bushman

Black frame and forks, chrome-plated headlamp, Bushfire orange tank upper rear and centre panels, white tank lower front and mudguards.

C15

As 1964 in Royal red or Sapphire blue except tank panels chrome-plated. All black option added during year.

C15 Sportsman

As previous SS80 in Flamboyant blue and black with chrome-plated headlamp. Change to silver hubs and back plates during year.

B44GP and B44 VE

Black frame, forks, oil tank on VE, air filter covers and hubs. Deep yellow tank.

1967
D10, C15, B44GP and B44VE

As 1966.

C25

Tank and side panels in Bushfire orange with white panels, chrome-plated mudguards and headlamp, black frame, forks and chainguard. Changed to blue and white during year.

B44VR

Similar to C25 in Royal red and ivory with identical chrome-plating and black paint.

1968

D14/4—as D10 Supreme.
D14/4S—as D10 Sports.
D14/4B—as D10 Bushman.
B25—as C25 in blue, black and chrome-plate.
B44VE—as 1967.
B44SS—as 1967 B44VR.

1969

D175 Bantam

As D14/4 in blue and chrome-plate, or Bushfire orange and white.

D175 Bushman

As D10 Bushman.

B25

As 1968.

Fleetstar

In black or white, chrome tank panels.

B44SS

Red petrol tank, oil tank and side cover, chrome-plated mudguards and headlamp, black frame and forks.

B44VS

As B44VE in 1966, with chrome-plated mudguards and petrol tank in polished alloy and yellow.

1970

D175, B25, B44SS and B44VS

As 1969.

1971

D175, B25, B44SS and B44VS

AS 1969 D14/4 in blue, black or red and chrome.
All frames for B25 and B50 models in Dove grey.

B25SS and B50SS

Petrol tank Flamboyant red or blue with black centre and side stripes, mudguards to match with black centre stripe, side panels to match.

B25T and B50T

Petrol tank polished alloy with black centre and side stripes, side panels and mudguards in red as on SS models.

B50MX

Petrol tank as B50T, mudguards in stainless steel. Side panels in race colour of yellow for England and white for USA.

All exhaust systems in heat-resistant black with stainless-steel heat shield fitted on SS and T models.

1972

All models with black frames, 8 in. brake back plate finished in black, hub left natural.

B50SS

Tank, side panels and mudguards in Hi-violet.

B50T

Polished alloy tank with Hi-violet sides and centre, white side panels, chrome mudguards.

B50MX

Tank as T model, mudguards stainless steel, side panels in Hi-violet and race colour as in 1971.

Engine and frame numbers

Before the Second World War BSA used a sequence of key letters which were followed by the model number and then the serial number. For the engine the model number used was the catalogue one but for the frame they used the first model number from the group as frames were common to several models. This arrangement was continued after the war but often a key letter would be used for more than one year.

Suffix letters were sometimes used after the model number, such as 'S' for spring frame, 'B' for battery fitted and 'P' for police model.

The Bantam engines were built as units to be sold as such in their early days and these had a letter 'U' at the front of the prefix. They also used a letter 'L' in the prefix

of both motorcycle and separate engines to indicate the use of the Lucas generator.

Generally the added letters follow a clear pattern as to their meaning but some confusion arises due to the many build standards often offered for particular machines. In the following tables this has been covered by bracketing sets of numbers as appropriate and reference to the model recognition points and the general text should assist in identifying machines.

The machines listed are what may be termed standard ones but in addition there were often export or special builds. Thus the C15, for instance, was built in nine models in more than one year, these including several for the USA, Police, racer and pastoral versions. In most cases the suffix letter indicates the use, even when C10 engines were fitted to AC invalid cars when the prefix used was ZC10AC-, for example.

Model	Engine	Frame
1937		
B20	HB20-101	HB20-101
B21	HB21-101	HB20-101
B22	HB22-101	HB20-101
B23	HB23-101	HB20-101
B24	HB24-101	HB24-101
B25	HB25-101	HB24-101
B26	HB26-101	HB24-101
M19	HM19-101	HM19-101
M20	HM20-101	HM19-101
M21	HM21-101	HM19-101
M22	HM22-101	HM19-101
M23	HM23-101	HM19-101

1938

as for 1937 except that the initial letter became J, e.g. JB23-101. Additional model:

Model	Engine	Frame
M24	JM24-101	JM24-101

1939

Similar coding to previous years but with variations to cater for 1938 models and mid-season changes.

Model	Engine	Frame
C10 standard	KJC10-	KJC10-
C10 de-luxe	KC10-101	KC10-101
C11	KC11-101	KC10-101
B21 standard	KJB21-	KJB20-
B21 de-luxe	KB21-101	KB21-101
B23 standard	KJB23-	KJB20-
B23 de-luxe	KB23-101	KB21-101

Model	Engine	Frame
B24	KB24-101	KB24-101
B25	KB25-101	KB24-101
B26	KB26-101	KB24-101
M20 standard	KMS20-101	KM20-101
M20 de-luxe	KM20-101	KM20-101
M21	KM21-101	KM20-101
M22 standard	KJM22-	KJM19-
M23	KM23-101	KM23-101
M24	KM24-101	KM24-101
1940		
C10	WC10-101	WC10-101
C11	WC11-101	WC10-101
C12	WC12-101	WC10-101
B29	WB29-101	WB27-101
M20	WM20-101	WM20-101
M21	WM21-101	WM20-101
M23	WM23-101	WM20-101

Wartime

War broke out just after BSA had started to build machines for the 1940 range and immediately the government requisitioned the entire stockholding which amounted to 690 bikes. These were quickly put into service alongside many other civilian machines but most were lost in the Dunkirk evacuation. Hence the scarcity of B29 and C12 models.

The bulk of the machines built for the services were M20s although some C10s, C11s and M21s were also supplied. While engine and frame numbers may have tallied on delivery, this seldom lasted as machines were rebuilt during their life without regard to this aspect. Many were sold off after the war and often wartime engines were fitted to later frames.

All models supplied to the services had the prefix letter W and some of the numbers and delivery periods are set out below.

Numbers	Date from	Date to
101– 4999	21. 9.39	
5000– 9719		17.11.39
9720–14439		15. 2.40
14440–18899		21. 5.40
19000–23039		8. 7.40
23040–27039		27. 9.40
27040–31879		3. 3.41
31880–36759	30. 1.40	
36760–40939	1. 4.41	29. 7.41
40940–45669	28. 7.41	20. 9.41
45670–50549	22. 9.41	4.12.41
50550–55429	5.12.41	28. 2.42
55430–60309	24. 2.42	14. 5.42
60310–70000	1942 estimated	
70001–90000	1943 estimated	
90001–110000	1944 estimated	

Model	Engine	Frame
1945		
C10	XC10-101	XC10G-101
C11	XC11-101	XC10G-101
B31	XB31-101	XB31-101
M20	XM20-101	XM20-101
1946		
C10	XC10-101 ⎫	⎧ XC10G-101 girder forks or
C11	XC11-101 ⎭	⎩ XC10T-101 with teles
B31	XB31-101	XB31-101
B32	XB32-101	XB31-101
M20	XM20-101	XM20-101
M21	XM21-101	XM20-101
1947		
C10	XC10-101	XC10T-101
C11	XC11-101	XC10T-101
B31	XB31-101	XB31-101
B32	XB32-101	XB31-101
B33	XB33-101	XB31-101
B34	XB34-101	XB31-101
M20	XM20-101	XM20-101
M21	XM21-101	XM20-101
1948		
C10	YC10-101	YC10-101
C11	YC11-101	YC10-101
B31	YB31-101	YB31-101
B32	YB32-101	YB31-101
B33	YB33-101	YB31-101
B34	YB34-101	YB31-101
M20	YM20-101	YM20-101
M21	YM21-101	YM20-101
M33	YM33-101	YM20-101
1949		
D1 motorcycle	YD1-101	YD1-101
C10	ZC10-101	ZC10-101
C11	ZC11-101	ZC10-101
B31	ZB31-101 ⎫	⎧ ZB31-101 rigid or
B32	ZB32-101 ⎪	⎩ ZB31S-101 plunger
B33	ZB33-101 ⎬	
B34	ZB34-101 ⎭	
M20	ZM20-101	ZM20-101
M21	ZM21-101	ZM20-101
M33	ZM33-101	ZM20-1021

Model	Engine	Frame
1950		
D1 Wico	YD1-20001 ⎫	⎰ YD1-20001 rigid or
D1 Lucas	YDL1-101 ⎭	⎱ YD1S-20001 plunger
C10	ZC10-4001	ZC10-10001
C11	ZC11-8001	ZC10-10001
B31	ZB31-9001 ⎫	
B32	ZB32-3001 ⎪	⎧ ZB31-9001 rigid
B32 alloy engine	ZB32A-3001 ⎬	⎨ or
B33	ZB33-4001 ⎪	⎩ ZB31S-5001 plunger
B34	ZB34-2001 ⎪	
B34 alloy engine	ZB34A-2001 ⎭	
M20	ZM20-4001	ZM20-7001
M21	ZM21-5001	ZM20-7001
M33	ZM33-3001	ZM20-7001
1951		
D1 Wico	YD1-40001 ⎫	⎧ YD1-40001 rigid or
D1 Lucas	YDL1-3001 ⎭	⎩ YD1S-40001 plunger
		⎧ ZC10-21001 rigid or
C10	ZC10-7001 ⎫	⎪ ZC10S-101 plunger or
C11	ZC11-16001 ⎭	⎨ ZC10S4-101 plunger frame and four
		⎩ speed gearbox
B31	ZB31-15001 ⎫	
B32	ZB32-4001 ⎪	⎧ ZB31-14001 rigid
B32 alloy engine	ZB32A-4001 ⎪	⎨ or
B33	ZB33-7001 ⎬	⎩ ZB31S-10001 plunger
B34	ZB34-3001 ⎪	
B34 alloy engine	ZB34A-3001 ⎭	
M20	ZM20-6001 ⎫	⎧ ZM20-10001 rigid
M21	ZM21-8001 ⎬	⎨ or
M33	ZM33-4001 ⎭	⎩ ZM20S-101 plunger
1952		
D1 Wico	YD1-63001 ⎫	⎧ YD1-64001 rigid or
D1 Lucas	YDL1-8001 ⎭	⎩ YD1S-64001 plunger
		⎧ ZC10-29001 rigid or
C10	ZC10-10001 ⎫	⎨ ZC10S-2601 plunger or
C11	ZC11-25001 ⎭	⎩ ZC10S4-2001 plunger and 4-speed
B31	ZB31-21001 ⎫	
B32	ZB32-5001 ⎪	
B32 alloy engine	ZB32A-5001 ⎪	⎧ ZB31-19001 rigid
B33	ZB33-11001 ⎬	⎨ or
B34	ZB34-4001 ⎪	⎩ ZB31S-17001 plunger
B34 sand cast alloy	ZB34A-4001 ⎪	
B34 die cast alloy	ZB34A-5001 ⎭	
M20	ZM20-10001 ⎫	⎧ ZM20-14001 rigid
M21	ZM21-10001 ⎬	⎨ or
M33	ZM33-5001 ⎭	⎩ ZM20S-301 plunger

Model	Engine	Frame
1953		
D1 Wico	BD2-101 ⎫	⎧ BD2-101 rigid or
D1 Lucas	BD2L-101 ⎭	⎩ BD2S-101 plunger
		⎧ BC10-101 rigid or
C10	BC10-101 ⎫	⎨ BC10S-101 plunger or
C11	BC11-101 ⎭	⎩ BC10S4-101 plunger and 4-speed
B31	BB31-101 ⎫	
B32	BB32-101	⎧ BB31-101 rigid
B32 alloy engine	BB32A-101 ⎬	⎨ or
B33	BB33-101	⎩ BB31S-101 plunger
B34	BB34-101	
B34 alloy engine	BB34A-101 ⎭	
M20	BM20-101 ⎫	⎧ BM20-101 rigid
M21	BM21-101 ⎬	⎨ or
M33	BM33-101 ⎭	⎩ BM20S-101 plunger
1954		
D1 direct	BD-101 ⎫	
D1 battery	BDB-101	⎧ BD2-14600 rigid
D3 direct	BD3-101 ⎬	⎨ or
D3 battery	BD3B-101 ⎭	⎩ BD2S-14600 plunger
C10L	BC10L-101	BC10LS-101
		⎧ BC11-101 rigid or
C11G	BC11G-101	⎨ BC11S-101 plunger or
		⎩ BC11S4-101 plunger and 4-speed
B31	BB31-6001 ⎫	⎧ BB31-1386 rigid or
B33	BB33-2001 ⎭	⎨ BB31S-5895 plunger or
		⎩ CB31-101 s/a
B32	BB32A-201 ⎫	⎧ BB32R-121 rigid or
B34	BB34A-201 ⎭	⎩ CB31-101 s/a
M20	BM20-1001 ⎫	⎧ BM20-1502 rigid
M21	BM21-1601 ⎬	⎨ or
M33	BM33-501 ⎭	⎩ BM20S-1192 plunger
1955		
D1 direct	DD-101 ⎫	⎧ BD2-34701 rigid
D1 battery	DDB-101	⎨ or
D3 direct	BD3-5138 ⎬	⎩ BD2S-34701 plunger
D3 battery	BD3B-5138 ⎭	
C10L	BC10L-4001	BC10LS-4501
C11G 3-speed	BC11G-11501	BC11S-4001 plunger
C11G 4-speed	BC11G-11501	BC11S4-8001 plunger
B31	BB31-15001 ⎫	⎧ BB31S-12001 plunger or
B33	BB33-5001 ⎭	⎩ CB31-6001 s/a
B32	BB32A-251	BB32A-201 rigid or
B34	BB34A-301	CB31-6001 s/a

Model	Engine	Frame
1955		
M20	BM20-2501 ⎤	⎡ BM20-4001 rigid
M21	BM21-4501 ⎬	{ or
M33	BM33-1301 ⎦	⎣ BM20S-4001 plunger

Note: a few C11G may have been built with rigid frames
as:
1954 BC11R4-101 rigid and 4-speed
1955 BC11-801 rigid and 3-speed
      BC11R4-501 rigid and 4-speed

Model	Engine	Frame
1956		
D1 direct	DD-4801	BD2S-55001
D1 battery	DDB-3301	BD2S-55001
D3 direct	BD3-10401	CD3-101
D3 battery	BD3B-12801	CD3-101
C10L	BC10L-7001	DC10S-101
C12	BC11G-23001	EC12-101 s/a or
		BC11S4-18001 plunger 4-speed
B31	BB31-22001	EB31-101
B33	BB33-7301	EB31-101
B32	BB32A-301 ⎤	⎡ CB34-101 s/a or
B34	BB34A-351 ⎦	⎣ B32R-301 rigid
M21	BM21-7501	BM20-7001 rigid or
		BM20S-8001 plunger
M33	BM33-2101	BM20S-8001 plunger
1957		
Dandy	DSE-101	DS-101
D1 direct	DD-	BD2S-
D1 battery	DDB-	BD2S-
D3 direct	BD3-	CD3-
D3 battery	BD3B-	CD3-
C10L	BC10L-	DC10S-
C12	BC11G-	EC12-
B31	BB31-	EB31-
B33	BB33-	EB31-
B32	BB32A-	CB34-
B34	BB34A-	CB34-
M21	BM21-	BM20- rigid or
		BM20S- plunger
M33	BM33-	BM20S- plunger
1958		
Dandy	DSE-11001	DS-11501
D1 direct	DD-8577	BD2S-65001
D1 battery	DDB-7849	BD2S-65001

Appendix

Model	Engine	Frame
1958		
D5 direct	ED5-101	FD5-101
D5 battery	ED5B-101	FD5-101
C12	BC11G-40001	EC12-16001
B31	GB31-101	FB31-101
B33	GB33-101	FB31-101
M21	BM21-11001	BM20-10001 rigid or BM20S-11001 plunger
1959		
Dandy	DSE-14462	DS-15165
D1 direct	DD-10812	BD2S-67581
D1 battery	DDB-10628	BD2S-67581
D7 direct	ED7-101	D7-101
D7 battery	ED7B-101	D7-101
C15	C15-101	C15-101
C15S	C15S-101	C15S-101
C15T	C15T-101	C15S-101
B31	GB31-1909	FB31-2572
B33	GB33-662	FB31-2572
M21	BM21-12033	BM20-10313 rigid or BM20S-12031 plunger
1960		
Dandy	DSE-17901	DS-18001
D1 direct	DD-12501	BD2S-70501
D1 battery	DDB-12501	BD2S-70501
D7 direct	ED7-1501	D7-8101
D7 battery	ED7B-7001	D7-8101
Scooter	S-101	4001
C15	C15-11001	C15-11101
C15S	C15S-301	C15S-501
C15T	C15T-301	C15S-501
B33	GB33-1001	GB33-101
M21	BM21-12901	BM20-10451 rigid or BM20S-12031 plunger
1961		
Dandy	DSE-21651	DS-21801
D1 direct	DD-14501	BD2S-73701
D1 battery	DDB-14501	BD2S-73701
D7 direct	ED7-3001	D7-18401
D7 battery	ED7B-15501	D7-18401
Scooter	S-6720	18801B
C15	C15-21251	C15-22001
C15S	C15S-2112	C15S-2701
C15T	C15T-1056	C15S-2701
SS80	C15SS-101	C15-27644

Model	Engine	Frame
1961		
B40	B40-101	B40-101
M21	BM21-14301	BM20S-14201
M21 alternator	BM21A-14301	BM20S-14201
1962		
Dandy	DSE-22164	BS-22268
D1 direct	DD-15481	BD2S-76680
D1 battery	DDB-16413	BD2S-76680
D7 direct	ED7-4501	D7-27450
D7 battery	ED7B-23001	D7-27450
Scooter	S-11407	30140B
C15	C15-29839	C15-31801
SS80	C15SS-1101	C15-31801
C15S	C15S-3101	C15S3601
C15T	C15T-1451	C15S-10001
B40	B40-3601	B40-3511
SS90	B40 BSS-101	B40-3511
M21	BM21-15453	BM20S-15061
M21 alternator	BM21A-15453	BM20S-15061
1963		
D1 direct	DD-16129	BD2S-78746
D1 battery	DDB-17606	BD2S-78746
D7 direct	ED7-5505	D7-33268
D7 battery	ED7B-26904	D7-33268
Scooter	S-12498	31825B
C15	C15-41807	C15-38035
SS80	C15SS-2705	C15-38035
C15S	C15S-4001	C15C-101
C15T	C15T-2001	C15C-101
B40	B40-4506	B40-5017
SS90	B40SS-180	B40-5017
M21	BM21-15588	BM20S-15159
M21 with alternator	BM21A-15588	BM20S-15159
1964		
Beagle	K1-101	K1-101
D7 direct	ED7-6887	D7-38400
D7 battery	FD7-101	D7-38400
Scooter	S-13263	33661B
C15	C15D-101	C15-42211
SS80	C15SS-3633	C15-42211
C15S	C15S-4373	C15C-853
C15T	C15T-2116	C15C-853
B40	B40-5275	B40-6668
SS90	B40SS-426	B40-6668

Model	Engine	Frame
1965		
Beagle	K1-3507	K1-3315
D7 direct	ED7-9001	D7-42878
D7 battery	FD7-3001	D7-42878
Scooter	S-13576	34300B
C15	C15F-101	C15-45501
SS80	C15FSS-101	C15-45501
C15S	C15FS-101	C15C-1601
C15T	C15FT-101	C15C-1601
B40	B40F-101	B40-7775
SS90	B40FSS-101	B40-7775
1966		
D7 Bantam de-luxe	ED7-101 ⎫	⎧ D7-49985 to 51960
D7 Silver Bantam	ED7-101 ⎬	⎩ direct or battery
D7 Silver and de-luxe	GD7-101	GD7-101 after frame 51960
C15	C15F-2089	C15-49001
C15 Sportsman	C15SS-2001	C15-49001
B40	B40F-1149	B40-9973
B40 modified engine	B40G-101	B40-9973
B44GP	B44-101	B44-101
B44VE	B44E-101	C15C-3137
1967		
D10	D10-101	D10-101
D10 4-speed	D10A-101	D10A-101
D10 Bushman	D10A-101	BD 10A-101
C15	C15G-101	C15G-101
C15 Sportsman	C15SG-101	C15SG-101
C25 Barracuda	C25-101	C25-101
B25 Starfire	C25-101	B25-101
B40	B40G-201	B40G-201
B44GP	B44-131	B44-267
B44VE	B44EA-101	B44EA-101
B44VR	B44R-101	B44R-101
1968		
D13 Supreme	D13B-101 to 780	D13B-101
D14/4 Supreme	D14B-781	D14B-781
D13 Sports	D13B-101 to 780	D13B-101S
D14/4 Sports	D14B-781	D14B-781S
D13 Bushman	D13C-101 to 780	D13C-101B
D14/4 Bushman	D14C-781	D14C-781B
B25	B25B-101	B25B-101
B44 Victor	B44B-101VS	B44B-101VS
B44 Shooting Star	B44B-101SS	B44B101SS

1969 onwards

A new coding system was adopted for all models comprising a date code, model code and serial number. The date code consists of two letters, the first giving the month and the second the year of manufacture. This year ran from August of previous year so that code JD is August 1969 not 1970 although for a 1970 model. Model code numbers were in the form already shown and agreed with catalogue numbers. The serial number began at 00100 each season and these were used without regard for the model.

First letter code—month:

A	January	D	April	H	July	N	October

A January D April H July N October
B February E May J August P November
C March G June K September X December

Second letter code—year:

C   August 1968 to July 1969
D   August 1969 to July 1970
E   August 1970 to July 1971
G   August 1971 to July 1972

Model recognition points

This section has been compiled for use with the data in the other appendices and represents a precis of the main text as applicable.

1937

'B' models used lighter frame and forks than 'M' models, all 'M' machines, except **M23**, had sidecar lugs. All toolboxes high on right of machine above rear wheel spindle, oil tanks on right, batteries on left, rear stand fitted. Horn bolted to lug on front down tube below tank. No push rod tunnel gland nut.

B20: 250 cc, sv, hand change, tubular silencer

B21: 250 cc, ohv, hand change, tubular silencer

B22: 250 cc, ohv, foot change, Brooklands silencer and fishtail

B23: 350 cc, sv, hand change, Brooklands silencer and fishtail

B24: 350 cc, ohv, foot change, Brooklands silencer and fishtail

B25: 350 cc, ohv, foot change, upswept tubular silencer and fishtail

B26: 350 cc, ohv, hand change, Brooklands silencer and fishtail

M19: 350 cc, ohv, foot change, Brooklands silencer and fishtail

M20: 500 cc, sv, hand change, Brooklands silencer and fishtail

M21: 600 cc, sv, hand change, Brooklands silencer and fishtail

M22: 500 cc, ohv, foot change, Brooklands silencer and fishtail

M23: 500 cc, ohv, foot change, Brooklands silencer and fishtail

1938

Push rod tunnel gland nut introduced on all ohv, engines, horn moved to front top engine mounting, idler gear bushes fitted. Otherwise, generally as 1937 models. Unchanged were **B20**, **B21**, **B22**, **B23**, **M19**, **M20**, **M22** and **M23**. **M21** had revised engine dimensions, otherwise unchanged. **B25**: with upswept Brooklands silencer and fishtail, crankcase shield but no toolbox. It. **B24** and **B26** fitted with horizontal Amal. **M24**: new model, 500 cc, ohv, footchange, tubular silencer, toolbox set in tank top, crankcase shield. **C10**: new model, 250 cc, sv, three-speed

gearbox, hand change, tubular silencer, oil tank combined with petrol tank, battery on left, toolbox on right above gearbox, rear brake pedal on right.

1939

Models **B20**, **B22** and **M19** deleted from range. New timing gear for all 'B' and 'M' models except **B21** standard, **B23** standard and **M22**. Generally as before for existing models, new de-luxe variants having slight changes.
B21 de-luxe, **B23** de-luxe, **B26**, **M20**, **M21**: with footchange and toolbox located between chainstays on right.
New oil tanks for most models and revised petrol tanks. No horizontal carburettors.
M24: new petrol tank, tank top instruments, toolbox between chainstays on right, four screw tappet cover, valanced rear mudguard, qd rear wheel, close ratio box standard.
C10 de luxe: footchange gearbox, rear brake pedal on left.
C11: new model, 250 cc, ohv, three-speed gearbox, footchange, generally as **C10** but 20 in. wheels.

1940

Models **B21**, **B23**, **B24**, **B25**, **B26**, **M22** and **M24** deleted from range along with de-luxe variants.
This left the **C10**, **C11**, **M20**, **M21** and **M23**, much as in 1939. Changes were made to the toolbox on the 'C' range, to tubular silencers for the side valve 'M' models, and to the shape of the rear number plate and the position of its lamp which became central on all models.
C12: new model, 350 cc, sv, based on **C10** design and using many common parts from **C** range.
B29: new model, 350 cc, ohv, hairpin valve springs, 'M'-type crankcase, Brooklands silencer with fishtail.

1945

C10, **C11**: as in 1939, except separate oil tank, oil lines from rear of crankcase, silencer parallel to ground, speedometer in petrol tank.
M20: as in 1939, except no tank top instruments, toolbox altered, mudguards not valanced, rear carrier fitted.
B31: new model, 'M'-type crankcase, teles, rigid, speedometer in tank.

1946

B32: new model, as **B31** except raised exhaust system, competition wheels, crankcase shield, magdyno or magneto to special order. **M21**: as **M20**.
'C' range: from April fitted with telescopic front forks.

1947

B33: new model, as **B31**, 3·50 rear tyre.
B34: new model, as **B32**.

1948

M33: new model, **M20** with **B33** engine, girder forks, built for sidecar use.
C11 de-luxe: new model, different finish.
'B' range: speedometer on fork top, not in tank.
'C' range: quick action throttle, drip shield on **C11**.
'M' range: toolbox, battery carrier, petrol cap as on **B** group, speedo central on forks.
Competition models: folding kickstart pedal.
All: domed headlamp glass, standard bars, drain plugs in oil tank and fork legs.

During June 1948: the **M** models were fitted with telescopic front forks. They retained the sidecar lugs as standard.
D1: new model, teles, rigid, flat silencer, deep valanced front mudguard, cable operated light switch.

1949

Sealed-beam headlight for all models, except **D1**.
D1 and 'M' range: continued.
'B' range: spring frame option.
'C' range: larger dynamo.

1950

'D' range: competition model added, plunger frame option, Lucas generator option, centre stand modified, gaiters on front forks.
B32 and **B34**: alloy engine option.
B31, **B33**, 'C' and 'M' ranges: unchanged.

1951

'C' range: plunger frame and 4-speed gearbox options, horn button in brake lever clamp; **C10** with alloy head, **C11** with more finning on barrel.
'M' range: plunger frame option, alloy head for side valve engines.
'B' and 'D' ranges: no change

1952

D1: new steering head gusset plate, light switch on headlamp.
'C' range: oil seal in 4-speed gearbox.
'B' and 'M' ranges: detail changes to brakes, dualseat option, new tank badges from March.

1953

D1: still with flat silencer, longer big end rollers, unsprung front mudguard without valance, chrome strips on tank welds, pillion footrest lugs on frame.

'**C**' range: boxed-in rear number plate with Lucas 525 Diacon lamp, round reflector at base of plate, speedometer mounted on fork top crown, underslung pilot lamp, dualseat option, 19 in. wheels for **C11**.

'**B**' range: number plate as '**C**' range, headlamp cowl, underslung pilot lamp, tank mountings changed, more finning on engines. 500 cc engines fitted with $\frac{1}{2}$ in. shorter con-rod and modified piston, **B33** fitted with 8 in. front brake and valanced front mudguard. '**M**' range: number plate, cowl and pilot lamp as '**B**' range; **M33** engine as for **B33**.

Winged Wheel: introduced in May.

1954

D1: big fin head and barrel, tubular silencer, heavier forks and flat silencer on competition models.

D3: new model, cowled headlamp, heavier forks, larger front brake, tubular silencer.

C10L: revised model, alternator, points in timing case, new frame with plunger rear suspension, **D3** type forks, shock absorber clutch, 3 speeds, **D3** front brake.

C11G: options of 3-speed rigid or plunger, or 4-speed plunger, alternator, points in timing case, shock absorber clutch.

B31 and **B33**: s/a frame for export, single bolt tank fixing, aluminium primary chaincase and new gearbox with new frame.

B32 and **B34**: s/a frame, new chaincase and gearbox, magneto only.

'**M**' range and **Winged Wheel**: no change.

1955

'**D**' range: new rear number plate, toolbox fixing changed, increased cylinder stud centres, 2 extra crankcase screws.

'**C**' range: ramp cams fitted, Monobloc, tank seam strip, altered pillion rests, plastic fuel pipe. **C11G** fitted with 7 in. front brake, deeper valanced rear mudguard.

B31 and **B33**: s/a frame option with Monobloc, new rear mudguard for **B31**, rubber air cleaner connection for **B33**, steering head lock, 2-lobe shock absorber cam.

B32 and **B34**: rigid, duplex frame.

'**M**' range: lock and cam as '**B**' range.

Winged Wheel: complete machine listed with cross-bar or drop frame, fitted with Webb girder forks.

1956

'**D**' range: s/a frame for **D3**, long silencer, dualseat standard.

D1 fitted with saddle as standard. Competition and rigid models discontinued.

C10L: more fins on light alloy head and iron barrel, damped forks, new 4-speed gearbox, separate lights and ignition switches, fitted with saddle.

C11G: discontinued.

C12: new model using **C11G** engine in s/a frame, damped forks, new 4-speed gearbox, full width hubs, switch panel on right behind oil tank, cowled headlamp, ammeter in headlamp, dualseat standard.

B31 and **B33**: s/a frame and dualseat standard, full width hubs, optional rear chaincase.

B32 and **B34**: no change, as 1955.

M20: discontinued.

M21: rigid and fitted with saddle as standard, plunger frame option.

M33: plunger frame standard with dualseat, 8 in. front brake, valanced front mudguard.

Dandy: initial showing, scooterette format.

1957

'**D**' range: no change, **D3** discontinued late in year.

'**C**' range: no change, **C10L** discontinued late in year.

B31 and **B33**: no change.

B32 and **B34**: duplex s/a frame, central oil tank, both models discontinued late in year.

'**M**' range: no change, **M33** discontinued during year.

Dandy: no changes.

1958

D1: change to main bearing lubrication.

D5: new model of 175 cc, similar to **D3**, discontinued late in year.

C12: no change, discontinued in year.

B31 and **B33**: ac electrics, alternator, coil ignition, points in place of magneto, clutch change, heavier rear chain, different headlamp cowl, cast-iron brakes, roll-on feet for centre stand.

M21: no change.

Dandy: revised gear change, centre stand, rear brake.

C15: new model, unit construction, distributor behind barrel, 17 in. wheels, cowled headlamp.

1959

D1: no change.

D7: new model as **D5** but with new frame, forks, mudguards, $5\frac{1}{2}$ in. brakes.

B31 and **B33**: no change, **B31** discontinued late in year.

M21 and **Dandy**: no change.

C15: no change.

C15T and **C15S**: new models, as **C15** with gaitered forks, no toolbox, modified for trials or scrambles use.

175 Scooter: new model.

1960

No changes to existing range, **B33** discontinued from middle of year.

B40: new model from late in year, based on **C15** with increased engine size, no push rod tube, valve lifter, heavier front forks, 7 in. front brake, 18 in. wheels.

1961

No changes to **D1**, **D7**, **C15**, **C15T**, **C15S**, **B40**, **M21**, **Dandy** or **175 Scooter**. **M21** fitted alternator during year.

SS80: new model, based on **C15**, 3 gallon tank, flat bars, polished cylinder head fins, roller big end.

1962

No changes to **D1**, **SS80**, **M21**, **175 Scooter** or **Dandy**, which was discontinued during year.

D7: needle roller small end.

C15: compression ratio raised to 7·5, new horn and ignition switch, 60 watt alternator.

C15T and **C15S**: primary chain tensioner added, roller big end, **SS80** camshaft fitted, increased section rear wheel rim, gearing altered, 7 in. front brake. During the year further changes were made to fit a 2 gallon light alloy tank, light alloy mudguards, 7 in. non-full width front brake, adjustable rear spring units, restricted ignition advance. The **C15S** was fitted with strutted bars and a special exhaust pipe.

B40: primary chain tensioner, roller big end, new horn and ignition switch, 60 watt alternator, floating shoes in front brake.

SS90: new model, based on **B40** on lines of **SS80**.

1963

No changes to **D1**, **D7**, **M21**, **C15**, **SS80**, **B40**, **SS90** or **175 Scooter**.

D1 discontinued during year, also **M21**.

C15T and **C15S**: revised frame, central oil tank, inboard exhaust system, new air cleaner, stronger s/a, new kickstart folding at lower end. **C15T** fitted with **C15**

camshaft and compression ratio up to 7·5. Rear wheel of **C15S** fitted with 4·00 × 18 tyre on WM3 rim.

1964

D7: new silencer and magnetic speedometer.

C15: primary chain tensioner, roller big end, compression ratio 8·0, magnetic speedometer, 3 gallon tank.

C15T and **C15S**: light alloy fork shrouds, fork gaiters, altered gearing and 8·0 compression ratio on **C15T**.

SS80 and **SS90**: blade mudguards, 16-tooth gearbox sprocket on **SS80**.

B40 and **175 Scooter**: no change.

Beagle: new model, 75 cc ohv single.

1965

D7: gearbox internal ratios changed and big end modified. De-luxe model introduced with rectified lighting, new tank and seat, changed handlebars, ball-ended levers. In August the standard **D7** was discontinued, the **de-luxe** fitted with a new carburettor, and the centre panels altered. The **Silver** model was introduced to the same specification.

All unit construction singles based on **C15** were fitted with points in timing cover, rack and pinion clutch mechanism, clutch cable stop on gearbox top, stub gear teeth, modified gearchange, new kickstarter mechanism.

C15: continued with above.

C15, **C15S**, **B40** and **SS90**: continued with above, all discontinued in middle of year.

SS80: continued with above, type number changed to **C15 Sportsman** in middle of year when fitted with humped dualseat, separate headlamp and standard gearbox ratios.

Beagle and **175 Scooter**: no change, discontinued in middle of year.

B44GP: new model for moto-cross use, special frame carrying lubricating oil in tubes, different crankcases, ball and roller main bearings, alloy barrel with hard chrome-plated bore, shuttle valve front forks, dual air cleaners, non-full width hubs, left-hand thread front wheel spindle, crinkle rear hub.

1966

D7: no change, replaced in middle of year by **D10** range.

D10 Supreme: contact breaker on right on outside of primary chaincase, larger alternator, 4-plate clutch, larger carburettor, oval connecting rod, mirrors.

D10 Silver: as Supreme.

D10 Sports: **D10** with 4-speed gearbox, sports bars, humped seat, full width hubs, high level exhaust, flyscreen, chrome-plated exposed rear suspension springs.
D10 Bushman: 4-speed **D10** unit with lowered gearing, undershield, trail tyres, 19 in. wheels, upswept exhaust.
C15 and **C15 Sportsman**: no change until middle of year. Then fitted with Victor type bottom half with strengthened crankcase and ball and roller main bearings.
C15 Sportsman discontinued at end of year.
B44GP: no change.
B44VE: new model, **B44GP** type engine but with liner in cylinder muff, **C15T** frame, shuttle forks, normal oil tank, trail tyres, trail exhaust, trail seat, direct lights, bulb horn. Late in 1966 two new models were introduced for 1967.
C25: new model, square-fin barrel, one-piece crankshaft with bolt-on webs, plain big end, 12 volt electrics, 7 in. brakes, 18 in. wheels, fibreglass petrol and oil tanks.
B44VR: as **C25** but with **B44VE** engine.

1967

D10, C15, C25, B44VR: as late 1966. **C15** discontinued in mid-year, **D10** and **C25** superseded at end of year.
B44GP: as 1966, WM1 front rim, 7 in. rear brake, rear chain size altered, discontinued in mid-year.
B44VE: as 1966, 7 in. rear brake, rear chain size altered.

1968

D14/4, Supreme: new model as **D10** Supreme but with larger diameter exhaust pipe.
D14/4S, Sports: new model as **D10** Sports, larger diameter exhaust pipe, heavier forks fitted with gaiters.
D14/4B, Bushman: new model as **D10** Bushman with changes as for **D14/4S**.
B25: was **C25** model.
B44VE: as 1967.
B44SS: renamed **B44VR** with 8 in. front brake, full width hub, spindle caps on fork legs, toggle light switch, gaitered forks, high-rise bars, side reflectors.

1969

D175: revised models in standard and Bushman forms only, new cylinder head, central plug, new crankcases, heavier forks, separate headlamp, exposed rear springs, unified threads.
B25 and **B44SS**: 7 in. twin leading shoe front brake, steel petrol tank of 3·25 gallons.
Fleetstar: low compression ratio version of **B25** with lowered gearing.
B44VS: renamed **B44VE** coil ignition, full lights, 8 in. front brake.

1970

D175: hard-chromed fork legs, Bushman discontinued late in year.
B25, B44SS, B44VS: new oil pump, oil pressure switch, hard-chromed fork legs, all discontinued at end of year.

1971

D175: no change, discontinued in March.
New range of 4-stroke singles in 250 and 500 cc capacities. Frame with oil tank in tubes, slimline forks, conical hubs, cam fork pivot adjuster for rear chain, 3 main bearings for 500 cc engines.
B25SS: 6 or 8 in. front brake, road tyres, unsprung front mudguard.
B50SS: as **B25SS** except 8 in. brake only.
B25T and **B50T**: as **B25SS** except 6 in. front brake, sprung front mudguard, trail tyres.
B25SS and **B25T**: discontinued in middle of year.
B50MX: motocross machine as **B50T** without lights or silencer, fitted with motocross tyres.

1972

No changes: all models discontinued early in year.

Carburettor settings

Model	Year	Type	Size	Main	Pilot	Slide	Needle Pos.	Needle Jet
Gold Star								
M24 500 cc	1938–39	10TT	$1\frac{5}{32}$	350		6	4	
B32	1949–54	TT9	$1\frac{1}{16}$	320		7	4	·109
B32 Clubmans	1953	RN	$1\frac{3}{32}$	450		6	4	·109
B32 Clubmans	1954	GP	$1\frac{3}{32}$	210		6	1	·109
B32 Scrambles	1954	TT9	$1\frac{3}{32}$	350		7	3	·109
B32 Clubmans	1955–61	GP	$1\frac{3}{16}$	280		5	4	·109
B34	1949–54	TT9	$1\frac{5}{32}$	360		6	4	·109
B34 Clubmans	1953	RN	$1\frac{3}{16}$	520		7	4	·109
B34 Clubmans	1954	GP	$1\frac{7}{32}$	260		7	2	·109
B34 Scrambles	1954	TT9	$1\frac{5}{32}$	360		7	4	·109
B34	1955	GP	$1\frac{3}{8}$	330		7	4	·109
B34 Clubmans	1956–63	GP	$1\frac{1}{2}$	350	25	4	3	·109
B34 Scrambles	1956–63	389	$1\frac{5}{32}$	320	25	3	2	·106
B34 Scrambles	1958–61	GP	$1\frac{5}{32}$	240		5	3	·109
B34 Scrambles (USA)	1961–63	389	$1\frac{3}{16}$	320	30	4	4	·106
'B' range								
B20	1937–38	74	$\frac{25}{32}$	80		4/5	3	
B21	1937–38	74	$\frac{25}{32}$	80		4/4	2	
B21	1939	75	$\frac{7}{8}$	120		5/4	3	
B22	1937–38	75	$\frac{7}{8}$	120		5/4	3	
B23	1937	74	$\frac{25}{32}$	80		4/5	1	
B23	1938	75	$\frac{7}{8}$	110		5/4	3	
B23	1939	75	$\frac{7}{8}$	130		5/4	3	
B24, B25 & B26	1937–39	76	1	160		6/4	3	
B29 (ex WD)	1940	76	1	160		6/4	3	
B30 (ex WD)	1940	276	1	170		6/4	2	
B31	1946–54	276	$1\frac{1}{16}$	150		6/4	3	
B31	1955–59	376	1	260	30	$3\frac{1}{2}$	2	·106
B32	1946–54	276	$1\frac{1}{16}$	150		6/4	3	
B32	1955–57	376	$1\frac{1}{16}$	260	25	4	3	·106
B33 & B34	1949–54	289	$1\frac{1}{8}$	200		4	3	
B33	1955–60	376	$1\frac{1}{16}$	260	25	$3\frac{1}{2}$	3	·106
B34	1955–58	389	$1\frac{1}{8}$	240	25	3	2	·106
'M' range								
M19	1937–38	76	1	150		6/4	2	
M20	1937–39	76	1	170		6/4	3	
M20 (ex WD)	1940–45	276	1	170		6/4	2	
M20	1946–54	276	1	170		6/4	3	
M20	1955–59	376	1	240	30	5	3	·106
M21	1937–39	76	$1\frac{1}{16}$	160		6/4	2	

Model	Year	Type	Size	Main	Pilot	Slide	Needle Pos.	Needle Jet
M21 (ex WD)	1940–45	276	$1\frac{1}{16}$	160		6/4	2	
M21	1946–54	276	$1\frac{1}{16}$	160		6/4	2	
M21	1955–61	376	$1\frac{1}{16}$	250	30	5	2	·106
M22	1937–39	76	$1\frac{1}{16}$	150		6/4	3	
M23	1937	89	$1\frac{1}{8}$	200		4	2	
M23	1938	89	$1\frac{1}{8}$	200		4	3	
M23	1939	89	$1\frac{1}{8}$	200		3	3	
M24	1938–39	10TT	$1\frac{5}{32}$	350		6	4	
M33	1949–54	289	$1\frac{1}{8}$	200		4	3	
M33	1955–60	376	$1\frac{1}{16}$	260	25	$3\frac{1}{2}$	3	·106
'C' range								
C10	1938–39	74	$\frac{25}{32}$	80		4/5	3	
C10 (ex WD)	1940–45	274	$\frac{25}{32}$	90		4/4	3	
C10	1946–53	274	$\frac{25}{32}$	90		4/4	2	·105
C10L	1954	274	$\frac{25}{32}$	90		4/4	2	·105
C10L	1955–57	375	$\frac{25}{32}$	120	25	$3\frac{1}{2}$	2	·105
C11	1939	74	$\frac{25}{32}$	80		4/4	3	
C11	1946–48	274	$\frac{25}{32}$	80		4/4	3	
C11	1949–53	274	$\frac{7}{8}$	80		4/4	3	
C11G	1954	274	$\frac{7}{8}$	80		4/4	3	
C11G	1955	375	$\frac{25}{32}$	140	25	$3\frac{1}{2}$	3	·105
C12 (250 cc)	1956–58	375	$\frac{25}{32}$	140	25	$3\frac{1}{2}$	3	·105
C12 (350 cc-sv)	1940	276	1	150		6/4	2	
'D' range								
D1	1948–50	261	$\frac{5}{8}$	75		5	2	·106
D1	1951–63	361	$\frac{5}{8}$	75		5	2	·106
D3	1954–58	523	$\frac{11}{16}$	90		5	3	·107
D5	1958	375	$\frac{7}{8}$	140	25	$3\frac{1}{2}$	2	·105
D7	1959–61	375	$\frac{7}{8}$	150	25	3	3	·106
D7	1962–66	375	$\frac{7}{8}$	140	25	$3\frac{1}{2}$	2	·105
D10	1967	626	26 mm	150	25	3	2	·105
D14	1968	626	26 mm	160	25	3	3	·105
D175	1969–71	626	26 mm	180		$3\frac{1}{2}$	2	·105
Flyweights								
Winged Wheel	1953–54	335	0·39	30		3	3	
Winged Wheel	1955–58	335	0·39	27		3	2	
Dandy	1956–61	365	$\frac{1}{2}$	35		3	3	
Beagle	1964–65	19	$\frac{19}{32}$	70	15	2	2	·104
175 Scooter	1958–60	363	$\frac{13}{16}$	130	15	3	5	·106
175 Scooter	1960–63	363	$\frac{13}{16}$	130	15	3	3	·106
Beeza Scooter	1956	363	$\frac{25}{32}$	100	20	4	3	·105

Model	Year	Type	Size	Main	Pilot	Slide	Needle Pos.	Needle Jet
Unit range								
C15	1959–67	375	$\frac{7}{8}$	140	25	4	3	·105
C15S	1959–60	376	$\frac{15}{16}$	180	25	3	2	·106
C15S	1960–63	376	$1\frac{1}{16}$	240	25	$3\frac{1}{2}$	2	·106
C15S	1963–65	376	$1\frac{1}{16}$	190	25	$3\frac{1}{2}$	2	·106
C15T	1959–65	375	$\frac{7}{8}$	140	25	4	3	·105
SS80	1961	376	1	180	25	$3\frac{1}{2}$	3	·106
SS80	1962–65	376	1	200	25	4	2	·106
C15 Sportsman	1966	376	1	200	25	4	2	·106
C25	1967	928	28 mm	200	25	3	2	·106
B25	1968–70	928	28 mm	170	25	3	1	·106
B25SS & B25T	1971	928	28 mm	190		$3\frac{1}{2}$	1	·106
B40	1960–65	376	$1\frac{1}{16}$	190	20	3	3	·106
B40WD	1967–68	398	28 mm	210	25			
SS90	1962–65	389	$1\frac{1}{8}$	200	30	$3\frac{1}{2}$	3	·106
B44GP	1965–7	389	$1\frac{5}{32}$	260	25	$3\frac{1}{2}$	3	·106
B44VE	1966	389	$1\frac{5}{32}$	330	25	$3\frac{1}{2}$	3	·106
B44VE	1967–68	930	30 mm	220	25	3	2	·107
B44VS	1969–70	930	30 mm	240	25	$3\frac{1}{2}$	1	·106
B44VR	1967–68	930	30 mm	230	25	3	2	·107
B44SS	1969–70	930	30 mm	240	25	$3\frac{1}{2}$	1	·106
B50SS & B50T	1971–72	930	30 mm	200		$3\frac{1}{2}$	1	·106
B50MX	1971	932	32 mm	250		3	2	·106
B50MX	1972	932	32 mm	250		$3\frac{1}{2}$	1	·106